Markets and Measurements in Nineteenth-Century Britain

Measurements are a central institutional component of markets and economic exchange. By the nineteenth century, the measurement system in Britain was desperately in need of revision: a multiplicity of measurement standards, a proliferation of local or regional weights and measures and a confusing array of measurement practices made everyday measurements unreliable. Aashish Velkar uncovers how metrology and economic logic alone failed to make measurements reliable and discusses the importance of localised practices in shaping trust in them. *Markets and Measurements in Nineteenth-Century Britain* steers away from the traditional explanations of measurement reliability based on the standardisation and centralisation of metrology; rather, the focus is on changing measurement practices in local economic contexts. Detailed case studies from the Industrial Revolution suggest that such practices were path dependent and anthropocentric. Therefore, whilst standardised metrology may have improved precision, it was localised practices that determined the reliability and trustworthiness of measurements in economic contexts.

AASHISH VELKAR is a lecturer in economic history at the University of Manchester. He won the 2010 Thirsk-Feinstein PhD Prize in economic history and the 2010 Coleman Prize for business history. Previously, Aashish held managerial positions at international consulting firms in South Asia.

Cambridge Studies in Economic History

Editorial Board

PAUL JOHNSON *University of Western Australia*
SHEILAGH OGILVIE *University of Cambridge*
AVNER OFFER *All Souls College, Oxford*
GIANNI TONIOLO *Universita di Roma 'Tor Vergata'*
GAVIN WRIGHT *Stanford University*

Cambridge Studies in Economic History comprises stimulating and accessible economic history which actively builds bridges to other disciplines. Books in the series will illuminate why the issues they address are important and interesting, place their findings in a comparative context and relate their research to wider debates and controversies. The series will combine innovative and exciting new research by young researchers with new approaches to major issues by senior scholars. It will publish distinguished work regardless of chronological period or geographical location.

A complete list of titles in the series can be found at:
www.cambridge.org/economichistory.

Markets and Measurements in Nineteenth-Century Britain

Aashish Velkar

University of Manchester

CAMBRIDGE
UNIVERSITY PRESS

CAMBRIDGE
UNIVERSITY PRESS

University Printing House, Cambridge CB2 8BS, United Kingdom

One Liberty Plaza, 20th Floor, New York, NY 10006, USA

477 Williamstown Road, Port Melbourne, VIC 3207, Australia

314-321, 3rd Floor, Plot 3, Splendor Forum, Jasola District Centre, New Delhi - 110025, India

79 Anson Road, #06-04/06, Singapore 079906

Cambridge University Press is part of the University of Cambridge.

It furthers the University's mission by disseminating knowledge in the pursuit of education, learning and research at the highest international levels of excellence.

www.cambridge.org
Information on this title: www.cambridge.org/9781107023338

© Aashish Velkar 2012

First published 2012

A catalogue record for this publication is available from the British Library

Library of Congress Cataloging in Publication data
Velkar, Aashish, 1969–
Markets and measurements in nineteenth century Britain / Aashish Velkar.
   p.   cm. – (Cambridge studies in economic history)
Includes bibliographical references and index.
ISBN 978-1-107-02333-8 (hbk.)
1. Weights and measures – Great Britain – History – 19th century.
2. Metrology – Great Britain – History – 19th century.   3. Great Britain –
Commerce – History – 19th century.   I. Title.
QC89.G8V45   2012
530.8′1309034–dc23   2012000782

ISBN 978-1-107-02333-8 Hardback

To my father, Deepak Velker (1944–1984),
for showing me the courage to be curious.

To my grandfather, K. S. Dhurandhar (1915–2003),
for teaching me that dreams can come true.

Contents

List of Figures

List of Tables

Acknowledgements

This book was inspired by the work I did between 2004 and 2009 as a doctoral researcher at the London School of Economics (LSE). My years at the LSE were spent exploring my interests at my own pace, unfettered by the responsibilities I previously had as a young corporate executive during the 1990s. I am indebted to the Department of Economic History at the LSE for giving me the freedom, in the form of a Carus–Wilson Research Studentship, to make this book possible in the first place.

The Economic History Society (EHS) provided generous support during my post-doctoral years, particularly in the form of the EHS Postan Fellowship (2008–2009). The fellowship allowed me to bring it all together and to extend my doctoral work in new directions. The Institute of Historical Research, London, provided me with an intellectual home during this fellowship. In 2010, the society's Thirsk–Feinstein Dissertation Prize Committee and their decision propelled me to follow up my doctoral work with a book project, and I am grateful for their support and encouragement. The Association of Business Historians was equally generous with its assistance and provided opportunities to present many elements of my work to its members during this period. Its decision on the 2010 Coleman Prize for doctoral dissertations simply reinforced my efforts to bring the doctoral research together in this book.

I am also grateful to my friends and colleagues on the 'How Well Do "Facts" Travel?' research project for including me in their activities. This project was funded by the Economic and Social Research Council and the Leverhulme Trust, and their financial support made my participation in the Facts project possible. The project team prompted me to think in many different ways about the things on which I was working at the time. I have many fond memories of our weekly meetings and all the workshops held at the LSE during those years.

I would like to acknowledge the support of the University of Sussex and my colleagues in the Department of Business and Management during

2010 and 2011, as this book was finally taking shape. I would also like to acknowledge Taylor and Francis, the publisher of *Business History*, and Oxford University Press, the publisher of *Enterprise and Society*, for agreeing to let me reuse some of the material I had previously published in articles in their journals.[1]

In many ways, the subject of this book was inspired by Ken Alder's colourful account of how the metric system was defined: *The Measure of All Things* (2003). Quite unknowingly, he set me thinking in a direction that eventually culminated in this volume. Many other scholars have knowingly and profoundly influenced my work since then. Martin Daunton and JoAnne Yates provided the initial encouragement and the subsequent intellectual support to transform my doctoral thesis into this monograph. My conversations with Ted Porter and Marcel Boumans were invaluable, inspiring and illuminating and provided unique perspectives for me to consider. Dudley Baines, Janet Hunter and Tim Leunig prodded me to think about the bigger picture during my early years as a graduate student at the LSE. More recently, collaborative work with Rajneesh Narula and David Higgins on other subjects has made me reflect upon the material for this book in different ways. Paul Strong, Roy Edwards and Xavier Duran frequently engaged in informal, friendly and challenging conversations about my work. Sabina Leonelli, Jon Adams, Ed Ramsden, Erika Mansnerus, Simona Valerani, Julia Mensink, Albane Forestier and others from the LSE Facts project kept the ideas flowing.

However, I reserve my greatest admiration for Mary Morgan and Peter Howlett, who patiently guided me through my doctoral research and beyond. They have had the most profound influence on this work and have encouraged me to push the boundaries of my abilities. They have given me personal, intellectual and moral support during these most challenging years of my life. The book may not have come to fruition if it wasn't for their constant and unwavering support.

My family has stood by my decision to pursue an academic career after eleven years in the corporate business world. Rashmi Velkar, Lata Dhurandhar and Minu and Kiriti Guha continue to extend unquestioning support to every decision I make. Elaine Morrison has unfalteringly

---

[1] A. Velkar, 'Caveat emptor: abolishing public measurements, standardizing quantities, and enhancing market transparency in the London coal trade c1830', *Enterprise and Society* 9 No 2 (2008): pp. 281–313, and A. Velkar, 'Transactions, standardisation and competition: establishing uniform sizes in the British wire industry c.1880', *Business History* 51 No 2 (2009): pp. 222–47.

stood by me in every way as this book was slowly taking shape: her patience remains immeasurable by any standard. I know I could show more appreciation for their support, especially that of Apara Guha, who, against all odds (and reason!), believed in my decision many years ago to pursue my dream. She lent me her strength to be bold. To her I owe everything.

1   Markets and measurements

An introduction

> As we trace the history of our metrology from the beginning we shall
> have ample evidence of [considerable] effort which ensured that the
> exchange of goods was equitable, with the consumer relying ultimately
> on kingly support of his claim for justice in the market-place.
>   — R. D. Connor, *The Weights and Measures of England* (1987)

Metrology, mensuration and measurement practices

Measurements defined the foundations of justice, safeguarded property
and ensured the rule of right, wrote Patrick Kelly in his book *Metrology*
(published 1816). Kelly, an accountant, a mathematics teacher, former
master of Finsbury Square Academy and an astronomer, argued that
measurements were fundamental to all commercial and economic activity, as 'productions of land and labour, or nature and art' were estimated
on the basis of weights and measures.[1] The diversity of weights and
measures that prevailed 'throughout the world' greatly concerned him.
As an expert on bookkeeping, currency exchange and other commercial
matters, he reckoned that diversity must be an 'interruption to trade
and commerce'.[2] This diversity was well documented in a parliamentary
report of 1820 that listed the immense variety of local and customary
weights and measures in a thirty-page appendix.[3] Kelly despaired that

---

[1] P. Kelly, *Metrology; or an exposition of weights and measures chiefly those of Great Britain
and France...* (London, 1816). Ashworth describes Kelly as an 'executive business astronomer' as he was among the several business-minded people, such as Francis and Arthur
Baily, Henry Colebrooke, Stephen Groombridge and Charles Babbage, who founded
and were dominant within the Astronomical Society in London. W. J. Ashworth, 'The
calculating eye: Baily, Herschel, Babbage and the business of astronomy', *The British
Journal for the History of Science* 27 No 4 (1994).

[2] Kelly, *Metrology*. See 'Introduction'. Kelly was also the author of *The universal cambist,
and commercial instruction* (London, 1811), a text on coinage and currency exchange,
and *The elements of book-keeping* (London, 1801), a text on single-entry and double-entry
bookkeeping.

[3] *Second report of the Commissioners on Weights and Measures*, [P]arliamentary [P]apers
Vol. VII 1820, pp. 475–509.

although there were numerous plans for correcting this diversity by adopting universal standards, the plans were as 'visionary and impractical as proposals to establish a universal language'.[4]

British historians have generally echoed Kelly's views. The overall consensus in the literature on the long nineteenth century is that diversity and nonuniformity of weights and measures tended to disrupt internal trade.[5] The presence of numerous local measurement units throughout the country is taken as evidence of how fragmented markets were in eighteenth-century England: 'a chain of local and regional markets at this date [rather] than as one emerging national economy'.[6] There is little dissension within the historiography of British markets that the diversity in its weights and measures had a detrimental impact on transactions and market exchanges, created uncertainties and costs, erected internal barriers to free trade and ultimately inhibited market integration.[7] In many other respects, late-eighteenth-century Britain may have been economically developed, but in terms of fragmented markets and diverse weights and measures, it was as undeveloped as the rest of Europe.

The confusing array of weights and measures was tidied up during the nineteenth century, especially through two major legislative reforms in the 1820s and 1870s. The Imperial system of weights and measures that was introduced in 1824 was the culmination of scientific, administrative and legislative efforts of scientists, MPs, civil servants and instrument makers in the late eighteenth and early nineteenth centuries. This reform of Britain's weights and measures, and the subsequent reform of 1878, eventually rid the statute books of duplicative and arcane acts, introduced a simplified and hierarchical system of measurement units and instituted a well-defined organisational structure to enforce this system nationally.

In many respects, this was a significant institutional change. Britain finally had a uniform system of weights and measures, a political quest that had been periodically attempted since the Magna Carta of 1225 had declared that 'there shall be one measure of wine, one measure of ale, and one measure of corn'.[8] Britain was one of the few nations in Europe to have a unified metrology in the first half of the nineteenth century.

---

[4] Kelly, *Metrology*, p. xi.

[5] J. Hoppit, 'Reforming Britain's weights and measures, 1660–1824', *The English Historical Review* 108 No 426 (1993): p. 82.

[6] G. V. Harrison, 'Agricultural weights and measures', in J. Thirsk (ed.) *The agrarian history of England and Wales*, Vol. VII, *1640–1750 (agrarian change)* (Cambridge, Cambridge University Press, 1985), p. 815.

[7] M. J. Daunton, *Progress and poverty: an economic and social history of Britain 1700–1850* (Oxford, Oxford University Press, 1995), p. 278.

[8] House of Commons Reports (1738–65) 1758 Vol. II, *Report of the Carysfort committee on weights and measures*.

The other major European powers would not achieve this until later: France (c. 1840), Germany (c. 1870), Italy (c. 1860), Russia (c. 1920). They adopted the metric system that was developed during the French Revolution in the 1790s. Britain narrowly rejected adoption of the metric measures in 1871, voting to retain the Imperial measures as the basis of its national measurement system for at least another century or so.[9]

The recalcitrant attitude of the British state towards metric measures was born partly out of resistance to change. Mr Fothergill, industrialist and MP, pointed out the insurmountable difficulties in adopting the metric system and was certain that

[it] would be met with strong disfavour of the working classes, who knew the present system perfectly well and understood all its working, [and would] have all their habits and notions in regard to work and wages upset by the introduction of a new system.[10]

Reforming Britain's weights and measures was fraught with tension between those who held fast to local, customary measures and those who were the proponents of uniformity and standardisation.[11] Efforts to enforce legislated measures had historically been unpopular and were often met with stiff local resistance. In the eighteenth century, people in the south-west of England led a popular revolt against the imposition of the Winchester bushel by the state.[12] Such resistance was replayed in the nineteenth century too: the Winchester bushel, which was outlawed in the 1820s, continued to be used to measure grain in the 1870s. Reforming legal measures meant striking a balance between scientific ideals, administrative practicality and local resistance. Consequently, nineteenth-century reforms of British weights and measures were generally conservative as the reformers wanted to ensure the success of reforms.[13]

The scientific principles underlying Britain's new metrology were also the subject of bitter disputes and disagreements. There were vociferous

9   E. F. Cox, 'The metric system: a quarter-century of acceptance (1851–1876)', *Osiris* 13 (1958). R. D. Connor, *The weights and measures of England* (London, HMSO, 1987). R. E. Zupko, *Revolution in measurement: Western European weights and measures since the age of science* (Philadelphia, American Philosophical Society, 1990).
10 *Hansard Parliamentary Debates*. Series 3 Vol. 208. 26 July 1871. 'Weights and Measures (Metric System) Bill.' cc295.
11 Hoppit, 'Reforming Britain's weights and measures'.
12 R. Sheldon et al., 'Popular protest and the persistence of customary corn measures: resistance to the Winchester bushel in the English west', in A. Randall and A. Charlesworth (eds) *Markets, market culture and popular protest in eighteenth-century Britain and Ireland* (Liverpool, Liverpool University Press, 1996).
13 Hoppit, 'Reforming Britain's weights and measures'. This is true of reforms in the 1820s well as in the 1870s.

arguments about the length standard and whether it should be taken as the distance between two lines engraved on a bar or between the ends of a line engraved upon it.[14] Joseph Whitworth and George Airy crossed swords on this issue more than once. Similarly, Whitworth's gauges, James Clerk Maxwell's electromagnetic measures or James Joule's measures of mechanical equivalent of heat were equally contestable and contested as scientific measurements.[15] Telegraph engineers debated whether the size of telegraph cables should be expressed in terms of mass-length or diameter and whether they should be arranged on a geometric scale. Britain's new metrology was supposed to challenge traditional measurements and practices, and yet this new metrology was also expected to confirm existing knowledge through expert measurements. This apparent paradox, Schaffer argues, could only be resolved when Britain's new metrology was conceived as being traditional. Tradition on which the new metrology was to be based had to be newly invented and forged through public controversy and painstaking labour.[16]

Notwithstanding the political and scientific debates surrounding the reforms, the question is, did the reform of Britain's metrology affect internal trade? Did the introduction of uniform weights and measures help business groups overcome the measurement problems that contributed to internal barriers, trade disruption and uncertainty in market exchange?

The historical consensus is that it did. The long process of standardisation of British weights and measures is taken as a clear indication of the emergence of an integrated national market. Such conclusions rest on a major assumption: that there exists a direct correspondence between 'measures' (i.e. the system of weights and measures units) and 'measurements' (i.e. the information that the act of measuring captures). Existing literature implies that this direct correspondence is why multiplicity, nonuniformity or incoherency of historical measures translated into multiplicity, nonuniformity or incoherency of measurements, which in turn had the disruptive impact on trade and market exchange – the corollary being that the introduction of uniform and invariable measures eliminated unreliability in measurements, simplified economic transactions and helped integrate markets.

There is little distinction in most historical accounts between standardising measures and standardising measurements, and the former is

---

[14] N. Atkinson, *Sir Joseph Whitworth: 'the world's best mechanician'* (Gloucestershire, Sutton, 1996). Chapter 5: 'The history of measurement'.

[15] S. Schaffer, 'Metrology, metrication and Victorian values', in B. Lightman (ed.) *Victorian science in context* (Chicago, University of Chicago Press, 1997).

[16] Ibid., p. 467.

expected to have translated into the latter. Ken Alder alluded to this distinction when he wrote that the scientifically motivated thrust of the French metric reforms of the 1790s was to replace an older economic system with a newer one based on measurements of value in terms of price.[17] Sidney Pollard captured the essence of this distinction when he remarked that 'the objectives of businessmen are not to attain perfection [of measurement units], but to keep down costs and increase efficiency'.[18] On the whole, however, most historical accounts fail to clearly emphasise the difference between the *abstract* systems of measures and the *practical* issues of making measurements – and why standardising the former helped to manage the latter.

This book investigates the practical problems that business groups – firms, merchants, entrepreneurs, and so on – faced in their daily commercial activities due to unreliable measurements. It explores why such measurement problems were historically significant and economically fundamental, why business groups sought solutions to such problems and what those solutions were. I refrain from making prima facie assumptions about the relationship between abstract measures and practical measurements. I highlight the difference between *metrology* (i.e. the system of weights, measures and other measurement units) and *mensuration* (i.e. the act of measuring).[19] This distinction between abstract principles and context-driven practices is important in understanding how historical businesses managed measurement problems in economic transactions.

My approach is similar to that of Graeme Gooday, who studies the persistent localisation of Victorian electrical measurement practices, or Bruce Curtis, who studies 'measurement hybrids' in pre-Confederation Canada. Gooday gives a detailed account of the development of electrical measurements by studying why specific experts, measurements and techniques were proposed as trustworthy and not others. He shows this by moving the focus away from laboratories and 'centres of calculation' and

[17] K. Alder, 'A revolution to measure: the political economy of the metric system in the ancien régime', in M. N. Wise (ed.) *The values of precision* (Princeton, Princeton University Press, 1995), p. 59.

[18] S. Pollard, 'Capitalism and rationality: a study of measurements in British coal mining, ca. 1750–1850', *Explorations in Economic History* 20 No 1 (1983): p. 125.

[19] The *Oxford English Dictionary* defines the two terms as follows: metrology, (*n.*) 1. A system of measures, *esp.* one used by a particular nation, culture, etc., 2. The study of systems of measurement; the science of measurement; the branch of technology that deals with accurate measurement; mensuration, (*n.*) 1. The action, process, or art of measuring; measurement, 2. The branch of geometry that deals with the measurement of lengths, areas, and volumes; the process of measuring the lengths, areas, and volumes of geometrical figures.

to the actions of practitioners.[20] In Bruno Latour's view, 'centres' enable scientists and bureaucrats to give the outside world a form through metrology. An 'enlightened network' links the powerful centre to the periphery via 'metrological chains', enabling scientific facts to survive in the outside world. Metrological chains also enable the bureaucratic 'centre' to act at a distance on the periphery and to translate what the periphery does back towards the centre. The chains make it possible to translate local relations into administratively pertinent forms, according to this view.[21]

While powerful scientific and bureaucratic metrological centres did emerge in the nineteenth century, I have steered the historical focus of this book away from such centres. I am interested in understanding what the new metrology did to the local measurements in historical markets and whether it made them reliable in the local context. I reflect on the relations between centralised metrology and diverse local measurement practices, as Curtis does in his sociological study of metrological reform in pre-Confederation Canada.[22] I argue that mensuration processes (i.e. the activities or steps through which particular information is captured at the local level) are responsible for shaping these local measurement practices. Chapter 3 offers a more complete discussion on the mensuration process and how the act of measuring can broadly be understood in terms of three distinct elements: observing and recording relevant information, comparing these observations to standards and eventually contextualising the comparisons. Several tools, instruments, standards and protocols (i.e. rules, norms or conventions) are essential in conducting this activity. 'Measurement', that is the information gathered from this act, is the end result of this activity. Through detailed case studies, I explore how business groups (merchants, firms, etc.) conducted this activity within different economic contexts, the distinct groups that shaped the measurement activity, the various measurement issues that they faced and the solutions that were proposed.

I show that historical markets actually faced two measurement problems. The first was undoubtedly the diversity in weights and measures – the proliferation of local or regional measurement units and the presence of a confusing array of weights and measures that potentially disrupted

[20] G. J. N. Gooday, *The morals of measurement: accuracy, irony and trust in late Victorian electrical practice* (Cambridge, Cambridge University Press, 2004). B. Latour, *Science in action: how to follow scientists and engineers through society* (Cambridge, MA, Harvard University Press, 1987).
[21] B. Curtis, 'From the moral thermometer to money: metrological reform in pre-confederation Canada', *Social Studies of Science* 28 No 4 (1998): p. 551.
[22] Ibid.

trade and economic exchange before the mid-nineteenth century. The second was an institutional problem stemming from the fundamental economic aspects surrounding measurements: markets may encounter transactional barriers because delineating *complete* information about any economic good is fundamentally costly. Information is normally based upon measurements of multiple attributes of an economic good. This forces the selection of a smaller (more manageable) set of criteria to measure. The selection, in turn, creates a potential for information asymmetry – a classic principal–agent problem.[23] In other words, measurement issues facing historical markets were not limited to the diversity of weights and measures but were of a more fundamental economic nature. The economic issues were manifest in questions such as what attributes should be measured, how they should be measured or who should measure them.

Metrological standardisation (i.e. the introduction of a uniform measurement system) solved the first problem of incompatible standards but not the second economic problem. By exploring how businesses solved the second problem, the historical studies featured in this book chart some of the profound institutional changes of the nineteenth century, in terms of both how people made measurements and the redefinition of economic relationships, within the context of the political economy of a reformed metrology.

This does not imply that the two aspects – metrology and mensuration – were historically independent. On the contrary, they tended to be inextricably linked within measurement systems as a whole. For Kula, systems of measurement include 'all the elements associated with measuring', including systems and instruments of counting, methods of using instruments, different methods of measuring in different social situations and the 'entire associated complex of interlinked, varied, and often conflicting social interests'. In Kula's definition, the system combines the various elements into 'an internally articulated structured whole', and the 'task of science is to investigate this system within the social reality that produced it and within whose framework it functions'.[24] Indeed, as Porter suggests, the bureaucratic imposition of standardised metrology notwithstanding, weights and measures were social measures and

[23] Y. Barzel, 'Measurement cost and the organization of markets', *Journal of Law and Economics* 25 No 1 (1982): p. 27.

[24] W. Kula, *Measures and men*, R. Szreter (trans.) (Princeton, Princeton University Press, 1986), p. 94. The National Measurement Office, UK, succinctly defines the national measurement system as 'the technical and organizational infrastructure which ensures a consistent and internationally recognized basis for measurement' (http://www.bis.gov .uk/).

predated any concern with science.[25] Legislation or standardisation of weights and measures was often an exercise in power that threatened the 'fragile margins of the budgets of poor' and amplified existing class struggles.[26] Measurements are often deployed outside the centres of metrology in the regulation of social and economic relations over large geographical areas.[27] This is starkly evident in the late-eighteenth-century metric reforms in France. The thrust of the French reforms was primarily to replace an economic system based on the measures of the ancien régime to one based upon value, that is, where everything that had economic value could be translated into the single, paramount variable of price (Chapter 2).[28]

British metrological reforms did not seek to dramatically replace existing economic relationships. Nevertheless, the case studies in this book show that disputes amongst the scientists and engineers, and amongst politicians and bureaucrats, were paralleled in the disputes amongst merchants, traders and business groups. Such disputes were resolved in their own microcontexts. They were not necessarily resolved by appealing to scientific ideals, by invoking political power or by imposing bureaucratic procedure. Resolution often required businesses to contextualise the significance of measurements in particular situations. In this context, the analytical distinction between metrology and mensuration – between abstract scientific systems and practical methods of measuring – is a useful one. I show why local measurement practices continued to remain crucially important in the British economy even when a unified metrology was successfully introduced in the nineteenth century.

What made measurements reliable?

The chapters in this book show that metrological standardisation at the centre solved the historical problem of multiple, potentially confusing measurement units but was incapable of solving the institutional problems of measuring multiple attributes. As a result, measurement practices that improved governance and monitoring remained crucially important

---

[25] T. M. Porter, *Trust in numbers: the pursuit of objectivity in science and public life* (Princeton, Princeton University Press, 1995), p. 23.

[26] Sheldon et al., 'Customary corn measures'. See also P. Linebaugh, *The London hanged: crime and civil society in the eighteenth century* (London, Allen Lane, 1991), p. 162, for the class struggle in the Atlantic tobacco trade as legislation was introduced in the American colonies to standardise the 'hogshead'. Similar class struggles can also be seen in the case measurements of coal in eighteenth-century London (p. 307).

[27] A. Barry, 'The history of measurement and the engineers of space', *British Journal for the History of Science* 26 No 4 (1993): p. 464.

[28] Alder, 'Revolution to measure', p. 59.

for ensuring measurement reliability at the local level. The historical quest for a unified and centralised metrology remained elusive until the nineteenth century. The state's repeated attempts to enforce uniform metrological standards had remained largely unsuccessful until then. Market transactions continued to be based upon a host of local, regional or customary measurement units which often bore little resemblance to other similarly termed units and which appeared confusing to the outsider.[29] But nonuniformity did not totally inhibit trade between markets using vastly different measurement units. Merchants, middlemen and dealers would regularly use published dictionaries or tables to convert between different weights and measures.[30] These merchants in fact acted as the translators between local measures, relying upon local norms or market rules to convert from one measure to another along established trade routes.[31] Additionally, other institutions emerged to ensure that proper measurements were meted during delivery or exchange of commodities. The institution of publicly measuring essential commodities such as coal and corn, called the metage system, was important in monitoring measurements and acted as a governance mechanism (Chapter 4). Rules of verification also emerged to manage measurement issues, particularly those related to measurements of quality. The practice of using the *counts* as a measure of fineness of silk thread or cotton yarn or the use of *natural weights* as a measure of grain quality transcended local or legal metrological standards (Chapter 6).[32] In such cases, reliability of measurements depended not so much upon uniformity as upon adherence to locally known market norms, customs and conventions. Markets depended upon such institutional methods to coordinate transactions, structure contracts and generally to avoid confusion.

---

[29] Sheldon et al., 'Customary corn measures'. N. Biggs, 'A tale untangled: measuring the fineness of yarn', *Textile History* 35 No 1 (2004). C. R. Fay, 'The sale of corn in the nineteenth century', *The Economic Journal* 34 No 134 (1924). Reports of various parliamentary committees on weights and measures in PP 1813–14 Vol. III, *Report from the committee on weights and measures*; PP 1819 Vol. XI, *First report of the commissioners on weights and measures*; PP 1820 Vol. VII, *Second report of the commissioners on weights and measures*; PP 1821 Vol. IV, *Report from the committee on weights and measures*.

[30] E.g. J. Hewitt, *The corn dealer's assistant* (London, 1736). E. Hodgkins, *A series of mercantile letters, with the weights, measures and monies reduced into the English Standard, etc.* (London, 1815). A. Bald, *The farmer and corn-dealer's assistant; or, the knowledge of weights and measures made easy, by a variety of tables, etc.* (Stirling, 1780).

[31] London coal merchants would convert from measures used in the north of England to those locally used on the basis of long-established market norms. R. A. Mott, 'The London and Newcastle chaldrons for measuring coal', *Archaeologia Aeliana* 40 4th Series (1962). See also Hoppit, 'Reforming Britain's weights and measures', p. 92.

[32] C. Poni, 'Standards, trust and civil discourse: measuring the thickness and quality of silk thread', *History of Technology* 23 (2001). S. Dumbell, 'The sale of corn in the nineteenth century', *The Economic Journal* 35 No 137 (1925).

The introduction of the Imperial measurement units in 1824 and the metric units in 1799 signalled a profound institutional shift. Unlike the local and customary units, these standards of weights and measures were supposedly abstract and decontextualised (Chapter 2). They could be employed across all economic contexts and across national and international geographies. In addition, they were arranged in a hierarchical manner, ensuring traceability and verification, and were centrally administered by the state bureaucracy, ensuring enforceability.

This centralisation and standardisation of metrology could not resolve the institutional choices involved in selecting – and limiting – the number of attributes to be measured and the various methods by which measurements could be made. Such choices remained highly contextual and local. Markets, businesses and firms had to adhere to particular measurement practices within microcontexts, which incorporated available metrological standards, governance mechanisms and other institutional rules.

Local measurement practices involved making various ex ante selections or choices (i.e. prior to the actual act of measuring). These included selecting the property or attribute of an object that was to be measured, choosing an appropriate measurement method, selecting the metrological standard, specifying the measuring instruments to be used and seeking agreement regarding measurement protocols (Chapter 3). These activities shaped the measurement practices at the local level. The choices that people made were shaped by the nature of the information that was required, the groups who required the information, their motivations and the purpose for which the measurements were required.

The key issue here is that such practices were localised, although they used so-called universal metrological standards. Often there was no single, uniform, *best* practice that everyone used. There seldom was an ideal or true way of measuring a product attribute. There was no reason why the measurement of wire diameter was inherently better than its weight per length to sort it into different sizes (Chapter 5), nor was there any inherent reason why weight measurements of dry goods represented ideal or true measurements compared to their volumetric measurements (Chapter 4).[33]

Practices depended upon the ease with which attributes could be measured. Thus, search attributes (e.g. colour, weight) were easier to measure at the time of transaction, whereas experience attributes (e.g. taste,

---

[33] Harrison, 'Agricultural weights and measures'. Marketing dry goods, such as grain or coal, by weight introduced complications which were not entirely appreciated at the time. See also Chapters 4 and 6 in this volume.

functionality) could usually be measured on an ex post basis. Credence attributes (e.g. method of production) could not be measured even on an ex post basis and were based upon trust, reputation or third-party certification.[34] Measurement practices also depended upon whether measurable attributes captured information about a product's condition (freshness or newness, colour, size, etc.) or composition (strength, purity, etc.) or functionality and performance ('does it do what it says on the tin?'). It was generally easier, and therefore less costly, to measure the product's condition rather than its composition or functionality (Chapter 6). Markets and businesses struggled to develop measurement practices that were relevant and suitable to their specific contexts rather than only conforming to an abstract ideal.[35]

Metrology and mensuration are two distinct sides of the same measurement coin. Metrology emphasised traceability and invariability of measurement units; the number of 'states' or 'values' the measurement artefact existed in was limited, fixed and derived from a primary standard. The mensuration processes and measurement practices worked effectively because they valued flexibility and incorporated several measurement standards and artefacts to render measurements reliable in given contexts. They shaped local practices and were less concerned with the universality of measurements. Metrology in the nineteenth century became highly centralised, codified and formalised. In this regard, they were de jure – especially the weights and measures standards – as their use was mandatory and exclusive, especially after circa 1824. Many local measurement practices also became codified during the nineteenth century. Some practices became codified in the form of legislation, as some medieval practices had been, such as the assize of bread or wine, but usually such legal practices were not strictly de jure as their use was not always mandatory or obligatory (Chapter 5). People could no longer choose whether to use the new uniform metrological units. They could no longer use the traditional, local or customary measurement units – all legal contracts had to be made using the legal Imperial measurement units. The choice of a *particular* legal unit in a given context, however, was determined by the interplay of economic, political and social forces. For instance, measuring coals according to their weight became enforceable by law in 1832 (Chapter 4), but wheat and other grains could be sold

---

[34] J. Tirole, *The theory of industrial organization* (Cambridge, MA, MIT Press, 1988).

[35] Metrologists continue to maintain that 'it is only by means of accurate measurements, ones that provide a close representation of nature, that the apparently simple requirement for comparability and long-term reproducibility can be met'. T. Quinn and J. Kovalevsky, 'The development of modern metrology and its role today', *Philosophical Transactions of the Royal Society of London, Series A* 363 No 1834 (2005): 2314.

either by weight or volume until 1921 (Chapter 6). Measurement reliability was not limited to providing public goods in the form of legal and standardised metrological units. It depended largely upon local practices that were embedded within the microcontext of economic relationships between individuals, businesses and firms and the state.

The State and the science of measurements

Nineteenth-century reforms to British metrology and efforts to make measurements in markets more transparent and reliable entailed an uneasy combination of depersonalising customary practices and defending traditional rights and moral values. The reformers of British metrology had recognised the difficulty of replacing local measurement units early on. In 1824 the new Imperial weights and measures were introduced, but they did not immediately replace the numerous and often incompatible local units. The reformers sought to overcome the relative nonuniformity of local units by connecting them to the primary standards of the Imperial system (Chapter 2). The use of local units was not expressly forbidden for nearly fifty years thereafter, and many markets continued to use the older measurement units. An additional layer of legal and traceable measurement units was added over the existing layer of local and customary units. This situation changed in 1878, when the Imperial measures were made the only legally recognised measurement units in Britain. Thus, for most of the nineteenth century, merchants, traders and business firms continued to operate under a relatively non-coercionary and decentralised metrological regime.

The state attempted to create a metrological system that appeared to be impersonal and reproducible. Its intention was to lend objectivity to the measurements made using the centralised metrology. Measurement procedures were established (and continue to be established) in scientific laboratories, trade association offices and public bureaus. Centralised metrology was a triumph of the rhetoric of objectivity that suited the nineteenth-century state very well.[36] Scott shows how measurements had historically been mired in the micropolitics of feudal rents, traditional measurement practices, measurement artefacts such as baskets and

---

[36] T. M. Porter, 'Objectivity as standardization: the rhetoric of impersonality in measurement, statistics, and cost-benefit analysis', in A. Megill (ed.) *Rethinking objectivity* (London, Duke University Press, 1994). Porter, *Trust in numbers*, p. 23. Wise, *Values of precision*, pp. 5–7; T. Frangsmyr et al. (eds), *The quantifying spirit in the 18th century* (Berkeley, University of California Press, 1990). J. A. Tooze, *Statistics and the German state, 1900–1945: making of modern economic knowledge* (Cambridge, Cambridge University Press, 2001).

wagons and so on.[37] Curtis argues that even though official codes may allow local practices to flourish, it is through state sovereignty that measurement practices produce social 'things which stick together' in an historical and objective sense. He considers the establishment of metrological systems after the eighteenth century to be 'a constitutive element of state formation'.[38] Ashworth demonstrates the length to which the state went to standardise metrology so that revenue extraction could become visible, calculable and predictable, or at least appear to become so.[39] Barry argues that there has been an increasing use of measurements and calculation within modern bureaucratic and industrial organisations, leading to a 'numericisation of politics'. That is, historically, there was a growing role for measurements and calculation in political decision making which ultimately relates to the ordering of social, economic and technoscientific activity. The history of metrology – measurement standards and techniques developed in central government laboratories – is one of the manifestations of this 'numericisation'.[40] Objectivity – as quantification – lent stability and predictability to the process of measurement, whereas objectivity in the form of impersonality made measurements more legible and defensible.

Notwithstanding the legibility, predictability and stability of measurements at the centres, people sought measurements they could rely upon and trust. Porter argues that although an element of personal trust is involved in commercial transactions, consumers and traders place a greater faith upon impersonal technological and regulatory mechanisms to make measurements precise and objective. In this regard, the culture of quantification changed radically when scientists collaborated with bureaucrats to develop metrological systems as 'technologies of trust'.[41] Even so, we must distinguish between the social and natural worlds as imagined by the political and scientific discourses – using their 'trustworthy' measurements – and the social and natural worlds as they are continually reinterpreted by individuals in the everyday course of social activity.[42] Gooday shows that trust in electrical measurements could not be reduced to 'well chosen metrology or shrewdly exercised power'.[43]

---

[37] J. C. Scott, *Seeing like a state: how certain schemes to improve the human condition have failed* (New Haven, Yale University Press, 1998), pp. 27–29.

[38] Curtis, 'Metrological reform', p. 548.

[39] W. J. Ashworth, *Customs and excise: trade, production, and consumption in England, 1640–1845* (Oxford, Oxford University Press, 2003), p. 262.

[40] Barry, 'History of measurement', p. 464.

[41] Porter, *Trust in numbers*, p. 23.

[42] Barry, 'History of measurement', p. 467.

[43] Gooday, *Morals of measurement*, p. 39.

For electrical measurements to be trustworthy in microcontexts, measurement practices had to be qualified with arguments about what constituted trustworthy conduct and trustworthy material culture. Trustworthy measurements had a complex socio-politico-technical character. Daunton shows how the material politics of consumption shaped the measurement reliability of the gas meters that validated the consumption of an invisible commodity. The legal definition of a cubic foot of volume was not sufficient to render measurements of consumption trustworthy for consumers.[44]

Measurement objectivity remained rhetorical precisely because it was shaped by the social and political context, as much as it was steered by intellectual thought. Objectivity, reified in measurement precision, for example, was a socially constructed value because it registered something that distinct groups considered valuable and agreed that it was so.[45] The transition from visual to photoelectric methods of measuring different colours of the spectrum depended upon the reconciliation between the physicalist interpretation valued by physicists and engineers and the physiological interpretation that psychologists and physiologists valued.[46] Temperature, too, had to be invented, as Hasok Chang argues, by reaching 'accuracy through iteration'; real values came into being as a result of successful operationalisation.[47]

As with scientific measurements, measurements involved in commercial transactions, too, required agreement and reconciliation. Whilst in theory, merchants and businessmen could trust quantified measurements made using precise instruments, which of the various measurements they made could be trusted? In practice, it was inconceivable that successive measurements of the same quantities were identical – a bane not only of the scientist in the laboratory but also of the trader or merchant. No two measurements of a bushel of coal or grain would yield the same results. Extremely precise wire gauges (using decimal measurements) would give hugely inconsistent results on successive occasions. Scientists deal with this problem by accepting a reasonable level of accuracy. One can distinguish between precision and accuracy: the difference between variability from the true values (precision) and what those true values are

---

[44] M. J. Daunton, 'The material politics of natural monopoly: consuming gas in Victorian Britain', in M. J. Daunton and M. Hilton (eds) *The politics of consumption: material culture and citizenship in Europe and America* (Oxford, Berg, 2001). For similar issues regarding the hydrometer and the excise on spirits, see Ashworth, *Customs and excise*.

[45] For various historical case studies, see Wise, *Values of precision*.

[46] S. F. Johnston, 'From eye to machine: shifting authority in color measurement', in B. Saunders and J. Van Brakel (eds) *Theories, technologies and instrumentalities of colour* (Lanham, Maryland, University Press of America, 2002).

[47] H. Chang, *Inventing temperature: measurement and scientific progress* (Oxford, Oxford University Press, 2004), pp. 212–13.

(accuracy).[48] Scientific measurements often have the benefit of expected true values predicted on theoretical grounds, but how was the merchant or trader to establish which measurements were accurate and which were not? As I show through the detailed cases in this book, it was often difficult to ascertain what the true values in commercial transactions were and what should be a universally true value about a quantity of coal or grain. This is one of the most fundamental problems of economic exchange. Different commercial groups may hold different conventions of what was true value, which in different situations led to disputes. Here the appeal to scientific ideals of objective metrological technology was not sufficient to resolve such differences.

If British metrology was an 'invention of tradition', as Schaffer suggests, then reliability of measurements depended not only upon the degree to which trust was transferred from the hand or the eye to the machine but also upon the extent to which the principal could trust the agent in economic relationships.[49] Creation of such trust, and the tensions involved in securing it, are clearly evident in the case studies presented in this book: who should measure, the buyer or seller (Chapters 4 and 6); what measurement instruments should be used (Chapters 4 and 5); to what extent can the state supervise and regulate measurement methods, and so on. They emphasise how British *metrology* became decontextualised but *measurements* continued to remain embedded within the historical context in which they were made.

Was Britain unique?

In terms of reforming its metrology during the nineteenth century, Britain was not unique. Most European nations successfully reformed, centralised and standardised their measurement systems. Germany, Italy, Spain, Portugal, the Netherlands, Belgium, the Swiss Cantons, Sweden, Norway and others began using the metric measures, on which their national measurement systems were eventually based. Russia systematically introduced reforms in the late nineteenth century, under the leadership of Dimitri Mendeleev (who had famously formulated the periodic table of chemical elements in 1869). But it was only after the Bolshevik Revolution that the Russian state imposed the metric system in 1918.

---

[48] Gooday, *Morals of measurement*, p. 57. M. Boumans (ed.), *Measurement in economics: a handbook* (London, Elsevier, 2007), p. 15. Wise, *Values of precision*, p. 9.

[49] Schaffer, 'Metrology'. J. Nasmyth, 'Remarks on the introduction of the slide principle', in R. Buchanan (ed.) *Practical essays on mill work and other machinery* (London, John Weale, 1841). J. Whitworth, *Papers on mechanical subjects* (London, E. and F. N. Spon, 1882).

While these industrialising nations chose to base their metrology on the French metric units, Britain's reformers based that nation's metrology on the incompatible Imperial units. Incompatibility was overcome to a large extent when the metric equivalents to the Imperial units were legally recognised in 1864. Other countries using the Imperial units included British colonies, such as Canada, Australia and India, and the United States.

Britain is unique amongst European countries because the state did not impose its metrology on its people, at least not initially and not in a coercive manner. Kula argued that Britain's weights and measures were relatively uniform compared to those of other European countries. This was why, he thought, Britain did not switch to the 'revolutionary' metric measures.[50] But this was not the case, and in fact, there was great diversity in customary measures in Britain, just as there was diversity in European weights and measures. Even so, initial reform that defined a significantly rationalised metrology in the form of Imperial measurement units (Figure 2.2) did not impose this system on local measurement practices.

This was contrary to French metric reforms in the 1790s which attempted to mould long-established local practices to the new enlightened way of thinking that the metre ushered in.[51] The role of the state in preserving local measurement practices was very different in Britain and France. The French metrological reforms on the whole had an immediate, profound and disruptive impact on local measurement activity. The British reforms did not. Social, cultural, political and economic factors were allowed to shape the local measurement practices within the microcontexts. As the historical studies in this book show, measurement practices did evolve and change quite significantly during this period. But change was not disruptive, sudden or led from the centre. This is a significant point of departure between Britain (and the other Anglo-Saxon countries such as the United States and Canada) and France and the other metric nations. This is yet another reason why the study of local measurement practices in Britain is both interesting and important for historians with an interest in measurements and markets.

The economy, markets and measurement practices

As the historical case studies in this book show, local measurement practices were being redefined at a time of significant economic growth in

---

[50] Kula, *Measures and men*, p. 280.
[51] For examples of how the French state sought to impose its 'enlightened' thinking and practices on ordinary people, see Alder, 'Revolution to measure'; J. L. Heilbron, 'The measure of enlightenment', in Frangsmyr et al., *Quantifying spirit*; Kula, *Measures and men*.

Britain. This period was also characterised by the changing structure and organisation of businesses and industries, discourses on political economy and the nature of markets and a redefinition of contract freedoms and liabilities.

Economic and industrial growth

From the eighteenth century onwards, there was a considerable expansion of domestic as well as international trade in Britain, both in terms of scale and scope. Britain's international trade grew at a compound annual rate of between 2.5 and 4.5 per cent during the nineteenth century.[52] This expansion was not limited to traditional commodities such as coal, corn, wine or woollens but included several New World commodities, such as cotton, sugar and tobacco, as well as luxury commodities, such as tea and spices. Trade along routes that linked traditional markets with newer distant markets increased, and commodities from newer sources in the Americas as well as the Orient found industrial applications in Britain. The expanding trade included both primary commodities and manufactures, including traditional products such as textiles and metalware, and engineered products made using new manufacturing techniques. Not only did improvements in production technology allow British firms to capture export markets with cheaper goods but demand for raw material from British firms created a huge new import trade. Improvements in transport infrastructure also made it easier to expand trade. Technological change on the whole had a considerable impact on developments in British trade during this period.[53] Expansion in trade also presupposed the development of legal, financial and commercial institutions that enabled the expansion in scope and scale of trade. The commercial revolution and the development of allied institutions thus supported industrial growth.

Expansion of industrial activity was accompanied by changes in the organisation of such activity. A growing proportion of output in many sectors, and especially in textiles, became factory produced in Britain during the nineteenth century. The number of workers in manufacturing

---

[52] P. Deane and W. A. Cole, *British economic growth: 1688–1959 – trends and structures* (Cambridge, Cambridge University Press, 1962), p. 29, Table 8; the percentage growth figures are decadal averages.

[53] For productivity increases in shipping, see C. K. Harley, 'Ocean freight rates and productivity, 1740–1913: the primacy of mechanical invention reaffirmed', *Journal of Economic History* 48 No 4 (1988); S. Ville, 'Total factor productivity in the English shipping industry: the north-east coal trade, 1700–1850', *Economic History Review* 39 No 3 (1986). For port infrastructure, see H. V. Driel and J. Schot, 'Radical innovation as a multilevel process: introducing floating grain elevators in the Port of Rotterdam', *Technology and Culture* 46 (2005).

activities, such as shipbuilding, blast furnaces, and so on, multiplied. There was also increased regional specialisation and concentration of manufacturing.[54] Even so, a vast majority of the firms engaged in industrial activity continued to be small in size, indicating a coexistence of a range of different firm sizes – large enterprises employing hundreds of people as well as smaller, workshop-based firms.[55] In fact, small firms also proliferated alongside large factories because of the widespread practice of subcontracting.[56] Thus greater specialisation and division of labour coexisted with integration of activities as merchant-manufacturers emerged by combining activities from merchanting, financing and entrepreneurship with manufacturing. The persistence of workshops during the years of industrial expansion indicates that the scale and location of industrial activity, and its dispersion, depended upon the relative costs of organising people, materials and information and the shifts in those relative costs.[57] Indeed, integration, agglomeration and specialisation in a range of organisational forms created newer interdependencies and relied upon expanding networks of information and trust – both existing networks and newly established ones.

Accompanying the concentration of industrial activity was the concentration of consumption centres with the rapid growth in the urban share of total population by the nineteenth century.[58] This had a significant impact on the occupational structure, with nearly two-thirds to three-quarters of the workforce employed in nonagricultural occupations. Real wages, on the whole, did increase during the nineteenth century, although the extent of increase appears to be more modest than previously thought.[59] Paralleling this, shifts in consumer preferences during the eighteenth century meant that commodities such as tea and sugar no longer remained luxuries but became necessities. The crucial shifts in consumer behaviour were also generated in the context of new goods and luxuries, and discerning consumers demanded a greater consistency of quality and novelty.[60]

---

[54] J. Langton, 'The Industrial Revolution and the regional geography of England', *Transactions of the Institute of British Geographers* 9 No 2 (1984).

[55] S. Timmins (ed.), *The resources, products and industrial history of Birmingham and the Midland hardware district* (London, Robert Hardwicke, 1866).

[56] G. Riello, 'Strategies and boundaries: subcontracting and the London trades in the long eighteenth century', *Enterprise and Society* 9 No 2 (2008).

[57] J. Mokyr, *The gifts of Athena* (Princeton, Princeton University Press, 2002), p. 119.

[58] E. A. Wrigley, *People, cities and wealth: the transformation of traditional society* (Oxford, Basil Blackwell, 1987), p. 158.

[59] C. H. Feinstein, 'Pessimism perpetuated: real wages and the standard of living in Britain during and after the Industrial Revolution', *Journal of Economic History* 58 No 3 (1998).

[60] M. Berg, 'From imitation to invention: creating commodities in eighteenth-century Britain', *Economic History Review* 55 No 1 (2002).

Business and industry: organisation and structure

Industrial organisations in the nineteenth century were confronted with several issues such as the organisation and management of expanding commodity chains, technological convergence and interdependence, the ability to generate competitive advantages, management and control of information and so on. Economic growth and the increasing sophistication of industrial activity in the nineteenth century made the organisation and management of complex value chains an important issue for British businesses. Specialisation and agglomeration meant sorting out how the interdependent relationships between various firms along the value chains were to be organised. The question of which economic activities (e.g. production, distribution, retailing) to integrate and which to disintegrate became relevant.[61] These considerations were particularly important in the case of heterogeneous industrial commodities, such as cotton, coal or wheat, but also in the manufacture and trade of manufactured goods such as wire products and textiles. Merchant-manufacturers were faced with decisions involving the organisation of production, storage and transportation; quality testing and assurance; enforcement of contracts; distribution of products to dealer-merchants and so on. The patterns of interactions between firms, suppliers and customers, and across firms in an industry, led to the creation of formal and informal organisations. Often such organisations co-evolved alongside industry structures. Trade associations, exchanges, technical societies and institutes and so on helped give an industry its form, lobby power and protection from outside competition.[62] Industries evolved distinct architectures, with each industry developing one or a number of distinct architectures, that is, different ways in which roles were distributed between interdependent firms (e.g. compare the industry structures described in Chapters 4 and 6).[63]

[61] M. Rothstein, 'Multinationals in the grain trade, 1850–1914', *Business and Economic History* 12 2nd ser. (1983). C. R. Fay, 'The London corn market at the beginning of the nineteenth century', *American Economic Review* 15 No 1 (1925). N. Hall, 'The emergence of the Liverpool raw cotton market, 1800–1850', *Northern History* 38 No 1 (2001). R. C. Feenstra, 'Integration of trade and disintegration of production in the global economy', *Journal of Economic Perspectives* 12 No 4 (1998). F. M. Santos and K. M. Eisenhardt, 'Organizational boundaries and theories of organization', *Organization Science* 16 No 5 (2005). G. Gereffi et al., 'The governance of global value chains', *Review of International Political Economy* 12 No 1 (2005).

[62] R. R. Nelson, 'Co-evolution of industry structure, technology and supporting institutions, and the making of comparative advantage', *International Journal of the Economics of Business* 2 No 2 (1995): p. 176.

[63] M. G. Jacobides et al., 'Benefiting from innovation: value creation, value appropriation and the role of industry architectures', *Research Policy* 35 (2006).

Expanding industrial activity was also intimately connected with technical changes and the introduction and maturing of new technologies. Although different organisational architectures emerged within industries, a *convergence* of technologies can be identified during the nineteenth century. Technologies employed along vertical dimensions in different productive activities converged towards similar skills, techniques and facilities in a process of 'technological convergence'.[64] This was especially apparent in metalworking and machinery industries, which involved the cutting of metal into precise shapes and forms using a relatively small number of operations: turning, boring, drilling, grinding and so on. Technological convergence is discernible in other industrial and commercial sectors.

Such convergence had two implications. First, it created complementarities and interdependencies between different firms, particularly in industries with higher degrees of specialisation.[65] This made the governance issues especially important as organisational interdependencies had to be managed alongside technological ones. Second, technological convergence reinforced the need for a given firm to develop new knowledge, new skills and new firm capabilities synchronous to other firms. Many of these new skills and capabilities developed alongside traditional or artisanal skills and shaped the manner and extent to which technologies matured.[66] Industry architectures both influenced, and were in turn influenced by, maturing technologies through a combination of market processes, collective bodies, governmental policies and political action. This co-evolution of technology, organisations and institutions was a complex process requiring actions at various levels (micro, meso, and macro) and between different groups.[67]

Firms also struggled to generate competitive advantages through innovations, and markets determined who stood to benefit from such advantages, and how.[68] Innovation may be defined in very broad terms

---

[64] N. Rosenberg, 'Technological change in the machine tool industry, 1840–1910', *Journal of Economic History* 23 No 4 (1963): p. 423.

[65] N. Rosenberg, *Perspectives on technology* (Cambridge, Cambridge University Press, 1976).

[66] R. B. Gordon, 'Who turned the mechanical ideal into mechanical reality?', *Technology and Culture* 29 No 4 (1988). K. Alder, 'Making things the same: representation, tolerance and the end of the ancien régime in France', *Social Studies of Science* 28 No 4 (1998). J. Mokyr, 'Technological inertia in economic history', *Journal of Economic History* 52 No 2 (1992).

[67] Nelson, 'Co-evolution of industry structure'.

[68] Michael Porter and David Teece had raised this issue in the 1980s but have focused mainly on technological innovations. D. J. Teece, 'Profiting from technological innovation: Implications for integration, collaboration, licensing and public policy', *Research*

and included the opening of new markets or new ways of marketing, new sources of materials, new ways of organising and so on, in addition to product or process innovation due to technological change.[69] Who stood to benefit from the innovation depended upon how the interdependent relationships were managed in an industry and how property rights were delineated along these relationships. On one hand, national factor endowments affected the competitive (or comparative) advantage that some firms secured, while on the other hand, market structure, managerial capability and firm-level behaviour were crucially (if not more) important in determining who benefited from the competitive advantage.[70] Nevertheless, the issue of who benefited from innovations is more complex than the factor endowment or the firm capability explanations suggest. It was also dependent upon the structure of the industry itself.[71] The set of rules which governed an industry architecture, and which were highly localised, not only defined the value creation and division of labour, that is, who could do what, but also how that value was to be appropriated and divided, that is, who got what.[72] Division of labour and value appropriation depended as much upon interdependencies as distinguishing oneself from others; competitive advantages were derived from conformity as well as differentiation.

Standardisation and the sameness of things

Economic and industrial growth, coupled with dynamic organisations and industrial structure, presented information and coordination problems for firms and business groups. Standardisation was one of the strategies that firms adopted to manage these issues. For manufactured products, there was a gradual but definite move towards interchangeability that involved 'making things the same'. The techniques of interchangeable manufacturing that originated in the state armouries of eighteenth-century France were similar to those adopted by engineers and businesses

Policy 15 No 6 (1986). M. E. Porter, 'Technology and competitive advantage', *Journal of Business Strategy* 5 No 3 (1985).

[69] J. A. Schumpeter, *The theory of economic development*, R. Opie (trans.) (Cambridge, MA, Harvard University Press, 1934), chapter 2.

[70] S. B. Saul, 'The market and the development of the mechanical engineering industries in Britain, 1860–1914', *Economic History Review* 20 No 1 (1967). R. C. Floud, 'The adolescence of American engineering competition, 1860–1900', *Economic History Review* 27 No 1 (1974). R. C. Allen, 'International competition in iron and steel, 1850–1913', *Journal of Economic History* 39 No 4 (1979).

[71] Nelson, 'Co-evolution of industry structure'.

[72] Jacobides et al., 'Benefiting from innovation'.

in Britain in the early nineteenth century. Such techniques were further refined and became known as the American system of manufacturing.[73] Interchangeability depended upon standardised design and specification in addition to standardised machining techniques and tools. This is what gave the products the sameness quality.[74]

Apart from sameness, businesses depended upon making things consistent. This was particularly apparent in situations in which a range of products and commodities were exchanged. Businesses had to make distinctions between products whilst ensuring individual products retained their sameness – after all, no business sold or purchased a single product! In the railways sector, for instance, the tension between distinctiveness and sameness is amply manifest. The Railway Clearing House, which introduced a standardised system of fares and charges across various railway companies, grappled with the unenviable task of distinguishing between different goods and passengers. The Railway Clearing House General Classification of Goods described thousands of separate items within various classes and filled a 129-page book.[75] Similar clearing house solutions to the sameness–distinctiveness tensions are evident in the quality grading systems that developed within international commodities such as wheat and cotton.[76]

The sameness–distinctiveness tensions were not only evident for tangible products and commodities. Intangible substances, such as gas and electricity, which were increasingly commodified in this period, generated a different set of standardisation issues. How to standardise, measure and thereby monetise utilities based upon electrical resistance, for example, telegraphy and electricity?[77] What was the illuminating power of gas? How to measure the passage of one cubic foot of gas and thereby

---

[73] K. Alder, 'Innovation and amnesia: engineering rationality and the fate of interchangeable parts manufacturing in France', *Technology and Culture* 38 No 2 (1997). Alder, 'Making things the same'. Saul, 'British engineering industries'. D. A. Hounshell, *From the American system to mass production 1800–1932: the development of manufacturing technology in the United States* (Baltimore, Johns Hopkins University Press, 1984). A. E. Musson and E. Robinson, 'The origins of engineering in Lancashire', *Journal of Economic History* 20 No 2 (1960).

[74] Nasmyth, 'Slide principle'.

[75] P. S. Bagwell, *The Railway Clearing House in the British economy 1842–1922* (London, Allen and Unwin, 1968), p. 75.

[76] A. L. Olmstead and P. W. Rhode, 'Hog-round marketing, seed quality, and government policy: institutional change in US cotton production, 1920–1960', *Journal of Economic History* 63 No 2 (2003).

[77] B. J. Hunt, 'The ohm is where the art is: British telegraph engineers and development of electrical standards', *Osiris* 9 (1994).

charge the consumer appropriately?[78] Such issues of quantification and standardised measurements brought together men of science and men of business – and at times even the state. The debates involving such measurements were not dissimilar to those involving accounting measures such as discounted cash flow techniques, risk-regulated rates of return or insurance risks.[79] Standardising measurements led to making products tradable and fungible through an institutional process: many of these products were not inherently tradable to begin with.

The sameness–distinctiveness–quantification tensions are manifest in the lengthy and heated debates surrounding seemingly mundane questions, for example, how much coal or wheat does one bushel contain? These tensions transcended considerations of compatibility, path dependency and lock-in. The development of measurement standards needs to be placed in the broader context of contractual liability and the politics of the market.[80] The changing attitudes and approaches to scientific thinking intersected with standardisation of measurements as an ex ante solution to problems of information and coordination.

Dynamics of contractual liability

The legal view of contractual liability in the nineteenth century was considerably different from the principles held in the eighteenth century, when the law and courts were usually concerned with the fairness in exchange, a principle congruent with traditional morality. The gradual rise of legal formalism in the nineteenth century implied that the 'protective, regulative and paternalistic' conception of law gave way to the expressions of individualistic desires and the economic and political organisation.[81] This is evident in the increasing application of the doctrine of caveat emptor by the courts from the early nineteenth century. The legal view resting upon this doctrine was that the consequence of

---

[78] Daunton and Hilton, *Politics of consumption*.

[79] S. Brackenborough et al., 'The emergence of discounted cash flow analysis in the Tyneside coal industry c1700–1820', *British Accounting Review* 33 No 2 (2001). R. Pearson, 'Moral hazard and the assessment of insurance risk in eighteenth- and early-nineteenth-century Britain', *Business History Review* 76 No 1 (2002). Porter, *Trust in numbers*.

[80] S. M. Greenstein and V. Stango (eds), *Standards and public policy* (Cambridge, Cambridge University Press, 2007). D. J. Puffert, *Tracks across continents, paths through history: the economic dynamics of standardization in railway gauge* (Chicago, University of Chicago Press, 2009).

[81] M. J. Horwitz, 'The rise of legal formalism', *American Journal of Legal History* 19 No 4 (1975). P. S. Atiyah, *The rise and fall of freedom of contract* (Oxford, Clarendon Press, 1979).

a bad bargain rested solely upon the buyer. The principle of good faith implied in this view meant that the seller

ought to disclose unusual facts known to him, but not known to the other party to the transaction . . . good faith forbids either party, by concealing what he privately knows, to draw the other into a bargain, from his ignorance of that fact and his believing the contrary.[82]

Caveat emptor in contracts for sale of goods did not require full disclosure by the seller, unlike insurance contracts. The mercantilist Joshua Child remarked in *A New Discourse on Trade* (c. 1868) that 'no man can be cheated except it be with his own consent; and we commonly say *caveat emptor*'.[83] The willingness of the courts to judge on the basis of this doctrine is considered as evidence by some to be a gradual move away from establishing the morality or fairness in exchange – an apotheosis of nineteenth-century individualism.[84]

While this doctrine moved away from providing legal protection against a bad bargain, it nevertheless intersected with the principle of protection against *deliberate* fraud or misrepresentation. As was the historical practice, the buyer continued to be accorded protection through legislation in instances when visual examination of a good was insufficient to highlight its defects such as incorrect measurement. If the use of false measurements, or giving 'short measure', was not evident from the buyer's due vigilance but rather depended upon the seller's assurance, then legislation tended to protect the buyer's reliance on the seller. Although this view potentially interfered with the right of freedom to contract, embodied in part within caveat emptor, protection against fraud was not to be equated with protection against poor quality. The statutes provided protection against fraud but not other means of opportunistic behaviour.

Thus the weights and measures legislation, in addition to establishing the metrological standards, was meant to prevent behaviour that facilitated fraud. In this regard, this legislation tended to be similar in principle to laws legislating adulteration of food and drink, hallmarking and assaying, general merchandise marking, licensing of doctors, protection of passengers in carriages and railways and so on. It did not, and could not, solve all problems of asymmetric information surrounding market transactions.

---

[82] Lord Mansfield's principle is cited in Atiyah, *Rise and fall of freedom of contract*, p. 168.
[83] J. Child, *A new discourse on trade* (Glasgow, 1751), p. 98.
[84] Horwitz, 'Legal formalism', p. 262. Atiyah, *Rise and fall of freedom of contract*, pp. 178, 464. The application of this doctrine in the United Kingdom may not have been as widespread as historically implied or even as commonly applied as in the United States. The stern severity of the principle was often tempered with the views of the older generation of judges and lawyers.

The solutions that emerged to the measurement problems, including the measurement practices that were developed, must be considered in the context of the sociopolitical tensions between caveat emptor and the prevention of fraud. Legislation making it compulsory to sell dry goods by weight, and an offence to sell them by volume (Chapter 4), needs to be considered in terms of the contractual freedom it limited, the protection against false measurements it provided and the extent to which it left other contractual issues (e.g. condition of the goods) to the due diligence of the buyer. Similarly, the legal but nonobligatory use of the standard gauge to measure wire sizes (Chapter 5) must be considered from the perspective of asymmetric information and the intent to defraud.

Another dynamic that shaped contractual liability was the movement away from litigation to arbitration in commercial disputes, particularly those involving trading and other business enterprises. Evidence suggests that after circa 1850, businesses and commercial concerns began to bypass the courts, as a trial forum, and relied instead on adjudication by commercial institutions such as trade associations, exchanges and chambers of commerce.[85] This form of adjudication depended upon the arbitration systems and machinery developed by the commercial institutions and was seen by the community as a quicker and less capricious method of settling disputes. Both economic (the relative costs involved in arbitration as opposed to litigation) and political factors (primarily concerning whether juries without the commercial acumen and experience could understand the evidence) appear to have shaped this dynamic.

In conjunction with the dynamics around the freedom to contract, this move towards more nonforensic methods of limiting or ensuring contractual liabilities shaped the solutions to measurement issues. Centralisation and standardisation of measurement practices (Chapter 6) is an example of how commercial institutions developed arbitration systems and mechanisms. This not only provided the institutions with efficient dispute resolution systems but also helped to standardise commercial practices that prevented disputes in the first place. This resulted in yet another socioeconomic boundary between the state and the market.

Politics of the market

Solutions to transactional and contractual issues, whether through standardisation, legislation or adjudication, were steeped in the wider politics of the market. While standardisation and legislation were ex ante

---

[85] R. B. Ferguson, 'The adjudication of commercial disputes and the legal system in modern England', *British Journal of Law and Society* 7 No 2 (1980).

solutions, aimed at preventing opportunistic behaviour, adjudication was an ex post remedy. They were shaped by how different groups conceived the market and the transactions within it. Paul Johnson argues that contemporary economists saw the market differently from others. While the economists viewed the market as made of a multitude of buyers and sellers 'all freely and frenetically competing', the lawyers viewed market interactions as between 'principals and agents', employing complex forms of contract and holding overlapping and conflicting duties and liabilities.[86]

Not all Victorians considered markets to be neutral or an arena for competitive exchange in which market principles operated untrammelled by authority. Indeed, the tensions between morality, equity, liberty (of exchange) and protection (against exploitation) were quite legitimate in creating and maintaining market relationships. This is not to imply that forces of demand and supply did not discipline market behaviour but rather to emphasise that the market was a legal and ideological construct, shaped by value judgements, promoting some interests and not others. This may seem inconceivable to many observers today – it did so to free market theorists then. Geoffrey Searle writes that several Victorian thinkers and writers questioned whether market forces were compatible with 'moral values', whether the two could be reconciled if they clashed and just how dangerous it was to promote market forces without having some 'authority' adjudicate when they did.[87]

The question was not if intervention in the market was legitimate but under what circumstances it was legitimate to intervene – a balancing mechanism if the market failed. Thus it was legitimate to intervene to set professional standards for doctors, lawyers and so on to protect the general public against exploitation by monopolies, fraudsters and similar persons to provide public goods or to protect against harmful externalities.[88] It was also considered legitimate to control competition when it was seen as excessive or misapplied or where its redistributive effects had undesirable social and political consequences.[89] The issues at stake here were the prevention of exploitative, fraudulent and opportunistic behaviour;

---

[86] P. Johnson, 'Market disciplines', in P. Mandler (ed.) *Liberty and authority in Victorian Britain* (Oxford, Oxford University Press, 2006), p. 215.

[87] G. R. Searle, *Morality and the market in Victorian Britain* (Oxford, Clarendon Press, 1998), pp. 255–56.

[88] Johnson, 'Market disciplines', citing J. S. Mill. Searle, *Morality and the market*, p. 254. Also Daunton, 'Material politics of natural monopoly'. Atiyah, *Rise and fall of freedom of contract*.

[89] A. Gambles, *Protection and politics: conservative economic discourse 1815–1852* (London, Royal Historical Society, 1999).

the establishment of the facts when such behaviour occurred; and the remedies for market failure, however it could be defined.

Proponents of protectionist and interventionist disciplining of the market from without for social, political and economic cohesion were nevertheless challenged by those who sought to establish an alternative political economy. The opponents were encouraged by the seemingly resilient and responsive markets, both during periods of exceptional crises and during less anxious and desperate periods.[90] Arguably the market was a sociopolitical construct rather than a natural phenomenon. Market relationships were shaped by opposing or divergent political views regarding fairness, morality, liberty and authority. The harsh discipline of the market was balanced by the authority of the politicians, bureaucrats or even the Church. These forces shaped the material politics of commodities and consumption. They defined relations between consumers and producers, between large and small businesses, between businesses and its stakeholders and between the different classes of consumers (e.g. large institutional buyers vs small individual consumers, men and women, etc.).[91]

The protectionist–interventionist discourse also shaped the boundaries between the state and business concerns – a particular focus of this book. Timothy Alborn defines modern companies as institutions that proactively employ a balance of political and economic means to achieve economic ends.[92] In fact, this view extends easily beyond the joint-stock company generally to other firms, businesses, entrepreneurs and merchants. The historical cases in this book show how merchants, firms, entrepreneurs and so on were able to command political resources to solve their particular economic and business issues. The historical material shows why and how businesses could successfully move Parliament to propose favourable legislation or lobby state departments to intervene on their behalf.

Conversely, the state occasionally considered its role to intervene in the market – if not to regulate then to adjudicate or arbitrate. T. H. Farrer, the permanent secretary of the Board of Trade, suggested that the board felt itself bound to act fairly as an arbitrator between consumers and companies.[93] The tensions between state action and market liberty surfaced where the state sought to protect businesses in instances when it felt the businesses were not competent to detect exploitation or maltreatment. The state also considered the extent to which it could, and should,

---

[90] Ibid., p. 19. Johnson, 'Market disciplines'.
[91] Daunton, 'Material politics of natural monopoly'.
[92] T. L. Alborn, *Conceiving companies: joint-stock politics in Victorian England* (London, Routledge, 1998), p. 2.
[93] *Report from Select Committee on the Metropolis Gas*, PP Vol. VI 1876, p. 12.

intervene to regulate or adjudicate and leave the market forces to limit or discipline opportunistic behaviour.

This clash of principles, ideologies and interests meant that similar problems had different solutions in different sectors born out of sociopolitical processes rather than the problem-solving, decision-making processes of a visible (or invisible) hand. Even when the state or business groups turned to men of science to help regulate or adjudicate, we can discern the rhetoric of objectivity and the presence of personal values that shaped expert validation.

Implications

The rich historical material presented in this book shows why markets and businesses continued to encounter fundamental measurement issues despite metrological standardisation in the nineteenth century. It reveals how solutions to those issues required a balance of economic logic and political power. It shows how networks of individuals – merchants and traders, engineers and entrepreneurs, scientists and technocrats, politicians and bureaucrats – argued, debated, fought, negotiated, bargained, lobbied and competed with each other to secure their own interests and goals, be they economic, political, social or personal. The material reveals how there was no coherent, coordinated or unambiguous effort to replace the inefficient with the efficient, the inferior with the superior, the fragmentary with the unified, the subjective with the objective or the personal with the universal. Realism was also shaped by conventions and norms and not driven entirely by values of precision and accuracy. Economic institutions persisted or emerged because they worked well with other institutions, not necessarily because they made markets and transactions more efficient. The standards that the institutions instituted at the meso-level tempered the more formal disciplining or control of markets from without; the public standards provided by these institutions were privately set and voluntarily adopted. On the whole, people used the new, unified and centralised metrological tools and weights and measures units to make measurements, but they continued to rely upon locally accepted practices to determine just how reliable those measurements were.

2   Inching towards the metre

Measurements, metrology and reform

A general uniformity of Weights and Measures is so obviously desirable
[that] its establishment has been a fundamental principle in the English
constitution from time immemorial . . . At the same time, it has commonly been considered as one of those objects which cannot [be] very
precisely defined, [and] there are many instances in which departure
from complete uniformity is not only tolerated, but established by law.

    – parliamentary report on weights and measures, 1819

Pre-Imperial measurement units were highly contextual. Their meaning,
significance and usage varied depending upon the context in which they
were used. The metrological reforms of the nineteenth century sought to
decontextualise these units and make them uniform across all contexts –
in their meaning, uses and significance. Kula refers to this as the transition
from 'representational' to 'conventional' units, that is, a transition from
those units that represented or expressed human conditions or values to
those that have no particular significance and are acceptable as a matter of
convention.[1] Historically, variability (as opposed to uniformity) was not
always undesirable, and variable measurements had specific economic
functions. In those situations, the variable weights and measures were
not considered unreliable. Formal and informal institutions (i.e. rules,
norms, etc.) helped to mitigate any unreliability or confusion according
to simple do-and-don't rules.

    Metrological reform affected the organisation of such institutions in
the nineteenth century. The state bureaucracy was intimately involved
in the British metrological reform. However, the initiative for it came
from private political as well as scientific and bureaucratic interests.[2]

---

[1] W. Kula, *Measures and men*, R. Szreter (trans.) (Princeton, Princeton University Press,
1986), p. 120.
[2] J. Hoppit, 'Reforming Britain's weights and measures, 1660–1824', *English Historical
Review* 108 No 426 (1993). R. Adell, 'The British metrological standardization debate,
1756–1824: The importance of parliamentary sources in its reassessment', *Parliamentary
History* 22 No 2 (2003).

In comparison, some of the pre-eminent scientific thinkers of the Enlightenment – Condorcet, Delambre, Lavoisier, Cassini and so on – drove the French metric reforms. These savants wished to replace the 'Babel of measurement' with a universal language of measures to bring order and reason to the exchange of goods and information.[3]

Other Western and Central European nation-states adopted the French metric system during the latter half of the nineteenth century.[4] The adoption of metric units in most nations coincided with major reforms that standardised, unified and replaced the disparate weights and measures in common use. In Italy and Germany, metrication coincided with political unification in the 1860s. Seventeen nations signed the Convention du Mètre in 1875, one of the first international treaties on scientific standards. This treaty established the metric units as an international standard system of measurements. Britain eventually signed the treaty in 1884. However, owing to fierce domestic resistance, metric units were not legally permissible in commercial trade contracts in Britain until 1898.[5]

Fundamentally, the issues of metrological reform transcended the battles between the proponents and opponents of the metric system. Metrological reform strengthened the scientific and bureaucratic centres of metrology. In fact, reform entailed the intersection of the interests of such centres. Reform also enabled metrological chains to tie local measurement practices to the centre more explicitly. However, as I argue in this chapter and the next, Bruno Latour's view of the centres and the chains is useful only to a certain extent.[6]

In Britain, reform did not impose the centre's – that is, the state's – view on all commercial sectors. This was despite efforts of several groups, including pro-metric groups, to impose a particular *type* of reform everywhere. This meant that many measurement practices in the nineteenth-century markets lay outside such Latourian chains, probably outside the view of the centres, and that not all practices were tied to the centre. This contrasts with the French experience, in which the scientific and bureaucratic centre sought to extend its influence everywhere. The 'action at a distance' view may be useful in understanding how the centre sought to manage the periphery through formal codes, but it does not completely

---

[3] K. Alder, *The measure of all things: the seven-year odyssey and hidden error that transformed the world* (New York, Free Press, 2003), p. 2.

[4] E. F. Cox, 'The metric system: a quarter-century of acceptance (1851–1876)', *Osiris* 13 (1958).

[5] R. D. Connor, *The weights and measures of England* (London, HMSO, 1987). R. E. Zupko, *Revolution in measurement: Western European weights and measures since the age of science* (Philadelphia, American Philosophical Society, 1990).

[6] B. Latour, *Science in action: how to follow scientists and engineers through society* (Cambridge, MA, Harvard University Press, 1987), pp. 250–57.

illuminate how people, merchants, businesses and so on accepted locally made measurements as reliable, trustworthy and actionable. To understand this requires a study of local practices. In Britain – and some of its colonies, such as Canada – local market practices were loosely tied to the centre. The view from the centre would obscure much of what went on in the periphery.

Nature and variability of historical measurements

Historical measurements were based on anthropocentric measurement units; they were based on the human form and in time evolved into units 'derived from the conditions, objectives, and outcomes of human labour'.[7] Such measurements were based upon social contexts and became representational in addition to being functional.[8] Often, measurement units were related to the method of production, such as those in the cloth trades used to measure the width of the cloth. The ell and the yard were both used to signify the breadth or width of cloth as produced on the looms.[9] Measurement units also represented the manner in which commodities were transported, reflecting the means as well as the method of transportation. Wagonloads and cartfuls represented the method of transportation, whereas sacks, scoops and vats signified the means of handling or distribution. Productivity signalling units included those that indicated the extent of land that could be ploughed in a day or by a team of oxen and horses.[10] Measurements based on such measurement units indicated human labours and were embedded in the context in which they were used.

This contextuality is especially evident in measurement units that were used in specialised occupations. In the production of coal on the estates of northern England, 'a baffling variety' of units were in use, including chaldrons, tens, keels, weys, tons, metts, vats, quarters, bushels, corves, scoops, rooks, dozens, fothers, loads (cart-, wain-, wagon-, horse- etc.)

---

[7] Kula, *Measures and men*, p. 5. He uses the term *anthropometric* to mean measures derived from the human body rather than measuring human form. The term is a translation of the Polish word *antropometryczne* (p. 24); I prefer to use the term *anthropocentric* to mean measurements centered not only on human form but also on human activities and occupations; cf. R. Tavernor, *Smoot's ear: the measure of humanity* (New Haven, Yale University Press, 2007), p. 2.

[8] The term *representational* is a translation from the Polish word for 'meaning' or 'significance' (*znaczenie* or *znaczeniowy*) and connotes 'to stand for', i.e. measurement units themselves signifying that which is being measured. For example, land was measured in units that signified how much land could be worked upon from sunrise to sunset. Kula, *Measures and men*, p. 3.

[9] Connor, *English measures*, p. 87.

[10] Ibid., p. 37. Kula, *Measures and men*, p. 4.

and others.[11] Units such as chaldrons and keels were fairly specific to the coal trade and signified measurements used in the delivery and transportation of the commodity. In the weighing of wool, the trade used units such as the sack of wool, which was to be composed of two weighs (weys), which in turn were to comprise twenty-eight stone or 350 pounds. A load or char of lead, wool, tallow or cheese was expected to be twelve weighs (weys).[12]

The highly contextual nature of historical measurement units implies that it is difficult to classify them neatly according to the physical property that they measured, that is, weight, volume, linear measure and so on. The bushel, for example, was a measurement unit that has been around at least since the thirteenth century. One of the earliest references to this unit links it to the gallon, a volumetric measure, which in turn is linked to the pound, a weight measure.[13] This chain of weight measure (pounds) defining a volumetric measure (gallons) in turn defining a volumetric measure (bushel) was reaffirmed once again in the late fifteenth century.[14] After the seventeenth century, the bushel was mainly used for the measurement of dry goods such as seeds, barley, malt, fruits and vegetables, grain and coal. But without a reference to some specific context, it was never unambiguously clear whether it was used as a unit of weight or volume (Figure 2.1).

A nineteenth-century survey of existing legal and customary units suggests that several different bushel units were in contemporary use.[15] Depending upon the commodity being measured, the bushel was defined using either a volumetric or a weight unit. Just as it was used to measure coal (the coal bushel), the bushel was also used to measure fruits and was equivalent to thirty-three quarts or four pecks. In contrast, the bushel used to measure wheat, rye, barley, oats, flour or salt was based on a unit of weight and was linked to the pound.[16] Not only did the nature of the

---

[11] J. Hatcher, *The history of the British coal industry*, Vol. 1, *Before 1700* (Oxford, Clarendon Press, 1993), p. 557.

[12] Connor, *English measures*, p. 130.

[13] Ibid., p. 151. Both the *Tractatus de Ponderibus et Mensuris* and the Assize of Bread and Ale of the mid-thirteenth century state that thirty-two grains of wheat make a *sterling* (penny) and twenty pence make an ounce and twelve ounces make a pound and eight pounds make a gallon of wine and eight gallons of wine make a bushel of London, which is the eighth part of a quarter.

[14] Ibid., p. 153.

[15] This survey was part of the second report prepared by the Royal Commission on Weights and Measures. *Second report of the commissioners on weights and measures*, PP Vol. VII 1820.

[16] Ibid., p. 483, appendix A. The pound equivalent of one bushel for these commodities was as follows: wheat (56 or 57), rye (55), barley (49 or 50; in Sussex it could be 53), oats (38), flour (or bread or biscuit; 42 or 45), salt (56, 65, 75 or 120; foreign salt could be 84).

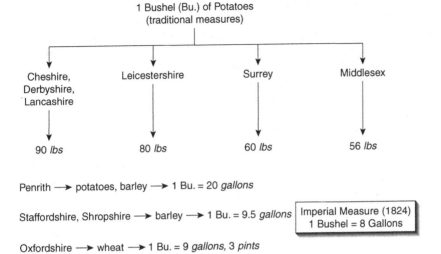

Figure 2.1. Diversity of measurement units, e.g. bushel. *Source*: PP Vol. VII 1820, pp. 477–509.

bushel unit depend upon the commodity being measured, it also varied between geographical locations. The bushel used to measure potatoes in Cheshire, Derbyshire and Lancashire was equivalent to ninety pounds, whereas in Leicestershire, it was equivalent to eighty pounds; in Surrey, it was sixty pounds; and in Middlesex, it was fifty-six pounds. Wheat was measured in Cheshire and Liverpool using a bushel of seventy pounds, but in Stockton, it was equivalent to sixty pounds. In Cheshire and Liverpool, barley was measured using a bushel of sixty pounds, whereas in Devonshire, it was measured using a bushel of fifty pounds. In Penrith, potatoes and barley were measured using a bushel of twenty gallons, whereas in Staffordshire and Shropshire, barley was measured using a bushel of nine and a half gallons. Barley was sometimes measured in Liverpool using a bushel of thirty-four and a half quarts or nine gallons (Winchester measure), whereas wheat was measured in Oxfordshire using a bushel of nine gallons and three pints (Figure 2.1). Although these practices were based on local usage and customary norms, most of them became codified by legislation over the years.

Another commonly used measurement unit, the ton, also exhibited similar variations. Although nominally equivalent to twenty hundred-weight or 2,240 pounds avoirdupois, in the early nineteenth century, a ton of wheat was equivalent to twenty bushels, a ton of lead was equivalent to nineteen and a half hundredweight, and a ton of linseed oil was equivalent to 236 gallons. Similarly, a ton of barley was equivalent to 1,709 pounds, whereas on the canals, a ton of oak or ash could be either forty or forty-eight cubic feet. There were regional variations to the ton and the context in which it was used. In Derbyshire, the ton used to measure bark, gypsum, lime, coal, straw, hay, lead ore and so on was the equivalent of twenty-four hundred pounds, whereas the ton used to measure grindstones was fifteen cubic feet, and that used to measure broken stones was twenty bushels. A ton of potatoes in Essex weighed 2,520 pounds, in Berwickshire they weighed twenty-eight hundredweight (or 3,136 pounds),[17] and in Kincardineshire they weighed four bolls.[18] A ton of timber in Devonshire or Wiltshire was forty cubic feet, whereas a ton of sifted gravel in Stratford, Middlesex, was twenty-three cubic feet. Portland stone in Dorset was sixteen cubic feet to the ton, whereas limestone in Leicestershire was forty bushels (five quarters) to the ton.

Variation in measurements

The contextuality and variability of measurement units are mirrored in measurements, that is, the information based on such units. Measurements were based on practices, norms and conventions that varied according to context and geography. For example, many dry goods, including grain, fruit, coal and so on, were measured for sale using volumetric units using vessels that were round in shape.[19] A common practice while measuring dry goods in this way was to form a heap such that the total quantity given would contain the amount within the vessel as well as in the heap on top. The practice of heaping was customary in England since the medieval period, and the method in which the heap was to be provided was sometimes regulated by legislation.[20] This was not a consistent practice, and dry goods were also measured using the stricken measure, that is, without the heap. A statute from the fourteenth century, while stating that corn should generally be measured without heap, required that measurements of corn relating to the rents and farms of lords be given according to the heaped measure. The extra quantity included in the heap differed according to the location and the type of commodity and according to trade.

---

[17] If shipped for London and assuming 112 pounds make one hundredweight.
[18] Equivalent to the standard English ton of twenty hundredweight.
[19] Connor, *English measures*, pp. 178–79.
[20] 12 Anne Stat. 2 C.17, 1713. Act for Ascertaining the Coal Measure regulated the coal bushel. The statute specified the shape of the container representing the measure as well as the size of the heap. See also Connor, *English measures*, pp. 179 and 56.

Rules regarding the heap changed between the fourteenth and eighteenth centuries. The extra amount included in the heaped bushel
increased from about one-eighth of the physical measure, during the time
of Henry VII, to about one-quarter, during the reign of Queen Anne. The
practice of heaping endured for centuries, initially as the privileges of the
lords, kings and even the universities of Oxford and Cambridge, eventually becoming a part of commonly used measurements. Such practices
meant that measurements were highly approximate even when nominally invariable measurement units were used. Eight heaped bushels could
contain the equivalent volume of ten, or more, or less, nominal bushels,
depending upon the extent of heaping. The custom and practice in the
market often differed from the legal provision. Market practice provided
eight heaped bushels as if they were nine stricken legal bushels. Over
time, the nine bushel measure had become common in usage and was
given a name, the fatt (or vat). As a consequence, nine heaped bushels, or
the fatt, became equivalent to ten stricken legal bushels.[21] Such practices
were common in many markets until the nineteenth century, particularly
in commodity trades using volumetric measures for dry goods such as
coal and grain (Chapters 4 and 6).

Another example of variable measurements is the variation in the size
of the bread loaf as regulated by the Assize of Bread and Ale.[22] The assize
specified different weights of loaves of bread for a fixed price of a farthing
(a quarter of a penny) in inverse proportion to the price of a quarter of
wheat. As the price of one quarter of wheat increased, the weight of a
farthing loaf was to decrease proportionately, as specified by the assize.
This mechanism ensured that a loaf costing a farthing would always be
available to the poorest customers, even though they would receive less
bread for a farthing when grain prices increased. Thus buyers would
in effect pay more for the same amount of bread, although they were
expected simply to reduce their bread intake when grain prices rose.[23]

The assize maintained a constant price for a loaf of bread, but it adjusted for changes in value by changing the quantity available per unit of
price. This mechanism established a relationship between grain price and
weight for each type of loaf of bread and ensured that bakers would make
a sufficient return despite the fluctuations in grain price, while the poor
could still afford to buy bread.[24] The assize existed until the nineteenth

[21] Connor, *English measures*, pp. 156–58.
[22] J. Davis, 'Baking for the common good: a reassessment of the assize of bread in medieval
England', *Economic History Review* 57 No 3 (2004): p. 468. The Assize was known as
the Assisa Panis et Cervisie.
[23] Ibid., p. 469.
[24] Ibid., p. 479, esp. table 3. Cf. Connor, *English measures*, pp. 193–227.

century; however, its enforcement had dwindled by the late eighteenth century, and the practice was eventually abolished in 1836.[25] Such a practice was not unique to medieval England but was common across medieval Europe.[26]

Some historians consider the variability of historical measurements as evidence of the existence of a moral economy of the poor (as opposed to the rich). E. P. Thompson, who is credited with the first use of the term, wrote that while measuring grain, the poor were given the right to shake the measure – 'so valuable was the poor man's corn that a looseness in the measure might make the difference to him of a day without a loaf.'[27] Other historians argue that such morality – to convey generosity – was not confined to the poor alone. Measurements that captured information about productivity, such as measures of land area, were used to allow farmers disadvantaged by poor soil fertility or climate to trade on equal terms with those farmers fortunate enough to till richer or more fertile lands.[28] Variation in customary measures is viewed as a 'system of handicapping, theoretically ensuring that everyone arrived at the finishing line together'.[29] Whether as charity to the poor, or as generosity towards the less privileged, such considerations cannot have failed to generate reciprocity and repetition. Measurement variability was reinforced and formalised, for better or for worse, and became accepted as market practice.

In the grain trade, merchants in several market towns would use a weighted bushel, where the grain measures were expressed in terms of density, that is, weight per volume or *natural weight*, as it was sometimes known. For example, around 1830, wheat brought into market towns such as Sheffield from other towns such as Gainsborough and Lynn was sold by the bushel weighing 63 pounds – or in equivalent terms, a quarter weighing 504 pounds – whereas wheat from Hull was to be delivered on the basis of 60 pounds per bushel (480 pounds per quarter).

[25] Connor, *English measures*, p. 215. S. Webb and B. Webb, 'The assize of bread', *Economic Journal* 14 No 54 (1904).

[26] Kula, *Measures and men*, pp. 72–75.

[27] E. P. Thompson, 'The moral economy of the English crowd in the eighteenth century', *Past and Present* 50 No 1 (1971): p. 102. R. Sheldon et al., 'Popular protest and the persistence of customary corn measures: resistance to the Winchester bushel in the English west', in A. Randall and A. Charlesworth (eds) *Markets, market culture and popular protest in eighteenth-century Britain and Ireland* (Liverpool, Liverpool University Press, 1996), p. 34. Shaking the measuring vessel while pouring the grain increased the amount of grain contained in the measure. See Chapter 6 in this volume.

[28] J. Hoppit, 'Income, welfare and the Industrial Revolution in Britain', *Historical Journal* 31 No 3 (1988): p. 90. Kula, *Measures and men*, p. 31.

[29] Hoppit, 'Income and welfare', pp. 89–90.

There is evidence of similar practices across medieval and early modern Europe (Chapter 6).[30] As a result, there may have existed a geography of measures, similar to a geography of prices, such that it is possible to distinguish different contours of measurements used to capture value in different ways.[31]

But measurement variability was based on opportunism as well as privileges or regard. Variable measurements were used for opportunistic reasons, as is evident from the custom of providing the ingrain in the coal trade (Chapter 4). This practice involved the provision of an additional unit given for every score of twenty units. Thus, when twenty chaldrons of coal were delivered, it was customary to provide an additional chaldron so that the total amount of coal delivered was twenty-one chaldrons instead of twenty. The seller would charge only for twenty chaldrons, in effect providing a discount of 5 per cent on the price.[32] The merchant seller would at times withhold the additional quantity in the score, a practice called *loading bare*, which created a host of monitoring and enforcement issues. Over the centuries, the practice of providing an ingrain became a statutory requirement: legislation in 1807 regulated exactly how the ingrain was supposed to be measured and the conditions under which it was to be provided.[33] Merchants in the coal trade, as in other trades where such practices were present, would benefit from the arbitrage the different measurements could provide – buy using a larger measure and sell using a smaller measure.[34]

Such examples illustrate the variability of measurements, on one hand, but also the institutional rules that emerged to manage them, on the other. The rules that specified, for example, the circumstances in which to provide the heap or the ingrain, or the size of the loaf of bread, served as mechanisms to manage measurements made within particular contexts. Many institutions were themselves the source of measurement variation, however, other institutions served to organise the measurements according to generally known do-and-don't rules. Thus institutions that

---

[30] *Returns from corn inspectors*, PP Vol. XLIX 1834, p. 262. Kula, *Measures and men*, pp. 105–8. S. L. Kaplan, *Provisioning Paris: Merchants and millers in the grain and flour trade during the eighteenth century* (Ithaca, Cornell University Press, 1984), pp. 52–53.

[31] Kula, *Measures and men*, p. 106. J. Thirsk (ed.), *The agrarian history of England and Wales*, Vol. VII, *1640–1750 (agrarian change)* (Cambridge, Cambridge University Press, 1985), p. 815.

[32] *Report of the select committee on coal trade*, PP Vol. VIII 1830, p. 361, appendix 4(h), for an example of deliveries made using the ingrain showing a ship meter's delivery bill.

[33] 47 George III, C.68, 1807, *Act for regulating the delivery of coals*, Para. LXII.

[34] Kula, *Measures and men*, provides examples of similar practices in the grain trade.

organised and managed variability in measurements coexisted with a multiplicity of highly contextual measurement units.

This situation changed during the nineteenth century, when metrological standardisation introduced decontextualised measurement units within the British economy. The introduction of the Imperial measures in 1824 was a historical watershed not only for British metrology but also for the British economy as it helped to redefine existing economic relationships over the next century and beyond.

Reforming Britain's weights and measures

Abstraction and decontextualisation of measurement units from their anthropocentric origins is historical fact and has occurred at different stages throughout history. Transitions from the concrete to abstract or notional measurement units – from the particular 'my bushel', 'your bushel' to the general 'the bushel' – are important turning points in the history of metrology.[35] Abstraction is a complex mental act demanding the ability to abstract a single common (physical) property from several qualitatively different objects and subsequently to use that property as a comparator. Thus, from the wine gallon and the ale gallon, two separate measurement units in use since the Middle Ages with slightly different cubic capacities, abstraction involved first selecting one particular attribute to measure: the property to occupy a given volume of space.[36] This then made it possible to define a single notional measurement unit, the gallon, to measure volume in any context (whether liquids or dry goods) and thereby replace all the other different types of gallons that were in use earlier. This abstracted measurement unit did not require any further qualification. Such units would signify only the information about the physical properties they measured, irrespective of the context in which they could be used: this made them decontextualised.

The Imperial measures, introduced in 1824, defined the various measurement units either as units of volumetric measure (or capacity), weight or linear measure. They were expressed purely on a notional basis without any reference to the geographic, occupational, functional or social contexts in which they were to be used.[37] In other words, they were decontextualised. The notionalisation of units, whether a result of anchoring

---

[35] Ibid., p. 24.

[36] The wine gallon equalled 231 cubic inches, whereas the ale gallon equalled 282 cubic inches. See Connor, *English measures*, p. 162.

[37] 5 George IV C. 74, 1824, *Act for ascertaining and establishing uniformity of weights and measures*, Para. VI.

them to some arbitrary artefact or to some artefact linked to a naturally occurring phenomenon, is an important event in the metrological standardisation of the nineteenth century.[38] In metrological terms, the period spanning a century and a half from circa 1750 can be segmented into four chronologically distinct periods. The period 1760–1824 was essentially characterised by the definition of the Imperial system of weights and measures, repealing all previous statutes and attempting to unify all measures and weights. Subsequent legislation modified and refined the standards defined in 1824. The next period, 1824–1850, was largely characterised by restoration of the physical standards that were destroyed by fire at the Houses of Parliament in 1834.[39] The great metric debates occurred after 1851, especially after the first International Exhibition held in London. This period lasted until about 1875, during which the 'battle of the standards' – Imperial versus metric – occurred. The last phase of the story in the nineteenth century ranged between 1875 and 1900, during which time metric measures were introduced in 1878 for purposes other than trade and eventually, in 1898, were permitted for legal use in trade and commercial contracts. During this period, British metrology literally inched towards the metre.

Imperial measures of 1824

Attempts to standardise British weights and measures have had a chequered history. The statutory efforts to unify the standards of weights

---

[38] S. Schaffer, 'Metrology, metrication and Victorian values', in B. Lightman (ed.) *Victorian science in context* (Chicago, University of Chicago Press, 1997), pp. 440–43. Cf. Kula, *Measures and men*, chapter 17. Kula wrote that the traditional measures were 'human' and that the modern measures (i.e. the metric measures) are conventional, 'dehumanized' and alienated (p. 123). Also K. Alder, 'A revolution to measure: the political economy of the metric system in the ancien régime', in M. N. Wise (ed.) *The values of precision*, (Princeton, Princeton University Press, 1995). Hoppit, 'Reforming Britain's measures', p. 90.

[39] I do not discuss this period in depth here. Connor, Zupko and others have given detailed accounts of important metrological developments during this period. Connor, *English measures*. Zupko, *Revolution in measurement*. Simpson provides a detailed account of the reconstruction of the length standards after they were destroyed in a fire in 1834 and describes how reformers gradually separated the primary standards from any natural basis. A. D. C. Simpson, 'The pendulum as the British length standard: a nineteenth-century legal aberration', in R. G. W. Anderson et al. (ed.) *Making instruments count: essays on historical scientific instruments presented to Gerard L'Estrange Turner* (Aldershot, Ashgate, 1993). This is echoed by Schaffer in his account of Herschel and the yard. Schaffer, 'Metrology'. The disputes involving Whitworth and the reconstruction of primary standards are recounted in N. Atkinson, *Sir Joseph Whitworth: 'the world's best mechanician'* (Gloucestershire, Sutton, 1996), chapter 5. For the parallel development of the French metric system during the 1790s, see Alder, *Measure of all things*.

and measures can be traced directly to the Magna Carta of 1225, which stated,

> There shall be [through] our Realm, one Measure of Wine, and one Measure of Ale, and one Measure of Corn; that is to say, the Quarter of London; and one Breadth of dyed Cloth, Ruffets and Haberjects, that is to say, two Yards Culne within the Lifts; And it shall be of Weights as it is of Measures.[40]

Efforts to derive measurement units from natural phenomena were made at various times since then. The Assize of Weights and Measures attributed to the year 1302 or 1303 stated that the 'English penny [shall] weigh thirty-two grains of wheat dry in the midst of the ear'.[41] A statute of Edward II from the fourteenth century states that three barleycorns, round and dry, make an inch, twelve inches a foot, three feet a yard and so on.[42]

Other statutes attempted to link measurement units to each other or to some arbitrary artefact rather than to a natural standard. The statute of Henry VIII from 1531 defined a beer barrel to be equivalent to thirty-six gallons. In the same statute, the barrel for measuring ale is defined as being equivalent to thirty-two gallons. Similarly, the firkin used to measure beer was to be nine gallons, whereas that used for measuring ale was to be eight gallons; and so also for the unit known as kilderkin – eighteen gallons for measuring beer and sixteen gallons for measuring ale.[43] An earlier statute from the fifteenth century had defined the barrel to measure wine to be equivalent to thirty-one and a half gallons.[44] Later, during the reign of Elizabeth I, physical artefacts were made that represented legal standards, such as the Exchequer standard

[40] Magna Carta (Great Charter) of Henry III, 1225, § 25, as reproduced in House of Commons Reports (1738–1765) 1758 Vol. II, *Report of the Carysfort Committee on weights and measures*, p. 413. Many customary British units are pre-Norman, Saxon and even Roman in origin. Connor, *English measures*.

[41] Connor, *English measures*, p. 320. See appendix A (d), which contains the text (in English) of the *Tractatus de Ponderibus et Mensuris* or the Assize of Weights and Measures (c. 1302). This phrase also appears verbatim in 51 Henry III 1266, which is referred to in the select committee report of 1814. *Report from the Committee on Weights and Measures*, PP Vol. III 1813–1814, p. 134. The entire text of the clause is 'that an English Penny called the Sterling, round without clipping, should weigh 32 grains of wheat, well dried and gathered out of the middle of the ear; and 20 pence to make an ounce, 12 ounces a pound, 8 pounds a gallon of wine, and 8 gallons of wine a bushel of London.'

[42] PP Vol. XI 1819, pp. 314–23, appendix B.

[43] *Carysfort Committee Report* (1758), p. 416.

[44] *Carysfort Committee Report* (1758). The statute of 1 Richard III C.13 1485, as reproduced in this report. The statute also defined other units to measure wine or oil such as the ton, which was to be 'twelve *score* and twelve *gallons*', a pipe, equivalent to 'six *score* and six *gallons*', a Tertian, composed of 'four *score* and four *gallons*' and a Hogshead, equivalent to 'sixty three *gallons*.'

gallon, which was a metal vessel stamped with a crown signifying its authenticity. This primary standard was defined as an arbitrary physical artefact with no apparent relation to any naturally occurring standard.[45]

Historically, standardising measurement units did not always involve rationalisation of the number of units in legal use. More often, it meant establishing equivalences between the various units in use. In the eighteenth century, the ale and beer barrels were unified and made equivalent to thirty-six gallons (43 George III).[46] Nevertheless, a barrel of anchovies was defined to be equivalent to sixteen pounds (27 George III), that of apples to be equivalent to three bushels (12 Charles II), that of barilla to be equivalent to 2 hundredweight (12 Charles II), and that of beef to be equivalent to 32 wine gallons (38 George III). A barrel of eels was to be equivalent to forty gallons according to 32 Edward IV but equivalent to thirty gallons according to 2 Henry VI. A barrel of honey was to be thirty-two wine gallons according to 23 Elizabeth but otherwise could be forty-two gallons of twelve pounds each. Various legislative efforts also attempted to enforce the use of particular measurement units to regularise the income of the Crown.[47] For instance, a revenue act of 1660 defined the barrel to be used for beer, ale and other liquors, whereas a finance act of 1701 made it obligatory for the malt trade to use the Winchester bushel.

Reformers in the eighteenth and nineteenth centuries interested in overhauling existing British measures bemoaned the 'despotic influence of custom', which they thought was responsible for the existence of the hundreds of measurement units in use. They argued that historical attempts to standardise measurement units were undertaken on a case-by-case basis and that the result of such uncoordinated and shabby attempts was that 'every new law gave room for exceptions [which] being a departure from the Principle of Uniformity, was probably a precedent for another [departure]'.[48] They also argued that errors in the construction of the physical artefacts, either deliberately or due to poor workmanship, were often perpetuated. Such variations, according to the reformers, crept into general use and were in turn repeatedly sanctioned by their adoption in legislation, leading to the vast diversity of measures.[49] The efforts to standardise measurement units from the eighteenth century onwards became rooted in attempts to reduce their diversity.

---

[45] Connor, *English measures*, p. 159. The Elizabethan standards in turn were derived from older standards of Henry VII.
[46] The following examples are taken from PP Vol. VII 1820, appendix A.
[47] Hoppit, 'Reforming Britain's measures', pp. 92–93.
[48] Ibid. *Carysfort Committee Report* (1758), p. 421.
[49] PP Vol. XI 1819, pp. 314–23, appendix B. *Carysfort Committee Report* (1758), p. 421.

Two parliamentary committees chaired by Lord Carysfort in 1758 and 1759 made a comprehensive study of legal units in force at the time and also made a detailed review of all the existing statutes and legislation regulating weights and measures. The committee recommended that all previous legislation relating to weights and measures be abolished and reduced into a single act. It sought to declare the yard promulgated by Elizabeth as the standard measure of length, to derive the measures of capacity and weight on the basis of this length measure, and to reduce all such measures into a hierarchical arrangement.[50] No legislative action followed this committee's reports in 1758–1759, and for the next half a century, no other official efforts were made to reform British metrology.[51] There were a few exceptions, such as the Act of 1791 regulating the payment of duty on import and export of corn, which allowed the trade to use customary measures while being taxed by the state on the basis of standardised measurement units.[52] Subsequent attempts by Parliament to define standards of weights and measures were made in the early nineteenth century with the appointment of the Select Committee of Weights and Measures, which reported in 1814. Various parliamentary and select committee reports were tabled between 1814 and 1821, and this process eventually culminated in the establishment of the Imperial standards by legislation of 1824.[53]

Between 1760 and 1800, reformers sought to construct more precise copies of the physical standards. Initial attempts revolved around comparing the existing standards kept with the Exchequer and the Royal Society to copies made with newer materials and greater precision. John Bird's copies of the standard yard, commissioned by the Carysfort Committee, were compared to those developed by General William Roy, Sir George Shucksburg and Edward Troughton.[54] Subsequent attempts tried to define the standard yard in comparison to an invariable natural phenomenon such as the arc of the meridian or the length of a pendulum.[55] The French metre was being defined around the same time

---

[50] *Carysfort Committee Report* (1758), p. 438. A copy of the medieval yard had been recently prepared by John Bird, an instrument maker and an acknowledged authority on scale division.

[51] Zupko, *Revolution in measurement*, p. 74. Simpson, 'British length standard', p. 180. Hoppit, 'Reforming Britain's measures', p. 95. A few individual parliamentarians, however, remained active in promoting the need to unify the weights and measures; see Adell, 'British metrology', and Hoppit, 'Reforming Britain's measures'.

[52] Adell, 'British metrology', p. 173. See also 31 George III C 30, 1791, *An act for regulating the importation and exportation of corn . . .* , Para. LVII.

[53] Zupko, *Revolution in measurement*. Adell, 'British metrology'. Hoppit, 'Reforming Britain's measures'.

[54] Simpson, 'British length standard', pp. 180–82. Connor, *English measures*, pp. 249–50.

[55] PP Vol. III 1813–1814, pp. 134–35.

as the ten-millionth part of the arc of the meridian stretching from the pole to the equator. On the basis of the recommendations of Dr W. Hyde Wollaston of the Royal Society and Professor Playfair from Edinburgh, the standard yard was redefined by the length of a pendulum that had a frequency of sixty vibrations per minute (or once every second).

Once the existing standard yard was pegged to a natural or abstract phenomenon, the standards of weight and capacity, too, were defined in a similar fashion. It was discovered that the specific gravity of distilled water was invariable at a given temperature and that one cubic foot of water would weigh one thousand avoirdupois ounces at 52.5 degrees Fahrenheit. In this manner, all the three primary standards of linear measure, weight and capacity could be linked together using some naturally occurring phenomenon, the reformers argued. The reformers were also keen to achieve economy in the number of units as well as simplicity in which units within a given hierarchy were calibrated with each other. In defining the equivalence between the different measures using the weight of water as a reference, the reformers suggested,

It is desirable that all minute fractions of weight should be avoided. There will be much less chance of error [if] only one or two weights are employed, than if a greater number were necessary, which would be the case if fractional parts were required.[56]

In this fashion, the 1824 act introduced legal standards that were devoid of significance in any particular geographic or occupational context and were linked to abstract and natural phenomena that were considered to be invariable (Figure 2.2). Or were they?

The new Imperial units were not completely devoid of any social context. The eighteenth-century attempts to define the standard yard were efforts to redefine an existing measurement artefact in invariable terms rather than defining a new measurement unit, as the French savants attempted with the metre.[57] The nineteenth-century attempts to peg the standard yard of thirty-six inches to the seconds pendulum was really an attempt to discover a natural phenomenon that would correspond to a measurement unit that had been arbitrarily determined and generally accepted through long usage and custom. The thirty-six inches of this standard yard could be linked to the pendulum in an invariable fashion only under some particular circumstances. The length of the pendulum

[56] Ibid., p. 135.
[57] Connor, *English measures*, p. 243. Simpson, 'British length standard', p. 179. Alder, *Measure of all things*.

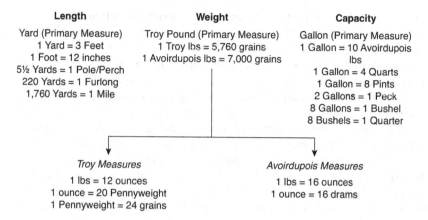

Length	Weight	Capacity
Yard (Primary Measure)	Troy Pound (Primary Measure)	Gallon (Primary Measure)
1 Yard = 3 Feet	1 Troy lbs = 5,760 grains	1 Gallon = 10 Avoirdupois
1 Foot = 12 inches	1 Avoirdupois lbs = 7,000 grains	lbs
5½ Yards = 1 Pole/Perch		1 Gallon = 4 Quarts
220 Yards = 1 Furlong		1 Gallon = 8 Pints
1,760 Yards = 1 Mile		2 Gallons = 1 Peck
		8 Gallons = 1 Bushel
		8 Bushels = 1 Quarter

Troy Measures	Avoirdupois Measures
1 lbs = 12 ounces	1 lbs = 16 ounces
1 ounce = 20 Pennyweight	1 ounce = 16 drams
1 Pennyweight = 24 grains	

Figure 2.2. Imperial system of weights and measures (1824). *Source*: *Weights and Measures Act*, 5 George IV C. 74, 1824.

vibrating sixty times a minute when measured in London at a temperature of 52.5 degrees Fahrenheit measured a little more than thirty-nine inches. The reformers equated the standard yard to thirty-six of these thirty-nine (and a bit) inches. Some extraordinary efforts were made to link an existing artefact to a natural phenomenon!

The primary objectives of the reformers were twofold. By relating an existing standard to a naturally occurring phenomenon, they were legitimising an already existing measurement unit. Simultaneously, they also intended to codify a method of reconstructing the primary linear standard from what was ostensibly a neutral, objective, natural and invariable phenomenon.[58] Even the definitions of the new standards of weight and capacity were attempts to relate existing customary units to natural phenomena rather than the other way around. In this manner, the British reformers mirrored the efforts of the French savants of the 1790s to define new metric measures with reference to natural phenomena.[59]

But were the new Imperial standards invariable or based upon a phenomenon that was invariable and reproducible? The reliability of the

[58] Simpson, 'British length standard', p. 182. Edward Troughton was able to define a complete system of weights and measures based on a very precisely constructed linear measure that was, in theory, independent of an arbitrary physical artefact.

[59] PP Vol. III 1813–1814. This would not be the first time that British and French concurrently made efforts to standardise weights and measures. In the mid-eighteenth century, there was an attempt to compare the weights and measures used in the two countries with a view to developing some way of standardising the conversion from one to another. Anon., 'An account of a comparison lately made by some gentlemen of the Royal Society, of the standard of a yard, and the several weights lately made for their use; etc.', *Philosophical Transactions (1683–1775)* 42 (1742): pp. 541–56.

seconds pendulum as the natural basis for the length standard depended upon the exact and unvarying relationship between its length and periodicity. But the periodicity of the pendulum is also affected by the local strength of the earth's gravitational field. The field shows sufficient variance across locations to necessitate the adjustment of the length to maintain a constant period. In other words, the invariability of the length of the pendulum to reconstruct the primary length standard could not be assured, a realisation that dawned upon the reformers after 1824.[60] Doubts regarding the reliability of the density of water and the accuracy with which it could be measured also surfaced around the same time.[61] This raised questions regarding the basis of reconstructing or redefining the primary weight and capacity standards. By the mid-nineteenth century, the reformers sought a complete separation from any natural basis of defining measurement standards.[62] The natural constants that had been so essential to earlier reformers were abandoned in favour of physical reference standards. The new basis for defining the standard of length, for instance, was in reference to the length of a piece of metal preserved in a prescribed fashion at a prescribed temperature.[63]

The entire exercise of initially basing the physical standards on some natural phenomenon had served to initiate an intellectual and institutional transition in British metrology. It created a legal metrology that was based mainly upon measurement units that were notional and devoid of any social context. Previously, the ton and the bushel were either a unit of weight or a unit of volumetric capacity, depending upon the commodity being measured and the geographical context (Figure 2.1). Some of this flexibility was due to usage; most of it had legal sanction. The Imperial ton and bushel that replaced these older units did not have this flexibility. Legally, the ton was defined as a unit of weight, whereas the bushel was defined as a unit of capacity. Also, the legal metrology was based upon

---

[60] Simpson, 'British length standard', p. 174.
[61] Zupko, *Revolution in measurement*, p. 190.
[62] Simpson, 'British length standard', p. 190. The primary standards of the 1824 Imperial measures were held in the Houses of Parliament and were destroyed in the fire that engulfed the building complex in 1834. The fire was caused by overstoking the furnaces that heated the House of Lords as some old papers and tallies held by the Exchequer were being incinerated. Connor, *English measures*, p. 261.
[63] Zupko, *Revolution in measurement*, p. 190. Coincidentally, the metre that had been defined on the basis of the length of the meridian was also detached from this natural standard and defined with reference to a physical artefact, after the variability of the meridian and errors in its estimation were exposed. Alder, *Measure of all things*. In the twentieth century, the metre was once again pegged to a natural phenomenon, the speed of light. BIPM now defines the metre as 'the length of path travelled by light in a vacuum during a time interval of 1/299792458 of a second'; http://www.bipm.org/en/si/base_units/.

measurement units that were traceable and linked with each other in a hierarchical manner. Traceability was intended to make the measurement units enforceable (assuming proper infrastructure and political will) as well as reconstructable (by linking them to the primary standards).

Initiatives for reform

Who initiated and led the metrological reforms, and why? Three distinct views can be identified in literature for this historical period. One view proposes the need for the state bureaucracy to standardise weights and measures to enhance governance and control of economic activities that generated fiscal revenue.[64] An alternative view presents the impetus for metrological reform to be private initiatives, either by individual parliamentarians or by the scientific community.[65] Other historians have stressed the primacy of technological innovation and the role of scientists and scientific societies in influencing metrological reforms.[66] These views need not be mutually exclusive. The key insight from this literature is that the bureaucratic and political needs coincided with the scientific quest for quantification. Metrological reforms were introduced when these interests intersected.

Ashworth and Scott both argue that effective central monitoring and the bureaucratisation of fiscal revenue required a standardisation of measurement units and suppression of local units.[67] The state's capacity to generate fiscal revenue, as a whole, had increased towards the end of the eighteenth century and gave rise to a fiscal–military state.[68] This required collection of extensive local knowledge of production and trading practices and surveillance and control of the common economy (pilfering, smuggling, adulteration etc.). Throughout the eighteenth century, the state sought ways to make the taxable commodities more amenable and conformable to its system of gauging. It tried to shape the production of taxed goods while centralising administrative functions such as installing a uniform method of gauging taxed goods predominantly at the source of production or distribution. In short, this view argues that achieving a uniform system of taxation, and a national market linked together by

---

[64] W. J. Ashworth, *Customs and excise: trade, production, and consumption in England, 1640–1845* (Oxford, Oxford University Press, 2003). J. C. Scott, *Seeing like a state: how certain schemes to improve the human condition have failed* (New Haven, Yale University Press, 1998).

[65] Hoppit, 'Reforming Britain's measures'. Adell, 'British metrology'.

[66] Zupko, *Revolution in measurement*. Schaffer, 'Metrology'.

[67] Ashworth, *Customs and excise*, pp. 7–8, 259. Scott, *Seeing like a state*, p. 30.

[68] P. K. O'Brien, 'The political economy of British taxation, 1660–1815', *Economic History Review* 41 No 1 (1988).

a uniform fiscal code, meant accounting for, and eventually reducing, the variations in and incompatibility of the weights and measures used in Britain. Consequently, local and regional units as well as packaging and production practices had to be suppressed as the state's revenue activities tried to 'recast such things to aid its own activities'.[69] To paraphrase Latour, the state (as a metrological centre) tied the outside economic world by metrological chains, a world that was given a particular form through the calculations that the reformed metrological tools (Imperial weights and measures) helped to create.[70]

The state bureaucracy turned to the rhetoric of quantification and the associated notion of objectivity to achieve these aims, and the standardisation of measurement units was sought within this context.[71] This reliance on quantification may very well be linked to the state's ability to legitimately generate fiscal revenue: 'a vital requirement in legitimating the excise was for the fiscal form of measurement to be perceived as objective and therefore just.'[72] If the public were unwilling to shoulder the increased fiscal burden through taxation, any changes to the key institution of legal metrology may have been possible only if they could be made to appear just and not unduly favouring any one particular group, that is, based on abstract principles and therefore objective.[73]

Such arguments may explain why the state bureaucracy sought metrological standardisation and why it supported the particular system of

[69] Ashworth, *Customs and excise*, pp. 7, 280.
[70] Latour, *Science in action*, pp. 250–57. B. Curtis, 'From the moral thermometer to money: metrological reform in pre-confederation Canada', *Social Studies of Science* 28 No 4 (1998).
[71] Ashworth, *Customs and excise*, pp. 261, 83. Ashworth views the eighteenth-century British state as one involved in centralisation of its administration, which turns to the values of quantification and precision to achieve this objective. The discussion on quantification and standardisation as a 'rhetoric of objectivity' is presented in T. M. Porter, 'Objectivity as standardization: the rhetoric of impersonality in measurement, statistics, and cost-benefit analysis', in A. Megill (ed.) *Rethinking objectivity* (London, Duke University Press, 1994). T. M. Porter, *Trust in numbers: the pursuit of objectivity in science and public life* (Princeton, Princeton University Press, 1995). See also M. N. Wise (ed.), *The values of precision* (Princeton, Princeton University Press, 1995). J. L. Heilbron, 'Introductory essay', in T. Frangsmyr et al. (eds) *The quantifying spirit in the 18th century* (Berkeley, University of California Press, 1990).
[72] Ashworth, *Customs and excise*, p. 261. In a reformulation of Thomas Paine's arguments, he writes that the fiscal–military state that had emerged in the eighteenth century was increasingly coming under criticism with allegations of 'greedy consumption of the people's wealth to fund a corrupt political system revolving upon an obsolete constitution'. A bloated bureaucracy, expensive wars and a new commercial world required a transparent, cheap and simple administrative system – one that required 'a different species of knowledge to direct its operations' (p. 341). See also O'Brien, 'British taxation, 1660–1815'.
[73] Ashworth, *Customs and excise*, p. 378.

decontextualised (and therefore objective) measurement units that comprised the Imperial measures. Notwithstanding this, efforts of *individual* parliamentarians drove the quest for a uniform metrology in the eighteenth century, and the state was initially reluctant to become involved in a complete reform of existing measures before the turn of the nineteenth century.

Nonstate initiatives to reform British metrology can be traced to the middle of the eighteenth century. In circa 1743, some members of the Royal Society attempted to compare the British measurement units, such as the yard and the pound, to their French equivalents, such as the French half-toise and the French two marc.[74] This was not an attempt to 'determine the absolute and legal' value of these measures but rather had more scientific motivations. Nevertheless, private support from trade and commerce for metrological standardisation was growing in strength at the same time. The support for the standardisation of the Winchester bushel in the early eighteenth century in corn markets of the Southwest had come from larger farmers and landholders, coinciding with the keenness of local officials in charge of setting the assize of bread for such standardisation.[75]

The first parliamentary attempt was the initiative by Lord Carysfort, who chaired two committees between 1758 and 1759. These committees reported on the various measurement units in use along with recommendations regarding their standardisation. The committees were funded by the Duke of Newcastle, and Carysfort, an Irish peer, acted largely on his own initiative.[76] Through these committees, Parliament 'was first made painfully aware of the gross inadequacies of [existing measures]'.[77] Towards the end of that century, another parliamentarian, Sir John Riggs Miller, was instrumental in keeping the problem of multiple and local measurement units alive before Parliament.[78] What motivated Carysfort and Miller to raise these issues in Parliament is difficult to establish, although it may have been some sense of social justice stemming from unreliability of measurements, particularly in the case of essential commodities such as corn.[79]

Private efforts to highlight the multiplicity of measurement units, particularly in agriculture, generated interest within certain government

[74] Anon., 'Comparison of standard yard'.
[75] Sheldon et al., 'Customary corn measures', p. 32.
[76] Hoppit, 'Reforming Britain's measures', p. 94. See also *Carysfort Committee Report* (1758).
[77] Hoppit, 'Reforming Britain's measures', p. 94.
[78] Ibid., p. 95. Adell, 'British metrology', pp. 173–74.
[79] Hoppit, 'Reforming Britain's measures'. Adell, 'British metrology', p. 173.

departments. The Board of Agriculture's county reports began to highlight the existence of variations between local units used in different counties, and in fact, one of the reports of 1795 suggested that the existence of so many local units was an 'incumbrance to the general intercourse of business [sic]'.[80] The board's involvement signalled the beginning of the government's interest in the problem of multiple units and the potential confusion that it may cause in interregional trade.

These private parliamentary efforts, motivated by commercial and mercantile interests, coincided with the Royal Society's quest for increasingly precise measurements. Experiments by General Roy, Wollaston, Playfair, Troughton, Henry Kater and others did much to improve the instrumentation and precision with which measurements for scientific purposes could be made.[81] Men of science interacted with men of commerce on this subject: Patrick Kelly, an authority on bookkeeping and the author of *Metrology*, published in 1816, was a close colleague of William Herschel the astronomer. Kelly and others like him believed that trade and commerce required durable standards for record keeping similar to those being adopted by astronomers. The reciprocal relationship between astronomers and accountants and bookkeepers is substantiated by the number of commercially oriented men, such as Kelly, who were active members of the Astronomical Society in London.[82] Many of them eventually served on the parliamentary committees that examined the practical issues in standardising Britain's metrology or testified before them. They served to nurture a view that a major reform of existing measurement units was necessary and that this required metrological standardisation based on decontextualised measurement units defined in relation to abstract, absolute, natural or astronomical phenomena.[83]

Parliament eventually appointed a series of committees and royal commissions to study the possibility of introducing a standardised metrology between 1814 and 1821. A broad consensual view emerged from these reviews that the establishment of a uniform metrology in Britain required a hierarchy of measurement units and a system of traceability based upon

---

[80] Hoppit, 'Reforming Britain's measures', p. 84. The chairman of the Board of Agriculture, Sir John Sinclair, was on the committee headed by John Miller to review weights and measures in 1790. *House of Commons Journals*, 1 April 1790, p. 359. H. John, *General view of the agriculture of the county of Lancaster* ... (1795; Repr. Newton Abbot Devon, 1969).

[81] Zupko, *Revolution in measurement*, pp. 69–75.

[82] Schaffer, 'Metrology', p. 440. W. J. Ashworth, 'The calculating eye: Baily, Herschel, Babbage and the business of astronomy', *British Journal for the History of Science* 27 No 4 (1994): pp. 422–23.

[83] Zupko, *Revolution in measurement*. Hoppit, 'Reforming Britain's measures'. Adell, 'British metrology'. Also PP Vol. III 1813–1814, and PP Vol. XI 1819.

measurement units that are related to each other through a system of comparisons and references:[84]

The simple connection [established] between the standard of weight and measures of capacity, will [preserve] the uniformity of those measures which are found to be most liable to error.[85]

Efforts to link existing measurement units to natural standards resulted in some strange relationships such as the standard avoirdupois pound being equivalent to the weight of water contained in 27.648 cubic inches.

Private individuals initiated the reform of the British metrology and the particular form of standardisation, that is, the Imperial measurement units. Parliamentarians sponsored efforts to bring what they considered to be the source of measurement problems, the existence of multiple legal measurement units, into public focus. Scientific experiments to develop precise physical measurement standards by private individuals helped to maintain the focus on metrological problems. The bureaucracy and the government, who had initially stayed away from these initiatives, gradually became involved in the early nineteenth century and sponsored efforts to define a new uniform and legal metrology to replace the older system. However, the state did not impose the new metrology on markets and businesses in the years following its introduction. Existing local units could be used permissively, unlike in the French metric reforms, where successive administrations sought to immediately replace all units used in the local economy by the new metrology, with disastrous consequences.[86]

[84] PP Vol. III 1813–1814. The reports concluded that an important reason preventing the establishment of uniform weights and measures before the nineteenth century was 'the want of a fixed standard in nature, with which the standards of measure might at all times be easily compared; [the] want of a simple mode of connecting the measures of length, with those of capacity and weight; [and] the want of proper Tables of Equalization [i.e. comparison]'. The National Institute of Science and Technology (NIST), US Department of Commerce, has adopted the following definition of traceability provided in the International Vocabulary of Basic and General Terms in Metrology: 'property of the result of a measurement or the value of a standard whereby it can be related to stated references, usually national or international standards, through an unbroken chain of comparisons all having stated uncertainties'. *International vocabulary of basic and general terms in metrology*, 2nd ed. (1993), definition 6.10; available online at http://ts.nist.gov/. Traceability is an important issue in modern metrological systems, such as the present UK National Measurement System (NMS), in which international traceability of standards forms one of NMS's key activities. *Review of the rationale for and economic benefit of the UK national measurement system* (Department of Trade and Industry, National Measurement System Policy Unit, 1999).

[85] PP Vol. III 1813–1814, p. 135. Connor, *English measures*.

[86] Alder, 'Revolution to measure'. J. L. Heilbron, 'The measure of enlightenment', in T. Frangsmyr et al. (eds) *The quantifying spirit in the 18th century* (Berkeley, University of California Press, 1990). Both give compelling accounts of the social and economic consequences of the enforcement of metric units on the local economy in France.

Further reforms

The reformers of British metrology had recognised the difficulty of replacing local measurement units early on. Although the first report of the Carysfort Committee in 1758 recommended that all local units be replaced by uniform and certain standards, by the following year, the committee's stance had softened somewhat when, in the second report, they acknowledged the propriety of preserving local measurement customs and measurement units.[87] Nearly sixty years later, another group of reformers were deliberating the same issues. A parliamentary report of 1819 stated,

[There is] great difficulty of effecting any radical changes, to so considerable an extent, as might in some respects be desirable.[88]

A subsequent select committee report of 1821 recommended that nonuniformity of local measurement units be remedied by connecting them in simple ratios to the primary standards of the Imperial measures.[89] The report recommended that existing subdivisions of weights and measures be retained and stated that the existing fractional units were better suited for 'common practical purposes than the decimal scale'.[90] Accordingly, the 1824 act contained a clause stating that generally, people

should be allowed to use the several weights and measures which they may have in their possession, although such weights and measures may not be in conformity with the Standard Weights and Measures established by this Act, [that] it shall and may be lawful for any person or persons to buy and sell goods and merchandize by any weights or measures established either by local custom or founded on special Agreement, [and] that the Ratio or Proportion which all such measures and weights shall bear to standard weights and measures established by this Act, shall be and become a matter of common notoriety.[91]

Thus the new notional Imperial measurement units did not immediately replace the local measurement units, although they introduced notional, traceable and legal metrological measurement units alongside those in local use. The new metrological standards were legal but not mandatory or obligatory for use. They could be enforced, and fraudulent uses of the

---

[87] *Carysfort Committee Report* (1758), p. 438. House of Commons Reports (1738–1765) Vol. II 1759, *Second report of the Carysfort Committee on weights and measures*, p. 456.
[88] PP Vol. XI 1819, pp. 309–12.
[89] *Report from the Committee on Weights and Measures*, PP Vol. IV 1821, p. 291. The ratios of local units to Imperial measures had to 'prove most accordant with generally received usage, and with such analogies as may connect the different quantities in the most simple ratios'.
[90] Ibid.
[91] 5 George IV C. 74, Para. XVI.

legal units could be punished, but it was not necessary to use the legal units in all contracts.

In the decades following 1824, various attempts were made to promote the use of the new Imperial units. Legislation passed between 1835 and 1858 established rules for weighing goods and carts in markets, directed market authorities to provide weighing houses and scales for general use by merchants and customers and encouraged the use of Imperial standards in markets.[92] The state attempted to abolish measurement practices that were 'liable to considerable variation' such as heaping or measuring dry goods by volume.[93] It also attempted to provide common access to reliable standards in cases of dispute and mandated that inspectors examine the weights and measures of anyone selling goods in streets and public places.[94] Zupko writes that the 'law was now extended to every conceivable commercial transaction' and that 'the web of law designed to protect buyers from unscrupulous sellers expanded more in this one decade [i.e. the 1850s] than it had over the previous thousand years'.[95]

Eventually, the Weights and Measures Act of 1878 abolished the use of all local measurement units, that is, units other than the Imperial units or their multiples, by making their use in commercial transactions illegal.[96] At the same time, the Board of Trade was given custody of the Imperial standards and control over the entire aspect of British metrology.[97] The process of introducing a standardised metrology was thus taken one major step ahead by making the Imperial measurement units the only legally recognised ones in Britain.

Concomitant to the legislative changes to encourage, facilitate or coerce people into using the Imperial measures, changes were made at an organisational level. This included the creation of a professional metrological officer corps. Zupko claims that monitoring and enforcement of legal standards had been the responsibility of 'thousands of nonqualified personnel who dominated these tasks since the Middle Ages'.[98] The nineteenth-century metrological reforms sought to centralise this

---

[92] Zupko, *Revolution in measurement*, p. 183.
[93] 5 & 6 William IV, C. 63, 1835, *Weights and measures (amendment) act*, Paras. VII & VIII. Connor, *English measures*, p. 180.
[94] Zupko, *Revolution in measurement*, p. 184. See n. 5, which lists weights and measures legislation enacted between 1824 and 1870 in relation to specific trades and products, esp. foodstuff and essential commodities such as coal.
[95] Ibid., pp. 183–84.
[96] 41 & 42 Victoria C. 49, 1878, *Weights and measures act*.
[97] Ibid., Para. VIII.
[98] Zupko, *Revolution in measurement*, p. 200.

function, wherein the task of verification and certification was no longer under the purview of local authorities but was to be conducted by centrally appointed inspectors who had 'entered into a "recognizance to the Crown"'.[99]

Yet Zupko may have overstated the novelty of this arrangement. In the Middle Ages, the Office of the Clerk of the Market effectively functioned as a medieval metrological corps. The principal clerk was of the King's household, and each shire and city had its own clerk. The principal clerk maintained the royal standard measures and would compare those in use throughout the kingdom with these royal standards.[100] This arrangement continued until about the seventeenth century, when livery companies, craft guilds and even local magistrates began verifying and certifying standards. Nevertheless, the nineteenth century witnessed the professionalisation of metrological inspectors, as some form of training and assessment became necessary to ensure that the inspectors were appropriately qualified to perform their functions.[101]

Despite the state's efforts to make the Imperial standards ubiquitous, many local units and practices persisted throughout the nineteenth century. The Winchester bushel, for example, which was abolished in 1835 and the use of which was made illegal, continued to be used in some market towns for measuring grain throughout most of the nineteenth century.[102] The use of non-Imperial units such as coombs, keels, pecks and firlots continued throughout the nineteenth century. Local units persisted alongside the newer, decontextualised, legal units of the Imperial system, although their use diminished over time. The practice of heaping continued for several decades after it was outlawed, and dry goods, such as grain, continued to be sold by volume rather than by weight.

The reform of British weights and measures was not unlike the late-eighteenth-century French attempts to introduce the metric system and to replace the metrology of the ancien régime. By abstracting measurements from the context of materials and labour, French reformers sought to break the custom of using local measurement units within local economies. And yet the way in which British measurement practices were reformed was quite unlike the way in which they were reformed in France.

[99] Ibid., pp. 204, 206.
[100] Connor, *English measures*, p. 325.
[101] Ibid., p. 334.
[102] Letter from the Clerk of the Peace, Lincolnshire, 19 February 1886, Board of Trade Papers, BT 101/138, [T]he [N]ational [A]rchives.

Reforming European metrology

The metric revolution (c. 1790–1840)

Heilbron writes that the metric system was produced in France when *l'esprit géometrique* – the quantifying spirit – united with the purposes of the Enlightenment and the Revolution. He argues that the system was an exemplar of eighteenth-century rationalism and was directed against 'the foggy and feudal metrology of the *Ancien Régime*'.[103] The metric reforms were supported by the rhetoric of the *philosophes* and realised through the politics of scientific societies and revolutionary tribunals. But they were resisted by the common man, in whose interest the reformers, *philosophes*, scientists and revolutionaries had claimed to act.

The rationality and quantifying nature of the metric system resonated with the demands of the *cahiers de doléances* for 'one law, one king, one weight, one measure'.[104] Kula wrote that standardisation of weights and measures was something that everyone in France wanted by the late eighteenth century, 'from peasants in different regions to the craftsmen in diverse trades to municipal leaders of virtually all towns'.[105] Apart from antiseigneurial motivations (quite evidently related to the opaque measures employed for rent collection), the *cahiers* reveal a strong commercial motivation for standardisation. The Physiocrats' arguments for 'a single [national] measure, binding upon all' mingled together with peasants' calls for 'one and the same measures [as] the present diversity of measures exposes people to swindlers'.[106] Buyers and sellers, merchants and peasants, craftsmen and nobility all stressed the need for standardisation of weights and measures on the eve of Revolution.

The metric reforms were meant to replace the hodgepodge of hundreds of thousands of customary measurement units with the universal language of metric measures. Universality was the central principle of the metric measures and guided its creators: 'a tous les temps, à tous les peuples,' or 'for all times, for all people'.[107] Zupko suggests that pre-Revolutionary France had more than 1,000 units of measurement accepted as standards in Paris, and a further 250,000 local variations of these units.[108] The rationality of the metric measures was to be combined with the nationality of its scope; that is, they were to replace entirely – without

[103] Heilbron, 'Measures', p. 208.
[104] Alder, 'Revolution to measure', p. 48. Kula, *Measures and men*, p. 215.
[105] Kula, *Measures and men*, p. 192.
[106] Ibid., p. 209.
[107] Ibid., p. 267. Cox, 'Metric system', p. 359.
[108] Zupko, *Revolution in measurement*, p. 113.

exception – the 250,000 local units that ordinary French people understood and used in their daily lives. Montesquieu's warnings about the 'seductive aesthetic' of uniformity were disregarded: 'so long as people obey the law, what does it matter if they obey the same one?'[109] Instead, it was Condercet's desire to realign inadequate human laws with universal principles that drove the direction of metrological reform in the waning years of pre-Revolutionary France. The French savants set about designing a system that unlocked the 'natural arithmetic' of the decimal system to make 'truth' accessible to all.[110]

As designed, the metric system was supposed to facilitate free exchange between French citizens by introducing a uniform language they could use in their daily economic lives. Calculating the price of cloth should no longer have to be a challenge fit for Archimedes![111] The metric units were supposed to remove obstacles to the national circulation of grain, to facilitate long-distance trade and, generally, to better integrate large sections of the national economy.[112] The universal language of the system was also supposed to enable the government to collect accurate information. This would have enabled, for instance, surveyor–geometers to ascertain exact measurements of changing land patterns.[113]

'The nation received what it wanted – only it was not what it wanted,' wrote Kula.[114] People rejected the metre and the other metric measures. Even though use of the new metric units became obligatory in August 1793, they hardly penetrated Parisian marketplaces in the years following their introduction. People largely disregarded the new units and resisted their use in daily economic life. The reformers had neglected to anticipate the disruption of existing market conventions that the new reforms would cause. The conventions that existed between economic groups, and the market relationships that depended upon these conventions, were built upon traditional, variable and trustworthy units (see the previous section).[115] The disruption to these conventions was severe. Market conventions that had historically been negotiated between various groups – peasants, artisans, shopkeepers, tradesmen, customers, merchants and so on – were threatened and had to be renegotiated, taking into account the new metric measures. Thinking from the older variable, value-adjusted

[109] Cited in Alder, 'Revolution to measure', p. 40.
[110] Heilbron, 'Measures'.
[111] Ibid., p. 212. Heilbron wrote that in pre-metric France, the calculation of a price of (English) cloth expressed in yards, feet and square inches and converting it into French *aunes, livers, deniers*, cubic king's feet etc. 'would have puzzled Archimedes'.
[112] Alder, 'Revolution to measure', pp. 54–55.
[113] Ibid., p. 47.
[114] Kula, *Measures and men*, p. 264.
[115] Ibid. Alder, 'Revolution to measure', pp. 43–46.

measures to thinking in invariable measures and variable prices amounted to a complete mental revolution.[116] Craftsmen, artisans and local merchants felt that their markets were now opened to outside competition. Consumers opposed the new units because they thought they gave unfair advantages to the shopkeeper. The shopkeepers, in turn, resisted them because they believed that they gave the customers undue advantage.[117] Shopkeepers took to illegally keeping two sets of weights and measures – old and new – as they were caught between the administration's insistence on the use of metric units and the customer's preference for the old measures. The resistance to the new metric measures came not only from the ordinary citizens, who, the elite assumed, opposed the new system owing to their ignorance. The bureaucracy, whose work the new measurement units were supposed to simplify, also found the new units just as inconvenient and resisted their use.[118]

Men of science had devised the metre, which was adopted by the rulers and bureaucrats and imposed upon the nation.[119] Alder concludes that the republican French scientists had reckoned that the language of the metric system would remake French citizens into rational economic actors. But this involved reshaping the mentality of the citizens, who were used to the traditional notions of economic value captured by variable units and variable measurements. The advocates of the metric system believed that state intervention was the only way they could transcend 'each individual's reluctance to surrender his or her own familiar measures'.[120] They had satisfied the nation's need for reform, but they had to subordinate the nation to their version of reform. Accordingly, the state initiated a program to educate its citizens about the new system. It printed tables, pamphlets and graphic illustrations showing how these units could be used in different economic contexts, how they could be converted from one to the other and how the older units could be translated into the newer units as well as a general explanation of the merits of decimal counting.

But the widespread hostility to the new measures continued. The republican scientists strenuously defended the system. The elite within the bureaucracy, who benefited from the centralisation and standardisation that the new metrological units afforded, also largely defended it.

---

[116] Kula, *Measures and men*, p. 252.

[117] Heilbron, 'Measures', p. 237.

[118] Kula, *Measures and men*, p. 252. Alder, 'Revolution to measure', p. 59.

[119] Alder, *Measure of all things*. Alder gives a compelling account of how the metre was defined, the scientific ideals that it was supposed to represent, how its scientific basis turned out to be erroneous and how the modern metric system that we now use had to abandon the scientific premise on which the metre was originally conceived.

[120] Alder, 'Revolution to measure', p. 54.

The government sought a compromise solution to this ardent defence by reformers and passive resistance by citizens.[121] Around the turn of the century, the Imperial state decided to temper its insistence on use of the new metric measures. The Napoleonic administration retracted the new metrological units and decimal division, and the succeeding administration of Louis XVIII forbade the use of the metric system for ordinary transactions. It was only after a second revolution that metric measures were readopted for compulsory use in France in circa 1840.[122] Even so, vestiges of pre-metric units remained in use in France until the end of the nineteenth century.[123]

International acceptance (1851–1875)

Between 1850 and 1875, the metric measures – 'the child of science, born of the dread French Revolution' – were transformed from the French system of weights and measures into an international metrological system. They were 'part and parcel of the growing internationalism' of the period.[124] As Appendix 2.1 shows, the international acceptance of metric measures during the nineteenth century resulted from a combination of international agreements, political integration and scientific and political cooperation. This combination enabled the system to be internationally accepted more or less in the form that was originally conceived in the late eighteenth century.

Until the mid-nineteenth century, nations had hesitated to adopt the metric measures. Their endorsement by the international scientific community and the French efforts to hand over the custody of the metrological units to an international body – the Bureau International des Poids et Mesures (BIPM) – elevated the metric measures from their nationalistic origins to an international system.[125] Seventeen nations, including Austria–Hungary, Belgium, Denmark, France, Germany, Italy, Norway, Russia, Spain, Sweden, Switzerland, and the Ottoman Empire, signed an international treaty – the Convention du Mètre – in 1875. This treaty established BIPM as a permanent organisational structure to coordinate all international matters relating to units of measurement. Portugal signed the treaty in 1876, with the United States following in 1878. Britain delayed acceptance of this accord until 1884 before finally becoming a signatory.

[121] Kula, *Measures and men*, p. 256.
[122] Alder, 'Revolution to measure', p. 61. Cox, 'Metric system', p. 361.
[123] A. E. Kennelly, *Vestiges of pre-metric weights and measures persisting in metric-system Europe 1926–1927* (New York, Macmillan, 1928).
[124] Cox, 'Metric system', pp. 376–77.
[125] http://www.bipm.org/. The website reports that as of 24 May 2011, fifty-five member states have signed the convention, along with thirty-three other associate member states.

Nations lacking a unified metrology found a ready-made answer in the metric system. Portugal, Brazil, Argentina, Norway and Switzerland initiated steps to make metric measures obligatory in their respective territories in the unmodified international form. Italy and Germany adopted the system as part of, and even to further advance, their respective political unifications. Industrialising nations found that an internationally accepted metrological system could aid in both domestic and foreign commerce. The Zollverin had adopted metric-based weights as part of the customs union even prior to Germany's political unification. In the United States, metric measures became permissible for use in commercial contracts by the end of the Civil War. However, in an exception to most other nations, the use of metric measures did not become obligatory or mandatory either in the United States or in the United Kingdom throughout the nineteenth and twentieth centuries.

Metric system and British defiance

In Britain, the Weights and Measures (Metric System) Bill was introduced in Parliament in July 1871 and was defeated by a slender majority of five votes: 82–77.[126] It was a private bill, sponsored by Mr J. B. Smith, Sir Charles Adderly and others, and was hotly debated during the Commons session. This event signified the closest that Britain had come to metrication in the nineteenth century. It is an example of the closely fought battle of the standards waged in Great Britain to secure the exclusive use of the metric units. The battle to retain the exclusive use of the Imperial measures as opposed to switching to the metric measures was fought on many fronts. Most commonly, though, the debates focused on the use of decimal as opposed to nondecimal measurement units and the practicality of using decimal numbers to manipulate everyday measurements. The preference to use decimal units was not universal, even though several groups had proposed their use within the Imperial measurement system itself, without adopting the metric units.

There were several prominent advocates of the decimal measures, including Leone Levi and Joseph Whitworth.[127] Levi was an ardent supporter of the metric measures and was a prominent force in trying to popularise their use in Britain in the latter part of the nineteenth century.

---

[126] *Hansard Parliamentary Debates*, Series 3, Vol. 208, 26 July 1871. Weights and Measures (Metric System) Bill, cc299.

[127] L. Levi, *The theory and practice of the metric system of weights and measures* (London, Griffith and Farran, 1871). See also Cox, 'Metric system'.

Whitworth, in contrast, sought the use of decimal divisions to Imperial measurement units:

Great and rapid progress would be made in many branches of the mechanical arts, if the decimal system of measures could be generally introduced. [Instead] of our engineers and machinists thinking in eights, sixteenths and thirty-seconds of an inch, it is desirable that they should think and speak in tenths, hundredths and thousandths. [The change from] fractional system [to] the more perfect decimal one is easy of attainment, and, when once made, it will from its usefulness and convenience amply repay any trouble which may have attended its acquirement.[128]

In the mechanical engineering sectors, the use of decimal divisions using Imperial measurement units, and measuring instruments based upon them, became widespread. An example would be cylindrical, flat surface and external plane gauges devised by Whitworth using decimal divisions of the inch. These gauges, in fact, were made into legal standards of length under the Weights and Measures Act of 1878.[129] Measurements used in the wire industry to gauge the diameter of wire became based upon decimal divisions of the inch rather than its fractional divisions. The engineering sectors valued the advantages of decimal manipulation of minute measurements in achieving the precision required. However, they generally rejected the use of the metric metre or its subdivisions, the centimetre or the millimetre, preferring to use the decimal divisions of the inch as the standard of measure.

Use of decimal measurement units was attempted in other sectors as well. Grain merchants in Liverpool, for instance, began using the cental, a unit of weight measure equivalent to one hundred Imperial pounds. The intention in this case was to replace the allegedly cumbersome hundredweight of 112 pounds. The cental's subdivision into smaller units was considered to be easier. The use of the cental, which became recognised as a legal measurement unit in 1879, did not extend much beyond the wheat trade in the immediate vicinity of Liverpool, although it experienced a brief surge in popularity in the United States between circa 1860 and 1900.[130]

British reformers had, from the beginning, argued against decimal division forming any part of the weights and measures legislation. The

---

[128] Whitworth, 'On a standard decimal measure of length for mechanical engineering work', *Proceedings of the Meeting of the Institution of Mechanical Engineers at Manchester*, 25 June 1857, pp. 45–55.

[129] TNA, BT 101/76, letter dated 28 December 1880. Also BT 101/182.

[130] L. D. Hill, *Grain, grades and standards: historical issues shaping the future* (Urbana, University of Illinois Press, 1990), appendix A. G. J. S. Broomhall and J. H. Hubback, *Corn trade memories: recent and remote* (Liverpool, Northern, 1930), p. 23.

reluctance in the use of decimal division predates the battle of the standards. However, undeniably, this was a reaction against the unpopularity
and unsuccessful promotion of decimal metric measures in France. The
1819 commissioners' report stated that

the [existing] sub-divisions of weights and measures [in Britain] appear to be
far more convenient for practical purposes than the decimal scale, which might
perhaps be preferred by some persons... We recommend that all multiples and
sub-divisions of the [proposed] standards to be adopted should retain the same
relative proportions to each other, as are at present in general use.[131]

This reluctance was refrained in a later report of 1869, which had claimed
that

the natural inclination of the mind [is] to halve and quarter continually... [The]
Metric system does not offer the same facility [for] continued binary subdivision.
[Any] attempt to force its use [would] probably be felt as a needless grievance.[132]

Similar arguments against decimal division were made in 1871 in the
House of Commons:

The decimal notation, with all its advantages, had points at which it broke down.
It was good in multiplication, but when it came to division their artificial nature
asserted itself. When it had to do with halving and quartering – processes, on
which a vast proportion of the transactions of ordinary life depended – then their
weakness was obvious. [The] notation rightly claimed to be scientific and strictly
mathematical, but it was not natural.[133]

The parliamentary committees, however, did admit to the convenience of
decimal division in large factories or in commercial transactions. But they
considered these to be decisions that were best left to the market rather
than requiring state sanction: 'owners of those factories can, however,
arrange such matters [i.e. use of decimal divisions to measure] to a great
extent without legislative assistance.'[134]

    The British industry selectively adopted the use of decimal divisions
within Imperial measurement units without express legislative backing.
The use of metric units per se did not catch on. It is important to consider
the reasons behind the increasing use of decimal units at the market level.
We would expect markets to switch to decimal units provided the benefits
accruing from this switch outweighed the costs of making the switch.

[131] PP Vol. XI 1819.
[132] *Royal commission to inquire into condition of Exchequer standards (of weights and measures)
second report*, PP Vol. XXIII 1868–1869, p. 736.
[133] *Hansard Parliamentary Debates*, Series 3, Vol. 208, 26 July 1871. Weights and Measures
(Metric System) Bill, cc271.
[134] PP Vol. XXIII 1868–1869, p. 736.

Such a trade-off was not universally favoured, but those sectors in which a greater degree of precision was required, such as in the engineering industries, made the transition some time during the latter half of the nineteenth century. The case of decimal measurements used in the wire industry illustrates this transition (Chapter 5).

Overall, the economic logic of universal measurement units had to be balanced with a political decision to abandon British units in favour of the French metric system, as it was seen in the United Kingdom. British reformers in the early nineteenth century had concluded that there was neither 'sufficient reason' nor 'practical advantage' in having a

quantity commensurable to any original quantity, existing, or imagined to exist, in nature, except as affording some little encouragement to its common adoption by neighbouring nations.[135]

The report's authors in this case were no doubt referring to the goals of the French savants to make the metric measures universal in this thinly veiled remark. This is despite their own efforts to link the existing Elizabethan standard yard to the motion of the pendulum (see the previous section). The reformers were of the opinion that adopting the metre and other metric units would lead to inconvenience in Britain's internal relations which could not be outweighed by the convenience in foreign trade that was in any case 'remunerated for their trouble by the profits of their commercial concerns'.[136]

As Appendix 2.1 shows, several UK societies and associations promoted the use of metric units in the 1850s and 1860s. The British branch of the International Association for Obtaining a Uniform Decimal System of Measures, Weights and Coins (IA) and the British Academy for the Advancement of Science actively campaigned against the government's recalcitrance and that of the antimetric groups.[137] Between 1863 and 1878, several parliamentary committees and royal commissions were set up to look into the merits (and de-merits) of adopting the metric units as the basis for the United Kingdom's metrology. MPs voted on several bills to make the use of metric units compulsory. Each bill was defeated, or if passed in one house, it failed to pass in the other.[138] The 1878 weights and measures legislation reaffirmed the obligatory use of the Imperial measures. This was a major setback for the pro-metric groups, although metric units were legally permitted for all purposes, except commercial

---

[135] PP Vol. XI 1819.
[136] Ibid.
[137] Zupko, *Revolution in measurement*, pp. 232–35. In the 1860s, the IA organised a series of public lectures to advertise the advantages of the metric measures.
[138] Ibid., pp. 238–46.

Table 2.1. *British exports to countries using various measurement standards*

	1847		1861	
To countries using metric units	23,692,811	40.5%	55,243,699	44.5%
To countries using Imperial units	16,261,568	27.8%	24,211,429	19.5%
To countries using other standards	18,536,482	31.7%	44,564,767	35.9%
Total value of British exports	58,490,861		124,019,895	

Note: Apart from France, Belgium and the Netherlands, no other European nation had legally adopted the metric units before 1850. Thus the figures reported for 1847 are for those countries that in 1861 had either fully or partially adopted the metric standard or were believed to be in the process of adoption. The percentage figures represent the proportion of total export value. Figures are in pounds sterling.
Source: Report from the Committee on Weights and Measures, PP Vol. VII 1862. Evidence given by Frank Perks Fellows on 16 May 1862, pp. 241–42.

contracts. The pro-metric movement did not subside and continued its campaign until the 1980s. In 1891, metric units began to be taught in schools, alongside units of the Imperial system. Despite Herschel's opposition to the metre, and his reverence for the Imperial measures as the national standards, metric units found general acceptance in the scientific networks and laboratories towards the end of the century. In trade and commerce, many groups supported the introduction of decimal measures; however, their preference was for decimal Imperial units rather than decimal metric units.[139]

The reaction of the state to the growing pressure to make the metric measures legal was to make them permissive, initially, in international contracts and eventually, grudgingly even, for regular use in domestic trade by 1898.[140] The metric units were never made obligatory, and their use formed a very small proportion of British trade by the close of the nineteenth century.[141]

Trade, empire and metrology

The need to use metric units was strongly promoted on the basis of using common measurement units in the expanding international trade of the period. British trade, particularly with countries that began using metric units after circa 1850, had expanded considerably by the mid-nineteenth century (Table 2.1). Notwithstanding the provenance of these statistics, they do reveal the expansion in Britain's overseas trade with

[139] TNA, BT 101/340.
[140] Connor, *English measures*, pp. 284–86. Zupko, *Revolution in measurement*, pp. 249–50.
[141] Connor, *English measures*, p. 286.

countries using either metric or other non-Imperial measures by the 1860s.[142] In any case, such evidence was used by the advocates of the metric system as sufficient justification for Britain to switch to metric measures. Trade with countries using Imperial measures – mainly the colonial countries and the United States – was a small proportion of Britain's international trade, they argued. They demanded that Britain adopt the metric units exclusively as the basis for its legal metrology. On the basis of the testimony of Leone Levi, Frank Perks Fellows and other supporters of the metric system, the 1862 select committee reported that

our system of weights and measures, being in this state of disorder and darkness, a sudden light was thrown upon it, and the advantage of a common international system fully brought to view.[143]

Such arguments were given a further boost with the Cobden–Chevalier trade treaty of 1860 and the explosion of economic openness that followed this treaty in Europe. The treaty led to an increase in Anglo–French trade as well as European trade in general.[144] Metric units, its proponents argued, would help to overcome the great inconveniences arising from metrological diversity in use in many of the European countries.[145] Scientists, such as William Thompson (later Lord Kelvin), generally supported the use of metric units in physics and related fields (e.g. electrical resistance). Others, such as Joule and Herschel, suspected a hidden agenda linked to metrication following the Cobden–Chevalier treaty. Joule expressed his doubt about the extent to which the metric units would be adopted internationally: 'it would be impossible to make 3/4 of the globe adopt the metre.'[146] Cobden and other parliamentarians, such as Ewart, did indeed attempt to push the adoption of the metric measures in the years following the treaty.[147] However, Herschel countered this by pointing out Britain's existing commercial and imperial superiority:

England is beyond all question the nation whose commercial relations, both internal and external, are the greatest in the world. Taking commerce, population, and area of soil then into account, there would seem to be far better reason for our continental neighbours to conform to our linear measure.[148]

[142] *Report from the Committee on Weights and Measures*, PP Vol. VII 1862. See the testimony of Frank Perks Fellows on 16 May 1862.
[143] PP Vol. VII 1862, p. 190.
[144] D. Lazer, 'The free trade epidemic of the 1860s and other outbreaks of economic discrimination', *World Politics* 51 No 4 (1999): pp. 470–72.
[145] Cox, 'Metric system', pp. 365–66. Zupko, *Revolution in measurement*, pp. 235–36.
[146] Cited in Schaffer, 'Metrology', p. 446.
[147] *Hansard Parliamentary Debates*, Series 3, Vol. 208, 26 July 1871. Weights and Measures (Metric System) Bill. cc263 and 273–74.
[148] Cited in Schaffer, 'Metrology', p. 449.

Although Britain's international trade relations were not to lead to changes to its existing weights and measures legislation, the British Empire did have a considerable influence on other aspects of her metrology.[149] For instance, Bruce Hunt has shown how the imperial context shaped the metrology and the scientific context of cable telegraphy and electrical physics. The cable empire (and the cabled empire) had a profound role in the definition and standardisation of the units of electrical resistance by combining the work done in the colonial outposts and in the metropolitan centres themselves.[150] The total length of submarine cables in the world increased more than eighty-six times between 1864 and 1880, as British firms laid cables to Gibraltar, Malta, Egypt, India, Singapore, Hong Kong and Australia. The expansion of the cable industry affected British electrical science and ensured that it was the British unit for electrical measurement – the ohm – that was adopted as the international metrological standard. As Hunt argues, this was because the British had submarine cables and the Germans (their rivals) did not.[151]

Metrology in the colonies, in turn, was shaped by the state's need to establish metrological chains, but only to an extent. Bruce Curtis has shown that the colonial government in Canada was able to link only certain activities with the metrological chains in the sense that Latour suggests, that is, linking local practices to official codes at the centre.[152] The pre-Confederation colonial governments made no attempt to link Canada's metrology to invariants in nature, in contrast to the French metric reformers. Neither did they attempt to establish a uniform set of metrological standards in the Canadian colonies. Pre-Revolutionary French metrological practices coexisted with versions of English metrological practices within the growing commercial sectors. The British colonial governments allowed such diverse practices to flourish until the 1860s, and consequently, Winchester, Troy and other English measures existed along with Canadian and Parisian units. Only after a new sovereign government was formed in 1873 was a common metrological system adopted. Advocates of the metric system were unsuccessful in getting the metric units to become part of the unified and centralised metrology, which was predominantly based upon the British Imperial measures.

---

[149] P. Palladino and M. Worboys, 'Science and imperialism', *Isis* 84 No 1 (1993).
[150] B. J. Hunt, 'The ohm is where the art is: British telegraph engineers and development of electrical standards', *Osiris* 9 (1994). B. J. Hunt, 'Doing science in a global empire: cable telegraphy and electrical physics in Victorian Britain', in B. Lightman (ed.) *Victorian science in context* (Chicago, University of Chicago Press, 1997).
[151] Hunt, 'Doing science', pp. 324–26.
[152] Curtis, 'Metrological reform'. Latour, *Science in action*, p. 250.

Thus, before the 1860s, the measurement practices continued to be tied to the thing being measured; that is, they remained highly contextual. Although the colonial governments were active in attempts to regulate the measurement and quality of individual commodities – and some practices of estimation and measurement were standardised – most local practices in pre-Confederation Canada varied according to the community. Consequently, many bureaucratic procedures and standards were decentralised and coexisted with 'messy and haphazard local practices'.[153] The only uniform metrological standard introduced by the colonial administration was money, which was centrally regulated and into which virtually all local practices could be translated.

Persistence of local measurement practices and their role in shaping centralised versions of metrology are also evident in former colonies such as the United States, which adopted the old English measures after 1776. For instance, to facilitate the government's revenue collection, the US Coast and Geodetic Survey obtained Edward Throughon's eighty-two-inch brass scale as the length standard from London.[154] John Quincy Adams's efforts to have the metric units adopted as part of the US metrology during the 1820s remained unfruitful. The weights and measures standards adopted by the US Treasury Department in 1832 were the Imperial standards of 1824. The exception was the Winchester bushel, which was different from the Imperial bushel, and which the Treasury retained as it 'represented more closely than any other English standards the average of the capacity measures in use in the United States'.[155]

This particular bushel measure would later be the centre of some fierce debates between grain merchants regarding the differences in the practices of measuring wheat and other dry substances.[156] The brief popularity of the cental in the United States – the British measurement unit peculiar to the grain trades – is another example of how local measurement practices were allowed to coexist along with standardised centralised versions (Chapter 6). Olmstead and Rhode find similar persistence of local measurement practices in the US cotton markets of the early twentieth century. The US National Bureau of Standards continued to recognise customary and commercial measurement units, which

[153] Curtis, 'Metrological reform', p. 558.
[154] 'The Mendenhall Order of 5 April 5 1893', *Report for 1893 of the US Coast and Geodetic Survey*. Reproduced in L. E. Barbrow and L. V. Judson, *Weights and measures standards of the United States: a brief history* (Washington, DC, US Department of Commerce, National Bureau of Standards, 1976), appendix 3.
[155] Barbrow and Judson, *US weights and measures*, p. 8.
[156] Hill, *Grain, grades and standards*, pp. 6–12.

were all derived from the centrally defined and standardised metrological standards.[157]

Importance of local measurement practices

The anthropocentric nature of historical measurement units reveals their high degree of contextuality, a major source of measurement variability. The metrological reforms of the nineteenth century introduced decontextualised measurement units in Britain and elsewhere. Metrology – that is, the system of weights, measures and other measurement units – was centralised during the nineteenth century. This was a historical watershed, as metrology moved further away from its anthropocentric origins towards an objective – abstract and decontextualised – hierarchical system based upon scientific principles borrowed from physics and astronomy. Traceability aided enforceability, which was further strengthened by administrative reorganisation. Existing centres of metrology were strengthened with bureaucratic teeth, and new ones were established. Legal and administrative institutions sought to extend the influence of these centres to all segments of society, especially the economic sectors. However, the centre's influence was never total or complete. In several cases, it was even absent. Understanding measurements in historical markets only from this perspective of metrology from the centre can thus be limiting.

In the case of Britain, especially, many local measurement practices were allowed to flourish throughout the nineteenth century. In several cases, such as the use of decimal measurements in industry, the centre – that is, the state – deliberately did not exert any influence. Such decisions were left to the market. This is not to say that the influence of the state was absent. On the contrary, in several instances, the influence of the state in shaping local practices was not inconsiderable, such as when it made it compulsory to measure all dry goods (e.g. coal, grain) by weight alone and not by volume for commercial contracts. However, it would be erroneous to generalise the standardising effect of the state on measurement practices across the board.

Reform sought uniformity of measures by eliminating the innumerable local measurement units in use before the nineteenth century. This solved one of the two measurement problems mentioned in Chapter 1. By eliminating variable weights and measures, and by centralising metrology, reform did not – or could not – address the second, institutional problem of measurements in historical markets. Britain's relatively unique

---

[157] Barbrow and Judson, *US weights and measures*, appendices 8 and 9.

approach not to extend the centre's complete control of local measurement practices – in contrast to the French reforms – makes it imperative to study local measurement practices. Such microstudies alone can reveal how institutional problems were resolved, how solutions to various measurement issues depended upon the microcontexts and the processes of finding those solutions. Without this perspective, our understanding of measurement problems that potentially contributed to internal trade barriers and uncertainty in historical markets would remain incomplete.

3   Mensuration and local measurement practices

> The standards of weights and measures being once determined, they are still liable to considerable modifications, according to the manner in which they are employed, and the state of the substances concerned; so that various directions for weighing and for measuring have been given.
>
> – parliamentary report on weights and measures, 1819

Metrological realism and measurement conventions

Alain Desrosières describes four attitudes to understanding reality based upon measurements. He particularly contrasts metrological realism (derived from measurement theory in the natural sciences) and conventional realism (based upon measurements of variables that are constructed, conventional or arrived at through negotiation).[1] Metrological realism is derived from the representational theory of measurement and, within the social sciences, relies upon sampling, low measurement error, precision and absence of systematic bias to make measurements reliable. Many measurements used in commercial transactions and economic activity, including those used in product specifications (e.g. measurements of design) or quality standards (e.g. measurements of product attributes) or contract amounts (e.g. volume of goods exchanged) embody the notion of metrological realism. This is evident in instances when repeated observations of a quantity have to conform to a prespecified value within an acceptable range of deviation. Realism on such bases is obvious in the sense that measurements that conform to such specifications or statistical laws can be transformed into generalisations, extrapolations or forecasts of economic or commercial activity.

Realism based on convention, in contrast, is less obvious in the sense that the quantities to be measured are arrived at through negotiation.

---

[1] A. Desrosières, 'How Real Are Statistics? Four Possible Attitudes', *Social Research* 68 No 2 (2001). Business statistics in this case are those supplied by national institutes to describe the activities of business enterprises and used by statisticians and subsequently by economists (pp. 339–40).

There is nothing obvious about the notion that the quality – and price – of tea is dependent upon the length of the tea leaves or that the fineness of cotton yarn should be dependent upon its length per weight expressed in terms of counts. Measuring these quantities is purely a matter of convention in the sense that agreement to measure these specific quantities is reached through negotiation or social construction.[2] Such measurements are nevertheless instrumental in rendering social phenomenon to be as real as any natural or statistically constructed phenomenon.

Pre-nineteenth-century measurements in daily economic activity tended to reflect reality mostly in the conventional sense. Metrological realism was a product of the Enlightenment that gave rise to metrological centralisation. Metrological realism eventually became the way in which Latour's metrological centres began to imagine the social reality, along with the construction and expansion of centralised statistics and databases.[3]

Nevertheless, many measurements in nineteenth-century markets continued to be based upon convention. *Mensuration* – a term signifying localised measurement practices – was often based upon conventional realism. In the microcontexts, measurement reliability was not understood in terms of *precision, bias* or *measurement error* – the vocabulary used in metrological realism. It had a more prosaic definition, usually involving differing notions of trust. In some contexts, trust in measurements was generated in the sense that Porter implies, that is, 'trust in numbers', because measurements were objectified and standardised.[4] In other contexts, trust was generated in the way that Gooday implies, that is, trust between the measurer (or an agent) and the instrument (or the principal), which is a nexus of sociotechnical and historical relations.[5]

---

[2] A reviewer of an article I once wrote remarked that socially constructed standards simply meant that people had to agree on the standards specifications and that this was 'obvious' – implying that the process through which agreement was reached was not worthy of analysis. If so, then we risk relegating much of economic analysis to the phrase 'people respond to incentives', which indeed we do not. S. E. Landsburg, *The armchair economist: economics and everyday life* (New York, Free Press, 1995), p. 3. There is nothing obvious about to what and how people agree ex ante. That is why 'social construction' of anything is a complex cultural and political process worthy of analysis, as the historical material in this book demonstrates.

[3] B. Latour, *Science in action: how to follow scientists and engineers through society* (Cambridge, MA, Harvard University Press, 1987).

[4] T. M. Porter, *Trust in numbers: the pursuit of objectivity in science and public life* (Princeton, Princeton University Press, 1995), pp. 27–29. T. M. Porter, 'Objectivity as standardization: the rhetoric of impersonality in measurement, statistics, and cost-benefit analysis', in A. Megill (ed.) *Rethinking objectivity* (London, Duke University Press, 1994).

[5] G. J. N. Gooday, *The morals of measurement: accuracy, irony and trust in late Victorian electrical practice* (Cambridge, Cambridge University Press, 2004), pp. 30–39.

These approaches to measurement reliability in the history and social studies of sciences are not entirely at odds with the language of economics with its notion of measurement costs. Barzel's discussion of measurements and measurement cost is strongly based upon the notion of metrological realism, with its emphasis on measurement error. This reflects the attitude evident in much of the economics literature, where measurement reliability is derived from low measurement errors, thereby implying higher accuracy and reduced measurement costs.[6] Literature on the economics of conventions acknowledges that measurements involving quality, for instance, have a conventional or constructed character.[7] Reliability in such contexts is a matter of trust (e.g. reputation, tradition) and not a matter of error-free measurements.

Historically, these notions of trustworthy and error-free measurements occasionally came into conflict, as in the case of measurements of wire sizes (Chapter 5). At other times, they formed a nexus that led to profound political and economic change, as in the case of measurements in the London coal trade (Chapter 4). Which particular notion prevailed when conflict arose was a function of the micropolitics and material culture that shaped measurement practices. The aim of this chapter is to reflect upon such complex constituents shaping such practices within microcontexts. I develop the view that the solution to the institutional problem of measurements in historical markets (an economic issue) required a reconciliation of metrological, scientific, sociocultural and political issues. The study of local measurement practices, within the framework of a mensuration process, can help deconstruct why and how a particular solution prevailed within a given microcontext.

Understanding mensuration

By mensuration I understand the art and science which is concerned about the measure of extension, or the magnitude of figures; and it is next to arithmetic, a subject of the greatest use and importance, both in affairs that are absolutely necessary in human life, and in every branch of the mathematics; a subject by which sciences are established and commerce is conducted.

– Charles Hutton, *A Treatise on Mensuration*, 1788

[6] Y. Barzel, 'Measurement cost and the organization of markets', *Journal of Law and Economics* 25 No 1 (1982): p. 28. L. Poppo and T. Zenger, 'Testing alternative theories of the firm: transaction cost, knowledge-based, and measurement explanations for make-or-buy decisions in information services', *Strategic Management Journal* 19 No 9 (1998).
[7] S. Ponte and P. Gibbon, 'Quality standards, conventions and the governance of global value chains', *Economy and Society* 34 No 1 (2005). O. Favereau et al., 'Where do markets come from? From (quality) conventions!' in O. Favereau and E. Lazega (eds) *Conventions and structures in economic organization* (Cheltenham, Edward Elgar, 2002).

The process of mensuration in a commercial or economic context can be understood in terms of its three broad aspects – observation, comparison and contextualisation. Observation involves several steps such as determining the nature of information required; selecting the property or attribute of an object to be observed to obtain that particular information; choosing appropriate measurement methods, metrological standards and measuring instruments; making actual observations and recording; and so on.[8] The first step – determining what information is required about an object – influences the rest of the mensuration process. For instance, suppose that we require information regarding the quantity of product being offered for sale in terms of its weight. The question is whether weight is directly observable (by using some sort of weighing scales) or whether it depends upon one or more other measurements (estimating weight by measuring the volume displacement of the object). The rest of the mensuration process will depend upon the answer to this question, which may be determined by sociotechnical rather than technical considerations.[9]

Many measurements in everyday economic life are not directly observable but are made with reference to other measurements. How do people decide which other measurements correspond closely with the measurement of interest? For this, the measurers must decide which other properties of an object associate closely with the property in which they are interested. They must also agree on the principle by which the two, or more, properties are correlated.[10] Suppose sellers and buyers are interested in obtaining information about the quality of a product that they wish to trade, say, tea. The quality of tea is not directly observable or measurable and requires the measurement of another property, say, the length of the leaf. To measure quality, in this case, using the leaf length measurements, requires making two distinct choices. The first choice is

[8] P. Kircher, 'Measurements and managerial decisions', in C. W. Churchman and P. Ratoosh (eds) *Measurement: definition and theories* (New York, John Wiley, 1959), p. 68.
[9] B. Ellis, *Basic concepts of measurements* (Cambridge, Cambridge University Press, 1966). See Chapter 4 for a discussion on direct and indirect measurements. Strictly speaking, the first type of measurement in the preceding example is not directly observable if we consider the definition of weight to be a function of mass of the object in conjunction with the gravitational force that acts upon it. However, for this illustrative example, we can disregard this strict definition.
[10] Ibid., p. 90. Ellis's distinction is based on N. R. Campbell's classification of measurement scales. A common example of associative measurement is temperature measurements (p. 183, appendix I). Ellis defines *associative measurements* as those that depend on a quantity p being associated with another quantity q such that when p is arranged in a particular order, under certain conditions, q is also arranged in a particular pre-specified order (p. 90). See also H. Chang, *Inventing temperature: measurement and scientific progress* (New York, Oxford University Press, 2004).

that the length of the leaf is an associative property of the quality of tea. The other choice is that a specific length of the leaf corresponds to a specific level of quality of tea. For any leaf-property: tea-quality or *specific leaf-length:specific* tea-quality correspondences, several different relationships could be established, and choosing one rather than the other is not always obvious.[11]

The associative decisions that sellers, merchants and buyers made were distinct compared to abstracting a set of attributes to measure from amongst all the attributes that could potentially be measured. The abstractive decisions were influenced by the ability to obtain information about different product attributes, for example, information about all possible attributes in addition to leaf length, to assess the quality of tea. Economists tend to link the abstractive decisions to the concept of measurement cost. The greater the number of attributes to be measured, the more potential measurement costs tend to increase.

There is a potential for conflict in both types of decisions – the associative as well as the abstractive. Which attributes to measure? Do the selected attributes associate well with the information required? If different groups (merchants, buyers, engineers, scientists etc.) have different preferences, whose preference will come to dominate? Answers to such questions can only be found and understood in microcontexts, as the historical cases of the following chapters show.

Comparison

The other important aspect of the mensuration process is the comparison of the observations to some comparator or standard to ascertain their reliability. Much of the literature in economics treats measurement problems in economic transactions as arising due to measurement error, which theoretically can be established by comparing observations to an accepted standard. This literature unmistakably follows the notion of metrological realism, as the following argument by Yoram Barzel suggests:

Measurements [in commercial transactions] are subject to error. The greater the variability of the measurement around the *true* value, the lesser the information about the commodity. The presence of random errors [in measurements] introduces the opportunity for costly transfers of wealth.[12]

Metrological realism also leads economists to argue that measurement errors, as a source of *inaccuracy*, lead to failed or ineffective markets:

---

[11] D. M. Forrest, *A hundred years of Ceylon tea: 1867–1967* (London, Chatto and Windus, 1967), appendix III. 'Orange Pekoe' grade (OP) may be defined as 'long, thin, wiry leaves', whereas 'Pekoe' grade may be defined as 'shorter leaves, and not so wiry as OP'.
[12] Barzel, 'Measurement cost', p. 28; emphasis added.

'accuracy in measuring asset values, both physical and human, defines the effectiveness of markets.'[13]

Accuracy, however, is an elusive and nebulous concept. It is often used interchangeably with *precision*. The economics literature generally does not distinguish clearly between the two terms, although they have very different meanings in the context of measurement reliability. As Ted Porter argues, precision requires nothing more than a 'tight clustering of the measurements', just like the bullet holes in a target made by the rifle of a marksman with a bias. The bullet holes (measurements) may be very near to each other but may be some distance from the bull's eye.[14]

It may be theoretically possible to identify the extent of precision desired in measurements through quantitative methods. In turn, precision may in fact mean minimising the measurement errors, that is, minimising the extent of variation in repeated observations. But achieving accuracy, according to Porter's notion, involves identifying and eliminating bias, which may not be a straightforward metrological issue but a sociological one. As Marcel Boumans puts it, precision can be objectively established for any chosen metric in a quantitative sense. However, accuracy depends much more on qualitative knowledge and cannot be assessed in the same objective or even in a quantitative way.[15]

Thus, by eliminating the bias, can we make measurements more accurate? Is the elimination of bias tantamount to eliminating measurement error, as Barzel suggests? The answer to this depends upon whether the standard with which the observations are compared has an intrinsic bias that could be established through the notion of metrological realism. For many measurements that people make every day in their economic activity – exchanging goods and services, buying and selling assets and products – ascertaining true value in a meaningful way may be practically difficult, if not impossible. In the language of economics, it could be 'costly'. To return to our example of the quality of tea, there is no natural law or theory that suggests that tea quality is necessarily dependent upon the length of the tea leaf or that a particular leaf length represents the true measure of tea quality. Different groups may measure quality using other attributes, such as colour, or may prefer different leaf lengths to indicate a particular kind of quality. In such microcontexts, accuracy – to mean reliability – may depend upon conventional realism based on a socially accepted version of the standard that people trust. Error reduction may

[13] Poppo and Zenger, 'Theories of the firm', p. 858.
[14] T. M. Porter, 'Precision', in M. Boumans (ed.) *Measurement in economics: a handbook* (London, Elsevier, 2007), p. 343. M. N. Wise (ed.), *The values of precision* (Princeton, Princeton University Press, 1995), p. 9.
[15] Boumans, *Measurement in economics*, p. 15.

help to make such measurements more precise – in metrological terms – but is less helpful in understanding their accuracy.

In a conventional sense, *reliability* could mean *conformity*. Do repeated observations closely resemble an acceptable or prespecified value? Historically, this notion became particularly important in the case of manufactured products, interlocking pieces of machinery, screw threads and metal strips or wire and in instances in which things had to be the same. The issue here was to determine whether several pieces of a product measured on a given attribute (length, weight etc.) all conformed to a preagreed value of length, weight and so on. Such measurements were useful tools in decision making: 'if measurements conform to specifications, then do *x*, otherwise do *y*.' The degree of observed variation (from the standard) may be due to instrument error or other random factors as well as to confusion, or disagreement, regarding the prespecified values or how to measure them. Chapter 5 describes a good example of this problem, where confusion or disagreement regarding whether wire size no 32 should be 0.009th or 0.0115th of an inch contributed to the *inaccuracy* in the measurement of wire sizes, regardless of the *precision* of the measurements. Confusion about metrological standards is also evident in the system of counts used to measure the fineness of cotton yarn. This system used a confusing variety of avoirdupois ounces and troy grains, each capable of being precisely measured and each clearly defined and standardised. As units of weight were used along with units of length, one contemporary observer claimed that the system was a 'disadvantage in so far that nobody understands it'.[16]

Another way of thinking about reliability is the extent to which measurements remained consistent over time; that is, were the measurements made in a given month consistent with measurements made a month ago, a year ago, a few years before, a decade earlier and so on? Heaped measurements (Chapters 2 and 4) are a case in point. As the amount contained in the heap, on top of the bushel measure, varied or changed depending upon the context or over time, the actual amount measured also varied, even though the nominal value of the bushel remained the same. In practical terms, whether grain was sold using the heaped measure or the stricken measure from one year to another in the same market affected the consistency of measurements.

William Beveridge described a stunning example of how the inconsistency in the use of the bushel for recording grain prices in Exeter in

---

[16] *Report of the Select Committee on Weights and Measures*, PP Vol. XIII 1895, p. 735. Testimony by H. E. Wollmer on 26 March 1895. N. Biggs, 'A tale untangled: Measuring the fineness of yarn', *Textile History* 35 No 1 (2004).

the seventeenth century creates the impression of a sharp drop in the price level in 1670.[17] The apparent drop in prices, upon closer examination, can be attributed to the local officials switching from recording the prices in terms of the customary bushel measure to the 'national' Winchester bushel in that year. The local bushel was one-fourth larger than the Winchester bushel, and the switch remained undocumented in official records. Local officials recorded prices in the nominal bushel both before and after the switch, giving the impression of consistency to the unwary historian. Consistent measurements were not entirely dependant upon less deviation from the nominal value of the measurement standard.

A third way to think about reliability is the *uniformity* of measurements across geographies or groups, that is, whether all groups use or make a given set of measurements in a uniform manner. Historically, dry goods such as coal, grain and fish were sold on the basis of their weight or by volume, depending upon the market. In the nineteenth century, almost three-fifths of British market towns sold wheat using volumetric measurements, slightly less than two-fifths sold it using a combination of weight and volume and the balance few towns sold wheat using weight measures.[18] For commodities like coal, different parts of the same trade route would use different ways of measuring the same commodity or would use different measurement units altogether.[19] Even when the same measurement unit was used, the value of that unit could differ. In the early nineteenth century, the Imperial bushel was equivalent to fifty-nine pounds if wheat was measured, fifty-one pounds if barley was measured, thirty-nine pounds if oats were measured, or sixty-four pounds if peas were measured (Chapter 6).[20] The question of unreliability arose when such variations in practices and local norms were either not generally known or difficult to ascertain. Naturally, merchants dealing in multiple markets with different conventions could exploit such informational asymmetries to their advantage.

The problem with equating reliability to stricter notions of variability (from a true value) is that, historically, variability of measurements was often a desired attribute (Chapter 2).[21] Variable measurements

[17] W. Beveridge, 'A statistical crime of the seventeenth century', *Journal of Economic and Business History* 1 No 4 (1929).
[18] *Returns from corn inspectors*, PP Vol. XLIX 1834, p. 251. Memo on 'Different customs or practices of selling corn and other grains.'
[19] S. Pollard, 'Capitalism and rationality: a study of measurements in British coal mining, ca. 1750–1850', *Explorations in Economic History* 20 No 1 (1983).
[20] PP Vol. XLIX 1834, p. 256.
[21] W. Kula, *Measures and men*, R. Szreter (trans.) (Princeton, Princeton University Press, 1986). K. Alder, 'A revolution to measure: the political economy of the metric system

had a social function, for example, a system of handicapping the less privileged.[22] Sometimes they had an economic function, for example, adjusting for changes in the market value without a corresponding change in monetary value, as with the Assize of Bread, where the weight of the bread loaf was altered according to the price of grain, without changing the price of the loaf.[23] At other times, variability was the result of persistence of local custom stemming from some symbolic meaning or communal memory: 'we have always measured it in this manner around here.'[24] Thus reliability in the sense of invariability, less deviation or error free was not universally desired in historic markets.

It is not evident that in any of the historical examples described earlier, variation in measurements resulted only from a lack of unchanging, invariable metrology, nor is it obvious that any of the measurements described earlier had to cluster around some true or ideal value – a value derived from some natural, physical phenomenon which could be indisputably ascertained. In this sense, measurement issues were not limited only to the invariability of the metrological units or to minimising the error around some true value. If reliability is considered in a broader sense to be derived from the sameness of measurements, then sameness could be achieved either through metrological or conventional notions of realism.

Contextualisation

The third aspect of the mensuration process involves contextualising the observations–comparisons to establish their significance within a particular context. Contextualisation enables people to make sense of the information that observations–comparisons convey about a particular economic activity. It enables them to make assessments and take decisions depending upon the significance of the observations–comparisons in a given microcontext. Practically, observations–comparisons can be classified or sorted on the basis of one or many

in the ancien régime', in M. N. Wise (ed.) *The values of precision* (Princeton, Princeton University Press, 1995).

[22] J. Hoppit, 'Reforming Britain's weights and measures, 1660–1824', *English Historical Review* 108 No 426 (1993).

[23] J. Davis, 'Baking for the common good: a reassessment of the assize of bread in medieval England', *Economic History Review* 57 No 3 (2004).

[24] R. Sheldon et al., 'Popular protest and the persistence of customary corn measures: resistance to the Winchester bushel in the English west', in A. Randall and A. Charlesworth (eds) *Markets, market culture and popular protest in eighteenth-century Britain and Ireland* (Liverpool, Liverpool University Press, 1996), pp. 34–35.

(qualitative) parameters: good–bad, acceptable–unacceptable, reliable–unreliable, adequate–inadequate and so on. Decisions can then be made on the basis of established if-then-else rules: if the outcome of the comparison is x, then the action taken should be A; otherwise, the action should be B. These are context-driven activities, where people take into account the sociocultural environment as well as institutional factors to make assessments or decisions.[25] Contextualisation helps to transform observations–comparisons into measurements through complex mental processes in addition to sociotechnical processes. In this sense, people are remarkably clever contextualisers.[26]

Historically, measurements had particular meanings that could only make sense in reference to particular contexts. Figure 2.1 illustrates this argument especially well: the meaning of a pre-Imperial bushel of potato, grain or other dry goods could only be made clear with reference to particular commodities, their geographical context, who measured them or on whose behalf the commodity was measured. In the example illustrated by Figure 2.1, the measurement of a bushel of potato must be contextualised in terms of a geographical location for it to be meaningful, especially since the meaning changes according to location in this case. Thus the measurement of a bushel becomes a *measurement* once it is placed in a relevant context (e.g. a bushel of potatoes in Cheshire, Leicestershire, Surrey etc.). Until then, it remains an observation, a recorded piece of information.

Contextualisation is important when we consider reliability in terms of conventional realism, more so than realism based on metrology. The manner in which individuals and groups contextualised observations–comparisons and turned them into measurements determined whether they were reliable. Historically, this became especially important when decontextualised metrological units were introduced in the nineteenth century (Chapter 2). Where previously the metrological units themselves had provided some of the context, groups using the new metrology had to recontextualise them along with the observations–comparisons. Recontextualisation is a complex mental ability which people undertake

[25] E. Hutchins, *Cognition in the wild* (Cambridge, MA, MIT Press, 1996). E. Hutchins, 'How a cockpit remembers its speeds', *Cognitive Science* 19 (1995). H. Artman and Y. Waern, 'Distributed cognition in an emergency co-ordination centre', *Cognition, Technology and Work* 1 (1999). A. T. Denzau and D. C. North, 'Shared mental models: ideologies and institutions', *Kyklos* 47 No 1 (1994): p. 4.

[26] G. A. Miller, 'Contextuality', in J. Oakhill and A. Garnham (eds) *Mental models in cognitive science: essays in honour of Phil Johnson-Laird* (Hove, Psychology Press, 1996), pp. 2–3. G. A. Miller, 'On knowing a word', *Annual Review of Psychology* 50 (1999): p. 11. G. L. Murphy, 'Comprehending complex concepts', *Cognitive Science* 12 (1988).

in many daily situations.[27] Consequently, the extent to which particular measurements were considered reliable depended upon the microcontext in which the mensuration process occurred.

Measurement tools: instruments, protocols and standards

Fundamentally, to make measurements, we require measuring instruments. They could be either physical artefacts or mental constructs. For instance, metrological units are often represented as physical objects or measuring vessels of particular dimensions, for example, the kilogram, metre, yard or bushel. Similarly, engineering gauges (such as cylindrical gauges, wire gauges and sheet metal gauges) are measurement instruments, just as thermometers or voltmeters are. Equally, metrological units are often just mental constructs, derived with reference to some physical phenomenon or object or other mental constructs but without a physical form of their own. For example, the ton, chaldron, acre and kilometre are all mental constructs of metrological units that have no representative physical artefacts but are understood with reference to some other artefacts. Measurement instruments also include accounting and auditing tools as well as economic models. In fact, any construct that enables us to observe and record phenomena of interest by 'picking them out in a particular way' is a measurement instrument.[28] This broad definition then includes metrological units – such as the Imperial units (pounds, bushels, inches etc.) and metric/SI units (kilograms, litres, metres etc.) – as well as weighing scales, measuring cups, foot rules and many other scientific and nonscientific instruments.

Historically, the existing level of measurement technology and development of certain measuring instruments had a profound impact on the emergence of several local measurement practices. For instance, improvements in weighing technology made it possible to directly observe the weight of bulky objects, an activity that was usually difficult and costly before the nineteenth century (Chapters 4 and 6). This made it more

---

[27] Miller describes how people recontextualise similar-sounding words to mean different things in different situations. Miller, 'Contextuality'. Miller, 'On knowing'. Sabina Leonelli describes how curators of scientific databases de-contextualise scientific facts, which are subsequently recontextualised by users of those databases; see S. Leonelli, 'Packaging small facts for reuse: databases in model organism biology', in M. S. Morgan and P. Howlett (eds) *How well do facts travel? The dissemination of reliable knowledge* (Cambridge, Cambridge University Press, 2010).

[28] M. S. Morgan, 'Making measuring instruments', *History of Political Economy* 33 Suppl. (2001): pp. 236–38. M. Power, 'Counting, control and calculation: reflections on measuring and management', *Human Relations* 57 No 6 (2004).

effective to begin weighing commodities such as coal and grain and had an impact on measurement practices in those markets. Similarly, the development of measuring instruments such as the chrondometer (for measuring the density of grain), the ohm (for measuring electrical resistance), the decimal measuring system and the micrometer gauge had a significant impact on local measurement practices.

Several measuring instruments capable of achieving a high degree of precision were developed during the nineteenth century. However, precision was not sufficient in itself to increase the reliability of measurements. For instance, Joseph Whitworth's millionth measuring machine was a very precise measurement instrument capable of achieving a precision of up to one-millionth part of an inch.[29] However, the reliability of the wire sizes did not increase with the precision with which wire diameters could be measured; machines capable of measuring wire sizes in the hundredth or thousandth parts of the inch were available in the nineteenth century. Reliability involved fixing a preagreed set of wire sizes: a process that involved standardising another measuring instrument, the wire gauge.

In fact, the manner in which measurement instruments could be used in local measurement practices was governed by rules, regulations and conventions, collectively termed here as *measurement protocols*. These are as much the tools within the mensuration process as the measurement instruments. Protocols may be formal legal rules and regulations, or they could be informal, de facto conventions that emerged through long usage, common knowledge or practical considerations. Thus metrological institutions regulated the construction of legally recognised measurement instruments; they specified the steps to be observed in their construction, the materials that the physical artefacts should be made of, the methods of testing their accuracy, the manner in which they should be calibrated and authenticated, the acceptable and unacceptable ways of using them and the penalties and recourse in the event of improper or fraudulent use. Sometimes legislation directed the use of particular metrological units in specific activities, for example, the use of certain kinds of weights for measuring dry goods.[30] Similarly, institutions, such as scientific or professional bodies, developed their own conventions and methodologies to govern the construction and use of other measurement instruments. At the other end of the spectrum, individual firms and organisations

[29] T. Kilburn, *Joseph Whitworth: toolmaker* (Cromford, Derbyshire, Scarthin Books, 1987), p. 24.
[30] 5 & 6 William IV, C. 63, 1835, *Weights and Measures (Amendment) Act*, and 11 & 12 Geo. V C. 35, 1921, *Weights and Measures in the Sale of Corn Act*. These statutes are examples of such legislation.

developed or adopted measurement instruments based upon their particular experience or manufacturing methods. The prevalence of wire gauges, which were often specific to individual workshops or regions (such as Birmingham and Lancashire), is an example of this. Protocols directed the manner in which the instruments were used: pouring the grain into a vessel from a particular height, drawing the wire through a particular sequence of holes on the wire gauge and so on.

Such protocols were institutions in the sense that they specified the 'rules of the game'.[31] They coordinated actions between individuals or between groups and organisations and included externally imposed rules (e.g. legislation) as well as conventions that emerged endogenously during interaction between individuals. Historically, there were different ways of organising or coordinating similar measurement activities across different microcontexts. Protocols within different groups making the same measurements or using the same instruments could be very different and potentially conflicting. Diversity in such cases was nontrivial and the product of socio-politico-cultural processes. There was no single set of rules that governed measurement protocols across all microcontexts.[32]

Standards

Standards used within the measurement practices are measurement tools, just as are protocols and measuring instruments. Apart from standardised metrological units, the measurement practices depend upon technical, design or product standards. A set of wire sizes is a measurement standard because it employs metrological units and uses specific measurement scales.[33] These same measurement standards are also product standards because they are a part of technical or design specifications such as 'the diameter of this wire must be six millimetres thick' or 'this product must

---

[31] D. C. North, *Institutions, institutional change and economic performance* (Cambridge, Cambridge University Press, 1990).

[32] This insight comes from convention theory that distinguishes between several modes of coordination by considering a variety of ways in which people coordinate between themselves. People create equivalences between themselves or between things and use a variety of cognitive as well as organisational forms to generalise these equivalences. Coordination depends upon the level of complexity involved in making things (and people) more general across contexts. J. Wilkinson, 'A new paradigm for economic analysis?' *Economy and Society* 26 No 3 (1997): p. 323. L. Thévenot, 'Organized complexity: conventions of coordination and the composition of economic arrangements', *European Journal of Social Theory* 4 No 4 (2001): pp. 406–7.

[33] The scales used could be nominal at one extreme, such as numerical quality grades, or they could be ratios, as in the case of numerical estimates of densities. See S. S. Stevens, 'On the theory of scales of measurement', *Science* 103 No 2684 (1946), for a discussion of the scales used in measurements.

weigh sixty pounds'. The fibre length of cotton staple is both a measurement standard and a quality standard for product grading. Similarly,
the counts system used for determining the fineness of yarn is a measurement standard as well as a product standard.[34] Is there an analytical
and meaningful difference between these standards – the metrological
units, measurement standards, technical or product specifications and
so on?

Tirole described a method of classification depending upon the
description of attributes of an economic good and the information about
the attributes that can be captured.[35] According to this classification,
some standards help in the selection of products by capturing information about their quality or diversity. These are standards based upon
search attributes that are ex ante, that is, relevant prior to exchange.
Experience attributes, in contrast, are evident ex post, and standards
that describe them (e.g. durability) are often relevant postconsumption.
Credence attributes are trickier to describe and may not be evident even
on an ex post basis. Standards that describe these attributes include those
that capture information about composition of materials, or presence of
(potentially harmful) substances, or manufacturing method employed
and so on. Establishing whether a product possesses the desired credence attributes is difficult and often requires third-party monitoring or
certification.

This classification helps in analysing how and why measurement and
monitoring costs differ across various standards. However, it does not
present a helpful framework to analyse differences between measurement
and product standards, if any, nor is it evident that the different types of
standards can be disentangled in any constructive manner. For instance,
suppose a contract grade specifies wheat density of No 2 spring wheat to
be sixty-three pounds per bushel. At best we can claim that the density
measurement acts as a search attribute, while the 'No 2' specification
is a credence attribute. Measurements such as density as well as several
other attributes are necessary to establish the credibility of a given wheat
sample to be No 2 type and no other. Analytically, the messiness of
classifying standards in this manner is difficult to resolve.

An alternative classification involves focusing on the public good characteristics of standards. Kindelberger argued that standards, especially
metrological units, are public goods due to their nonrivalrous nature:
'they are available for use by all and use by any one does not reduce

[34] A. H. Garside, *Cotton goes to market: a graphic description of a great industry* (New York,
Frederick A. Stokes, New York, 1935), p. 68. Biggs, 'A tale untangled'.
[35] J. Tirole, *The theory of industrial organization* (Cambridge, MA, MIT Press, 1988).

the amount available to others.'[36] He argued that several standards with public goods characteristics in fact began life as privately set standards by merchants, professional associations or companies. Thus standards are public goods, even though they may be privately set either to reduce transaction costs or to improve compatibility.

Romer provided a qualification to this argument of nonrivalry by claiming that some standards, such as a design standard, could be made excludable even though they remain nonrivalrous. He argued that rivalry is a technological attribute, whereas excludability is a function of both the technology and the legal system, that is, institutions. A nonrival good having the property that its use by one firm or person in no way limits its use by another could be rendered excludable if the owner can prevent others from using it. Conventional economic goods (products or services) are both rivalrous and excludable, whereas public goods by definition are both nonrival and nonexcludable. However, some economic goods, such as designs or standards, can be nonrivalrous yet excludable. This nonrivalrous yet excludable nature of some standards renders them nonpure private goods, that is, somewhere between public and private goods.[37]

In this classification, metrological units are evidently closer to the public goods end of the spectrum (they are not excludable), whereas product standards are clearly closer to the private goods end of the spectrum. Their nonrivalrous nature makes them nonpure private goods. Measurement standards, if they form part of design standards, also tend towards nonpure private goods if they are made excludable. However, this framework is still insufficient as it does not reveal the motivations and mechanisms by which nonrivalrous standards are made excludable. While metrological units are clearly very different from measurement and product standards, the framework does not allow us to make useful distinctions between product and measurement standards, if any.

Classifying standards by the manner in which they are established enables us to place de facto standards at one end of a spectrum and de jure standards at the other. Economists have by and large considered standards to emerge either de facto, that is, as a result of market exchanges, or through a de jure process of regulation and legislation.[38] However,

[36] C. Kindelberger, 'Standards as public, collective and private goods', *Kyklos* 36 No 3 (1983). P. A. Samuelson, 'The pure theory of public expenditure', *Review of Economics and Statistics* 36 No 3 (1954).
[37] P. M. Romer, 'Endogenous technological change', *Journal of Political Economy* 98 No 5, Part 2 (1990). See also C. Antonelli, 'Localized technological change and the evolution of standards as economic institutions', *Information Economics and Policy* 6 Nos 3–4 (1994).
[38] D. J. Teece and E. F. Sherry, 'Standards setting and antitrust', *Minnesota Law Review* 87 No 6 (2003). H. Spruyt, 'The supply and demand of governance in standard-setting:

many standards have historically been developed by standard-setting committees in an explicit form of nonmarket coordination at a meso-level but without the legislative obligation of de jure standards.[39] Many standards promulgated by standard-setting bodies such as the International Standards Organization (ISO), the American National Standards Institute, the British Standards Institute or the Bureau International de Poids et Mesures are collaborative standards. Such standards are sometimes referred to as voluntary consensus standards as they are voluntarily adopted by market and firms.[40] Farrell and Saloner had argued that standard setting through a combination of committees and market coordination closely resembles how several standards actually emerge.[41] Historical evidence presented in this book confirms that standards set by committees often are the result of consensus requiring explicit negotiation (not de facto) and have governance-promoting ability even though they are voluntary (not de jure).[42] As the following chapters reveal, it is difficult to apply this classification strictly across different contexts. However, this classification helps to distinguish between the different types of standards in a relevant and useful manner. Metrological units (inches, metres, litres, gallons etc.) are usually de jure standards that emerged

insights from the past', *Journal of European Public Policy* 8 No 3 (2001). Antonelli, 'Standards as institutions', pp. 196–97. H. Koski and T. Kretschmer, 'Entry, standards and competition: firm strategies and the diffusion of mobile telephony', *Review of Industrial Organization* 26 (2005). P. A. David and S. Greenstein, 'The economics of compatibility standards: an introduction to recent research', *Economics of Innovation and New Technology* 1 Nos 1–2 (1990).

[39] R. N. Langlois, 'Competition through institutional form: the case of cluster tools standards', in S. M. Greenstein and V. Stango (eds) *Standards and public policy* (Cambridge, Cambridge University Press, 2007). M. B. H. Weiss and M. Sirbu, 'Technological choice in voluntary standards committees: an empirical analysis', *Economics of Innovation and New Technology* 1 No 1 (1990). K. T. Hallström, *Organizing international standardization: ISO and the IASC in quest in authority* (Cheltenham, Edward Elgar, 2004).

[40] C. N. Murphy and J. Yates, *The International Organization for Standardization (ISO): global governance through voluntary consensus* (New York, Routledge, 2009). Literature on voluntary standards further distinguishes between public and private voluntary standards, whereby voluntary standards set by non-state actors may be adopted by the state and invested with legislative powers without making them mandatory. See S. Henson and J. Humphrey, 'Understanding the complexities of private standards in global agri-food chains', paper presented at International Workshop on Globalization, Global Governance and Private Standards, Leuven (2008), p. 2, esp. figure 1. Also T. Havinga, 'Private regulation of food safety by supermarkets', *Law and Policy* 28 No 4 (2006). S. Henson and T. Reardon, 'Private agri-food standards: implications for food policy and the agri-food system', *Food Policy* 30 No 3 (2005).

[41] J. Farrell and G. Saloner, 'Coordination through committees and markets', *RAND Journal of Economics* 19 No 2 (1988).

[42] Mattli has used the term *institutional standards* to describe such standards. W. Mattli, 'The politics and economics of international institutional standards', *Journal of European Public Policy* 8 No 3 (2001).

in the nineteenth century through a political process of centralisation. Other metrological units (electrical resistance, wire sizes etc.) are voluntary consensus standards that emerged in local or microcontexts. Still other standards used in measurement practices tended to be set either through de facto market interactions or on the basis of voluntary consensus. Such de facto or voluntary consensus standards may eventually become codified as legislation. However, they are privately set public standards whose use is optional rather than obligatory; they are 'optional laws'.[43]

Whether set through de facto, de jure or voluntary consensus, standards fulfil a variety of functions. Compatibility standards help to make a variety of products and technologies compatible with one other (capture network externalities), reference standards are useful in monitoring performance, while variety-reducing standards help in reducing diversity and confusion.[44] Whatever function they fulfil, standards (metrological, technical, product, quality etc.) are critical measurement tools that are integrated within local measurement practices.

Standard setting and standardisation

Standardisation is potentially one of the strategies to prevent what economists term as opportunistic behaviour, overcome informational and coordination problems and capture externalities through its network effects. It provides ex ante solutions to counter fundamental problems of economic exchanges – as described by Greif, Barzel and others – compared to costlier ex post solutions of adjudication and arbitration.[45] How do standards emerge? What determines whether certain standards achieve a lawlike or regulatory status? To what extent are they influenced by historical choices that people make? Do superior standards replace

---

[43] N. Brunsson and B. Jacobsson, 'The contemporary expansion of standardisation', in N. Brunsson and B. Jacobsson (eds) *A world of standards* (Oxford, Oxford University Press, 2000).

[44] P. Swann et al., 'Standards and trade performance: the UK experience', *Economic Journal* 106 No 438 (1996). Antonelli, 'Standards as institutions', p. 197; David and Greenstien, 'Compatibility standards'. Teece and Sherry, 'Standards setting and antitrust'. G. Tassey, 'The role of government in supporting measurement standards for high-technology industries', *Research Policy* 11 (1982). Spruyt, 'Governance in standard-setting'.

[45] A. Greif et al., 'Coordination, commitment, and enforcement: the case of the merchant guild', *Journal of Political Economy* 102 No 4 (1994). A. Greif, 'The fundamental problem of exchange: a research agenda in historical institutional analysis', *European Review of Economic History* 4 No 3 (2000). Barzel, 'Measurement cost'.

inferior standards? These are important questions in the context of local practices, which may determine whether measurements in microcontexts are considered reliable.

The extensive literature on the economics of standards describes several approaches to standardisation. An influential view suggests that standardisation is highly contingent upon accidents of history. W. Brian Arthur gives an excellent precis of this view. According to him, if two or more technologies compete for dominance, then insignificant events may by chance give one of them an initial advantage in terms of the number of people adopting it. This technology may then improve more than the others, making it more appealing to a greater number of potential adopters. This in turn may lead to this technology being further adopted and further improved. Thus 'a technology that by chance gains an early lead in adoption may eventually corner the market of potential adopters, with the other technologies becoming locked-out.'[46] Under different circumstances, a different technology might achieve sufficient adoption and become the dominant one, thereby setting the standard.

The standardisation of the keyboard design – QWERTY – is often cited to be the result of such an historical selection process.[47] Another example cited is the emergence of the market for nuclear power reactors using light water technology.[48] These examples stress that the standardisation of particular designs or technologies occurs in the presence of competing and perhaps more efficient alternatives. Path dependency has a considerable influence on the standardisation process.

Puffert, writing about path dependence in the standardisation of railway gauges, has shown how particular preferences, both in initial gauge selection and subsequent conversion processes, resulted in the spatial diversity of gauges. This diversity, he argues, has persisted even after concerted efforts to capture network externalities through track conversions. He considers track selection to be a product of both systematic influences (i.e. predictable, measurable and fundamental such as technological changes and economic costs) and nonsystematic elements (i.e. transitory circumstances and idiosyncratic choices of individuals).

---

[46] W. B. Arthur, 'Competing technologies, increasing returns, and lock-in by historical events', *Economic Journal* 99 No 394 (1989).

[47] P. A. David, 'Clio and the economics of QWERTY', *American Economic Review* 75 No 2 (1985). S. J. Liebowitz and S. E. Margolis, 'The fable of the keys', *Journal of Law and Economics* 33 No 1 (1990).

[48] R. Cowan, 'Nuclear power reactors: a study in technological lock-in', *Journal of Economic History* 50 No 3 (1990).

Thus initial preferences and path dependency may result in diversity preventing a one-size-fits-all standard from emerging.[49]

The economics literature generally tends to analyse standard setting as a strategic action that firms adopt to secure a competitive edge over other firms. Besen and Farrell discuss several strategies that firms adopt, particularly in technology or network industries, that involve making choices between competing or cooperating with other firms to set standards. They describe circumstances in which dominant firms compete with other firms in strategic standard-setting 'games'. The returns to winning a standards battle are potentially large, but the risks of losing are costly.[50] Nonetheless, it may be more effective for firms to cooperate with other firms to set standards rather than compete and let the market set a dominant standard. Indeed, firms enter into standard-setting alliances, coalitions or standardisation 'clubs', and the emergence of a standard is the result of a deliberate decision-making process. Such coalitions are formed between producer groups or user groups or indeed between producer and user groups.[51] Coalition forming is tricky and may be riddled with agency problems, time inconsistency, free-riding and so on. Such problems could potentially be solved through state intervention and de jure standardisation, according to this literature.[52] However, there is a lack of overall consensus on the exact trade-offs involved in public policy intervention in standards setting, from the perspective of both efficiency and competition policy.[53]

Following Farrell and Saloner's normative work on mixed strategies of standard setting through markets and committees, Murphy and Yates

[49] D. J. Puffert, *Tracks across continents, paths through history: the economic dynamics of standardization in railway gauge* (Chicago, University of Chicago Press, 2009).

[50] S. M. Besen and J. Farrell, 'Choosing how to compete: strategies and tactics in standardization', *Journal of Economic Perspectives* 8 No 2 (1994). C. Shapiro and H. R. Varian, *Information rules: a strategic guide to the network economy* (Cambridge, MA, Harvard Business School Press, 1998). C. Shapiro and H. R. Varian, 'The art of standards wars', *California Management Review* 41 No 2 (1999).

[51] Antonelli, 'Standards as institutions', p. 205. Teece and Sherry, 'Standards setting and antitrust', pp. 1934–42, 1987. M. A. Cusumano et al., 'Strategic maneuvering and mass-market dynamics: the triumph of VHS over beta', *Business History Review* 66 No 1 (1992).

[52] D. Foray, 'Users, standards and the economics of coalitions and committees', *Information Economics and Policy* 6 Nos 3–4 (1994). Cf. R. Axelrod et al., 'Coalition formation in standard-setting alliances', *Management Science* 41 No 9 (1995). Kindelberger, 'Standards', p. 388. Also K. A. Konrad and M. Thum, 'Fundamental standards and time consistency', *Kyklos* 46 No 4 (1993). Teece and Sherry, 'Standards setting and antitrust'. S. Berg, 'The production of compatibility: technical standards as collective goods', *Kyklos* 42 (1989).

[53] J. Farrell, 'Should competition policy favor compatibility?' in S. M. Greenstein and V. Stango (eds) *Standards and public policy* (Cambridge, Cambridge University Press, 2007). Koski and Kretschmer, 'Standards and competition'.

show how the ISO has historically emerged as an organisation nestled within a large network of voluntary consensus standard-setting bodies.[54] This process of standardisation allows powerful bodies (dominant firms, organisations or even states) to defect from a standard-setting process coordinated by committees before formal policy is reached. Voluntary consensus effectively enables the groups to retain the flexibility of standard switching that a formal policy does not allow (de jure standardisation). At the same time, it provides an environment to avoid costly standard wars by setting a standard ex ante that de facto standardisation process does not allow. In this sense, standard setting by firms is often a political process motivated by strategic considerations. Several studies of standard setting in information technology, electronic components or telecommunications support this view.[55] Weiss and Sirbu's study of eleven standard decisions made by voluntary standard committees in the telecommunications and information technology sectors found that in addition to firm size, political processes dominate the choice of technology standards for committees; that is, the degree and manner in which large firms support one standard over another greatly influence the standard-setting process.[56]

Invariably, the process of standardisation or switching from one standard to another has to overcome resistance to change. The literature on the economics of standardisation defines resistance in terms of inertia, that is, the tendency to remain unchanged. This tendency occurs due to the effects of lock-in and technological interrelatedness. According to this view, if the use of an existing standard depends upon compatibility with complementary standards or upon its use by a sufficiently large number of users, then 'there are benefits to doing what others do'.[57] Switching from this standard to a newer standard would not make sense to any single user unless all users, or a large majority of users, switch to the new standard. In this situation, there is a socially excessive reluctance to switch to a new standard, even if it is superior to the existing one. Society

[54] Farrell and Saloner, 'Coordination'. Murphy and Yates, *International Organization for Standardization*. Hallström, *International standardization*. W. Higgins and K. T. Hallström, 'Standardization, globalization and rationalities of government', *Organization* 14 No 5 (2007).
[55] Axelrod et al., 'Coalition formation'. Langlois, 'Cluster tools standards'. J. Farrell and C. Shapiro, 'Standard setting in high-definition television', *Brookings Papers on Economic Activity: Microeconomics* 1992 (1992). M. T. Austin and H. V. Milner, 'Strategies of European standardization', *Journal of European Public Policy* 8 No 3 (2001).
[56] Weiss and Sirbu, 'Voluntary standards committees'.
[57] J. Farrell and G. Saloner, 'Installed base and compatibility: innovation, product preannouncements, and predation', *American Economic Review* 76 No 5 (1986): p. 940.

could become locked in on an existing standard, even though demonstrably superior standards or technologies may exist (as in the example of QWERTY cited earlier), and any changes to the existing standard could be path dependent.[58]

Path dependency of standards could also be the result of stubborn resistance to change, not just lock-in or technological interrelatedness, as historical studies of popular protests against standardisation of metrological units amply demonstrate.[59] Such resistance must be understood in its local or regional context and may be closely related to questions of communal memory.[60] The diversity of local measurement units is matched by their persistence in the face of standardised metrology. So great could be the resistance at times, and so great a desire to perpetuate historical practices, that users would seek to measure commodities, such as grain, to yield measurements of the same size and weight as before the measures were standardised.[61]

Another source of persistence or resistance to change is the ideology and cultural symbolism associated with measurement technologies and artefacts. The influence of culture can be understood in terms of symbolic meanings that are relative to specific cultural contexts. For instance, decimal units came to represent progress in the nineteenth century compared to fractional units, even though some others considered decimal units to be artificial and unnatural. Similarly, fixed, abstract and immutable metrological units based on scientific principles came to symbolise objectivity and rationality in the late eighteenth and nineteenth centuries in Britain: in France, the metric units symbolised a break from the feudal units of the ancien régime. Symbols form systems of meaning and become ideologies that exert a powerful influence on (technical) change.[62] Metrological units have historically acted as symbols

[58] David and Greenstien, 'Compatibility standards', pp. 5–9. Farrell and Saloner, 'Installed base and compatibility'. M. L. Katz and C. Shapiro, 'Network externalities, competition and compatibility', *American Economic Review* 75 No 3 (1985).

[59] Kula, *Measures and men*, pp. 111–13.

[60] Kula refers to the term *mémoire collectif* used by M. Bloch, who in turn has used Durkheim's terminology to claim that persistence of measures is bound up with questions of communal memory. Ibid., p. 111.

[61] Sheldon et al., 'Customary corn measures', pp. 34–35.

[62] E. Schatzberg, *Wings of wood, wings of metal: culture and technical choice in American airplane materials, 1914–1945* (Princeton, Princeton University Press, 1999), pp. 11–19. Staudenmaier reminds us that humans repeatedly report feelings of awe, aesthetic delight or fear as part of their conscious experience of different technologies – suggesting that technological cognition is an important aspect of understanding cultural symbols. J. Staudenmaier, 'Problematic stimulation: historians and sociologists constructing technology studies', in C. Mitcham (ed.) *Social and philosophical constructions of technology* (London, Jai Press, 1995).

of culture, identity and ideology that can become powerful sources of resistance.

The standardisation process must be understood in its sociological sense as well as in the context of economic and technological imperatives. On this point there is broad consensus within the diverse literatures from economic history, public policy and the history of science and technology.[63] The process of standardisation is highly contingent upon the material politics of consumption, production and exchange. It involves the selection of one standard from among several alternatives through some selection process. This process is greatly affected by initial preferences and path dependency, which influence people's decisions in terms of selecting some standards over others. Standardisation may be the result of coordinated or negotiated efforts between groups or coalitions – not only strategic interactions between competing firms. This process does not always result in the dominance of the most efficient standards, and superior standards need not always replace inferior standards. Multiplicity of standards and incompatibility between them are quite common in product and commodity markets rather than an exception.

Historically, standardisation of measurement practices involved standardising both the process and the tools that people used in the process of measuring. To be specific, standardising observations involved standardising the property or attribute of the object that is measured in a given context (e.g. weight or volume, colour or composition), the recording instruments that were used in making the observations and the method of making observations (e.g. method of stretching cotton staple to observe its length, pouring grain into a measuring vessel from a specific height, measuring the diameter of the wire from the middle of the strand etc.). Standardising the comparisons involved making prior decisions about the choice of standard to be used to compare the observations (metrological standards, product specifications, quality classes and grades etc.), methods of making the comparisons (sorting, ranking, pair-wise etc.), the groups or individuals responsible for making these comparisons and

---

[63] David, 'QWERTY'. Weiss and Sirbu, 'Voluntary standards committees'. M. J. Daunton, 'The material politics of natural monopoly: consuming gas in Victorian Britain', in M. J. Daunton and M. Hilton (eds) *The politics of consumption: material culture and citizenship in Europe and America* (Oxford, Berg, 2001). Sheldon et al., 'Customary corn measures'. G. V. Thompson, 'Intercompany technical standardization in the early American automobile industry', *Journal of Economic History* 14 No 1 (1954). Mattli, 'Institutional standards'. Austin and Milner, 'European standardization'. B. J. Hunt, 'Doing science in a global empire: cable telegraphy and electrical physics in Victorian Britain', in B. Lightman (ed.) *Victorian science in context* (Chicago, University of Chicago Press, 1997). Gooday, *Morals of measurement*. Havinga, 'Private regulation'. Henson and Humphrey, 'Private standards'.

conditions under which they are made and so on. Similarly, contextual-isation involved developing prior decision rules for anticipated outcomes of the comparisons (e.g. 'if x, then y, else z' rules) and monitoring mechanisms to ensure their compliance.

The process of standardising measurement practices should be viewed as part of a larger institutional change demanding not only that the individual standards were established or altered but also that other components connected to it were established or altered.[64] Institutional change of this nature had to be shaped by the interaction between individuals, groups, organisations and institutions at various levels.[65] The different, sometimes conflicting objectives of the different groups involved no doubt caused tensions between those groups that supported standardisation (i.e. uniformity) and those groups that were content to continue using existing measurement practices. These tensions had to be resolved locally. It is only through the study of such local or microcontexts that we are able to understand and appreciate how path-dependent standards emerged through socio-politico-cultural processes and were often difficult to anticipate ex ante. The historical case studies of measurement practices in the following chapters illustrate this salient point.

Mensuration and local measurement practices

The mensuration process as I have explained here, that is, observation, comparison and contextualisation, is a complex social activity. It links measurement tools, that is, the instruments, protocols and standards, in a particular way within a microcontext. Such links are established through historical (social, political, cultural etc.) processes as different groups involved in the commercial and economic activity exert their influence on the instruments, standards and protocols and thereby shape local measurement practices.

Conventions played a large and important part in shaping these links, despite the rise of metrological realism during the nineteenth century. Measurement reliability, thus, was not exclusively based upon error reduction, minimising deviation or tight clustering of measurements around a true value – the vocabulary of metrological realism.

---

[64] C.-F. Helgesson et al., 'Standards as institutions: problems with creating all-European standards for terminal equipment', in J. Groenewegen et al. (eds) *On economic institutions: theory and applications* (Cheltenham, Edward Elgar, 1995), pp. 165, 171–72. Antonelli, 'Standards as institutions', p. 214.

[65] North, *Institutions*, pp. 7–8. S. Ogilvie, '"Whatever is, is right?" Economic institutions in pre-industrial Europe', *Economic History Review* 60 No 4 (2007).

Conventional ideas of accuracy – as distinct from metrological precision – continued to guide people's perceptions about measurement reliability. In this sense, measurement practices developed as sociological constructs within microcontexts. They were the result of different historical processes, as compared to metrological reforms occurring at the centre during the nineteenth century. Such practices played a crucial role in rendering measurements reliable in the local contexts, notwithstanding the centralisation and standardisation of metrology.

This thesis can be truly appreciated by examining specific cases of how merchants and businesses struggled to make measurements reliable in everyday economic activity. The case studies featured in the following chapters highlight the sources of measurement problems in different contexts and the different kinds of solutions that emerged. The case of the London coal trade circa 1830 explores the factors that led to three significant reforms of long-established measurement practices: the abolition of the public measurement system, the abolition of the heaped measures and the switch from using volume measures to weight measures (Chapter 4). These reforms were introduced to address a fundamental measurement issue facing this trade: were the measurements regarding quantities (i.e. amount) used for delivering the product during market exchanges reliable? In other words, could the buyers rely upon measurements used in the trade such that the amount of coal that they received was actually the amount of coal they purchased?

The case of the wire-making industry focuses on the incentives facing buyers and sellers of wire products in the nineteenth century and how these incentives gave rise to different notions of reliable measurements (Chapter 5). The case study highlights the struggles to define a standard one-size-fits-all gauge to measure wire sizes, which could be legally enforced and would overcome the disputes arising from incompatible and multiple gauges. In other words, it studies the rationalisation of multiple standards into a uniform metrological standard.

The case of the international wheat trade highlights how the measurement of quality became a complex, centralised and sophisticated process involving measurement of numerous product attributes using multiple standards (a standard in this case being an arbitrary reference point to which individual observations were compared). The measurement issue that the trade faced was which 'summary criteria', that is, a set of product attributes, could capture ex ante the important aspects of product quality – in terms of the product's composition, condition and functionality (Chapter 6).

Each of the three cases has been chosen to highlight different aspects of the mensuration process. Chapter 4 discusses the changes that occurred in the measurement protocols as a consequence of the efforts to make measurements in the delivery of coal in London more reliable. Chapter 6 explores the decisions regarding the choice of product attributes to measure and how markets developed solutions to deal with situations when this aspect was not standardised across trade routes. Chapter 5 analyzes standard-switching behaviour, the convergence towards uniform standards and the development of a standardised measuring instrument. Overall, all three cases explore the correspondence between the different aspects of the mensuration process – observation, comparison, contextualisation – and the tools used in the process, including instruments, protocols and standards.

The three case studies highlight in some detail how people actually made measurements in various economic and commercial contexts. The influence of different groups of people on the measurement practices is explored on the basis of their incentives or the particular interest they had in the measurements. These groups comprised merchants, traders and middlemen; producers, buyers and consumers; state departments, legislatures and local government authorities; trade and industry associations, commodity exchanges and chambers of commerce; scientific societies and trade journals; and so on. The differences in the incentives and, consequently, the extent to which the different groups influenced measurement activities are specifically highlighted through the cases.

For instance, the case of coal measurements in London investigates how various groups – local London merchants, producer–merchants in Newcastle and Durham, Corporation of London, Houses of Parliament, state departments (e.g. the Treasury) and so on – resolved the measurement problem through lengthy debates on various measurement issues (Chapter 4). The debates raised the following questions: were public measurements necessary within the trade? Could the inefficiencies of the existing metage system be reformed? Would a switch of standards – from volume to weight – enable the buyers to effectively monitor transaction quantities?

The case of the wire sizes investigates how entrenched interests within buyer and producer groups resulted in a stalemate with neither group willing to accept the other's notion of reliable wire sizes (Chapter 5). These interests stemmed from different incentives: the buyers desired sizes that would enable them to use wire products more effectively in their applications, and the producers desired sizes that would economise their production costs. The stalemate – between producer associations, chambers of commerce and buyer associations – was overcome once the state was asked to intervene on behalf of the industry: the Board of Trade acted as an arbitrator between the various industry groups.

The case of the wheat trade investigates how the markets addressed the problem of measuring the quality of a highly heterogeneous commodity by selecting different sets of summary criteria for use in different contexts and by different groups (Chapter 6). The grading process was a responsive activity: a universal attribute set could not be used across all trade routes, and the grades (and consequently the measurement standards) had to be reviewed periodically. Commodity exchanges developed numerical grades to help manage complex quality measurements using different attribute sets. Even so, not all measurements were made by associations or third-party organisations. The buyers often had to rely on their own sets of measurements. The millers developed specific quality measurement methods and used different sets of measurements to determine product quality.

On the whole, the cases explore how local practices were shaped by cultural, economic, political and technological factors. By exploring how such factors shaped the incentives and decisions of various groups, the cases explore how different groups influenced different aspects of mensuration, for example, selection of attributes to measure (Chapter 6), selection of measurement tools (Chapter 4), standardisation of metrology versus measurement practices (Chapters 4 and 5) and so on.

The three case studies highlight how different solutions emerged to address the different mensuration issues: metrological standardisation (Chapters 4 and 5), standardising protocols (Chapters 4 and 6), third-party monitoring of measurements (Chapters 4 and 6), coordination by trade associations (Chapters 5 and 6) and so on. The case of the coal trade shows how standardising practices through regulation was a way to solve transparency issues in market transactions. The case of the wire industry investigates how standardising both wire sizes (metrological standardisation) and wire gauges (measurement instrument) was a solution to make measurements of wire diameters reliable. The efforts of heterogeneous buyers and producers were coordinated through trade associations, and in fact, the coalition of large manufacturers was able to influence the eventual standards to be fairly close to their desired specifications. The case of the wheat trade shows how market institutions and third-party monitoring by commodity associations were able to guarantee the reliability of measurements. Standardisation of measurement practices, in this instance, did not involve the rationalisation of numerous standards, that is, a decrease in the number and variety of standards. In contrast, protocols were developed to make it possible to use several specialised standards.

In all three cases, there is no evidence of a true value or a universal measurement criterion to which measurements had to conform. There was no true way of measuring grain quality or an ideal wire gauge or the perfect way of measuring the amount of coal delivered. Markets found different solutions to measurement issues, standardisation being one of them. The cases explore the role of market institutions and demonstrate that a narrow focus on metrology cannot uncover how markets managed measurement issues.

4 Governance and regulation

Standardising measurements in the London coal trade (c. 1830)

> If bread be the staff of life, coals are its clothing.
> — *The Times*, 28 March 1829

The long-distance trade in 'sea coles' existed in the United Kingdom ever since the Company of Woodmongers and Coal Sellers was established in London around 1330.[1] There was a fair amount of traffic in the commodity by the fourteenth century, which continued to grow steadily until the nineteenth century. In 1369 the City of London appointed *coal meters*, who were city officials responsible for measuring coal. Public measurement of coal was a method devised 'to ensure fair measure for the consumers'.[2] The Crown had also begun to levy taxes on coal to finance its activities: a tax on coal in 1362 helped finance the Black Prince's campaign in France.[3] By the nineteenth century, a highly structured and elaborate trade route involving coastwise coal shipments, a portfolio of taxes and fiscal charges on this trade and a public system of delegated monitors to measure the commodity had existed for more than half a millennia – long-established institutions in the history of the metropolis.

In this chapter, I explore the links between the structure of the London coal trade, the state's fiscal interest in this trade and the changes to the local measurement practices in the early nineteenth century. I investigate the factors that led to three significant reforms around 1830: the abolition of the public metage system, the abolition of the heaped measures and the switch from using volumetric metrological units to weight units. I show that ensuring reliability of measurements in this important industrial sector involved fundamental changes to centuries-old measurement

---

[1] H. B. Dale, *The fellowship of woodmongers: six centuries of the London coal trade* (London; repr. from the *Coal merchant and shipper*, 1923), p. 1.

[2] R. Smith, *Sea-coal for London: history of the coal factors in the London market* (London, Longhams, 1961), p. 2. Dale, *Woodmongers*, p. 1. Dale claims that the coal meters were formed c. 1330.

[3] Dale, *Woodmongers*, p. 1. Also J. T. Taylor, *The archaeology of the coal trade* (Newcastle, Frank Graham, 1858), p. 13.

practices. Measurement instruments and protocols were altered or substituted, and existing standards were replaced. Such changes were motivated by the need to increase governance and improve coordination along the distribution channel. The initiative came from coal merchants and trading firms, and the state's involvement was ensured by the opportunity to solve certain political economy issues. Overall, changing measurement practices was a major institutional change as it redefined traditional roles, responsibilities and rights of the various economic groups involved in the industry.

Specifically, the case study explores the following questions: why were traditional measurement practices considered unreliable by circa 1800? Why were public measurements necessary before the nineteenth century? Why was this medieval practice replaced? Why were London merchants accused of using the wrong measurement standards? What was the significance of the changes to the local practices? Did these changes make the measurements more reliable?

The London trade faced several governance issues as the traffic in the commodity increased significantly in the early decades of the nineteenth century (Figure 4.1). It took nearly a hundred years for the traffic in this trade to double compared to circa 1700 levels. The same quantum of growth was achieved in only thirty years in the early years of the nineteenth century. Several institutions regulated the sale and delivery of the commodity in London, including the public measurement system, the various layers of duties and charges and the *turn system* that guided the loading and unloading of colliers. With increased traffic, these institutions came under severe strain, creating several complications in the governance of the trade. Addressing these complications implied resolving distribution bottlenecks due to increased congestion, improving the port infrastructure and docking facilities, reforming the turn system and restructuring the public measurement or metage system.[4]

The public metage system had traditionally acted as a mechanism to govern and manage the measurement activity within this trade. It was an important mechanism for monitoring the amount of coal that was exchanged during all trades in the market. It was also a crucial mechanism for determining the fiscal income that would accrue to the government from this trade. The measurements certified by the public measurers were used as a basis for determining the rights of the sellers, buyers *and* the state. The reformation of the metage system was part of efforts to

---

[4] Smith, *History of coal factors*, pp. 195–229. S. Ville, 'Total factor productivity in the English shipping industry: the north-east coal trade, 1700–1850', *Economic History Review* 39 No 3 (1986): p. 364.

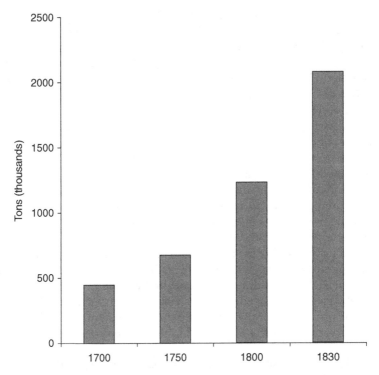

Figure 4.1. Quantity of coal transported to London (1700–1830). *Source*: Based on figures reported in M. W. Flinn, *The history of the British coal industry*, Vol. 2, *1700–1830* (Oxford, Clarendon Press, 1984), table 8.1.

strengthen governance within the London trade and, in the process, to reform or alter a mechanism that was considered by some groups to be inadequate and/or nontransparent.

At a broader level, the trade reforms reflected the changing political economy of British taxation. As was discussed in Chapter 2, the state increasingly sought ways to make the taxable commodities more conformable to its system of measurement. As part of its efforts to centralise administrative functions, it had progressively installed a uniform method of gauging taxed goods predominantly at the source of production or distribution.[5] This was achieved for most of the commodities by the eighteenth century, with the exception of coal. Fiscal revenues

[5] W. J. Ashworth, *Customs and excise: trade, production, and consumption in England, 1640–1845* (Oxford, Oxford University Press, 2003), p. 383.

from coal were substantial by the end of the eighteenth century, accounting for more than 3 per cent of the state's total revenue.[6] Nevertheless,
the state's capacity to continue taxing this essential commodity, with an
inelastic demand, was contested in the early decades of the nineteenth
century. The trade reforms, according to some historians, such as Paul
Sweezy, T. S. Ashton and Michael Flinn, represent the 'triumph of [free]
trade and rational taxation'.[7]

The issue that lay at the core of the metage reforms was the standardisation of quantity, or rather, a method of estimating reliable quantities.
The state's fiscal, administrative and regulatory functions required a reliable method of accounting for the quantity of coal traded; the metage
system was originally meant to be a part of that method. Consistency of
measurements was an important issue in this case. The market sought
reliable measurements to ascertain 'who got what'. Thus conformity of
measurements to some prespecified value was an important consideration for determining the income and property rights of various economic
groups along the value chain (sellers, factors, buyers etc.). The quantity
of coal exchanged during each trade in the London market – and particularly the use of heaped measures using volumetric metrological units to
determine that quantity – became the key issue in the early nineteenth
century, upon which the reform of the metage system and measurement
practices hinged.

This problem of reliable quantities was not unique to the coal trade
around this period. Historically, quantities reflected the socio-politico-
economic relationships, particularly feudal rents, and were highly sensitive to the use of local measurement artefacts (e.g. the shape of baskets)
as well as local practices such as heaping and striking.[8] Efforts to standardise quantity measurements in the spirits, liquor or salt trades in the
eighteenth century were protracted and involved considerable debate and

---

[6] M. W. Flinn, *The history of the British coal industry*, Vol. 2, *1700–1830* (Oxford, Clarendon
Press, 1984), p. 284. In 1789, revenues from the coal trade contributed £552,000 of the
total state revenue of £16.7 million.

[7] P. M. Sweezy, *Monopoly and competition in the English coal trade: 1550–1850* (Cambridge,
MA, Harvard University Press, 1938), p. 55. He remarks that the 'cloying fetters of
mercantilist trade and fiscal policy were swept away with one stroke'. T. S. Ashton and
J. Sykes, *The coal industry of the eighteenth century* (Manchester, Manchester University
Press, 1929). Ashton and Sykes wrote that the 'remedy for the evils lay not in the increase
of state and municipal supervision, but in the abolition of duties, the substitution of weight
for measure [and] developments of transport', pp. 224–25. Also, Flinn, *Coal Industry*,
p. 285, who writes that the reforms were symbols of the victory of free trade and the
triumph of capitalism and were manifested in the London case by a 'growing willingness
on the part of the government to listen to free trade arguments'.

[8] J. C. Scott, *Seeing like a state: how certain schemes to improve the human condition have failed*
(New Haven, Yale University Press, 1998), pp. 27–29.

negotiation between the state and the trade.[9] Debates involving stand-ardisation of quantity are evident in the grain trade in other historical periods as well as geographical locations (see Chapter 6).

Sidney Pollard had highlighted the significance of the measurement changes and their importance in helping the coal mining industry to standardise quantities. He argued that the increasing complexity of mar-ket transactions in the nineteenth century, both in scale and in geograph-ical scope, induced owners of coal mines to adopt fewer and standardised metrological units in place of the multiplicity of units that had worked well in the past.[10] This case study shows that rationalising the number of measurement units was not sufficient to standardise quantity. In fact, the multiplicity of metrological units per se was not the cause of measure-ment problems at the London end of the trade route. Standard switch-ing is a path-dependent and nonergodic process. Even though the coal merchants likely realised the benefits of switching to uniform measure-ment standards, coordinating between the collective benefits of uniform measurements and the private benefits of nonstandardised or even non-compatible standards was not straightforward. Pollard did not account for the potential inertia in switching from one standard to another.

The industry had begun to use a range of standards and standardised measurement tools. For instance, the colliery owners of the north-east had adopted cost and management accounting practices such as dis-counted cash flow techniques and risk-adjusted rates of return on their estates by the turn of the eighteenth century.[11] The demands for reliable measurements were likely a reflection of these changing values of quan-tification, particularly amongst the coal owners and merchants from the north-east. This raises several questions. To what extent could coal own-ers, who used the ostensibly more reliable weight standards, impose their preferences on measurement practices used by the London merchants? Why were the units of weight considered to be more reliable than the units of volume? Was the decision to switch from volumetric measurements to weight measurements linked to the abolition of the public measurement system? Answers to such questions depend upon the competition and complex negotiations between the different groups of merchants and the

[9] Ashworth, *Customs and excise.*
[10] S. Pollard, 'Capitalism and rationality: a study of measurements in British coal mining, ca. 1750–1850', *Explorations in Economic History* 20 No 1 (1983).
[11] R. K. Fleischman and R. H. Macve, 'Coals from Newcastle: an evaluation of alternative frameworks for interpreting the development of cost and management accounting in Northeast coal mining during the British Industrial Revolution', *Accounting and Business Research* 32 No 3 (2002). S. Brackenborough et al., 'The emergence of discounted cash flow analysis in the Tyneside coal industry c1700–1820', *British Accounting Review* 33 No 2 (2001).

various levels within the state (bureaucracy, legislature, local government etc.) as well as the ability of coal owners to exert their influence on the state and the London market.[12] This case study traces how the notions of reliable practices held by coal merchants at the production end of the trade route travelled to and influenced the local practices in a major consumption centre.

Structure of the London coal trade

London was precocious in its use of coal. Since the Middle Ages, the metropolis was supplied by coal from the coalfields of Northumberland and Durham, mainly around the river Tyne and the Wear. The abundant outcropping seams of coal and direct water connections favoured this trade route, and the traffic along this route grew substantially over the centuries.[13] In the early nineteenth century, even as the other coal-producing regions, such as Wales and the Midlands, increased their output of coal in proportion to Northumberland, this region dominated the supplies to London. Virtually all of London's coal came from the ports of Newcastle and Sunderland, and more than half of the coal shipped out of these ports was delivered to London.[14] The north-east–London trade route that dominated the trade in London was as old as the trade in coal in the metropolis.

Almost all of the coal that was sold in London until the nineteenth century was brought via the coastal sea routes. A negligible amount of coal came into London via inland routes. For instance, in 1810, out of the 1.25 million tons of coal brought into London, about 1.24 million tons were shipped via coastal routes, and only about 8,000 tons were delivered via inland routes, mainly canals. This proportion remained more or less constant until the 1840s, when the proportion of deliveries via inland routes increased steadily, and by 1866, the proportion delivered by inland routes, primarily by the railway networks, was about 50 per cent of the total quantity delivered to London.[15] Thus, before 1840, London's supplies of coal came primarily from the north-east via coastal routes on ships known as *colliers* (Figure 4.2).

---

[12] W. J. Hausman, 'Market power in London coal trade: the limitation of the vend, 1770–1845', *Explorations in Economic History* 21 No 4 (1984). Sweezy, *Monopoly and competition.*

[13] J. Hatcher, *The history of the British coal industry*, Vol. 1, *Before 1700* (Oxford, Clarendon Press, 1993), p. 25. Smith, *History of coal factors*, pp. 5–6.

[14] *Account of coals shipped from the ports of Great Britain*, PP Vol. XIV 1818, pp. 165–69.

[15] *Account of coals brought coastways and by inland navigation*, PP Vol. LXIV 1867, p. 642. Of the 6 million tons of coal delivered in 1866, about 3 million were delivered by the coastal routes, and nearly 3 million were transported via the railways.

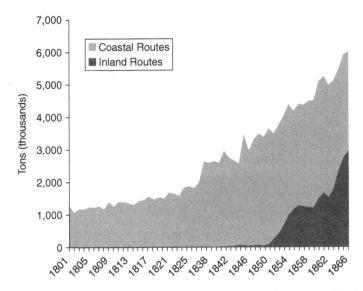

Figure 4.2. Quantity of coal delivered by mode of transport. Excluding foreign imports. Quantities between 1801 and 1827 reported in London chaldrons (LCh) and converted to tons on the basis of 1 LCh = 25.5 hundredweight and 20 hundredweight = 1 ton. Quantities from 1837 onwards are reported in tons. Almost all of the coal transported via inland routes after c. 1860 was by rail. *Source*: Data from various parliamentary reports (see main text).

The London trade route consisted of complex structures organised around numerous distinct economic groups (Figure 4.3).[16] As Figure 4.3 shows, the coal passed through several hands before reaching the ultimate consumer. At the north-east end of the trade were the coal owners, who owned or leased estates producing a high-quality coal that had a strong demand in London. They were a highly organised group and were able to form several combinations or associations that were essentially monopolistic in nature. During the sixteenth and seventeenth centuries, groups of dominant coal owners were organised as the Grand Lessees and later the Company of Hostmen. These groups combined to apportion between themselves the vend or quantity of coal that would be delivered to the market in each period, and there is evidence of such combinations

---

[16] The following account of the supply chain is based on the select committee reports on the coal trade. See House of Commons Reports (1785–1801) Vol. X 1800, *Second report from the Committee on Coal Trade.*

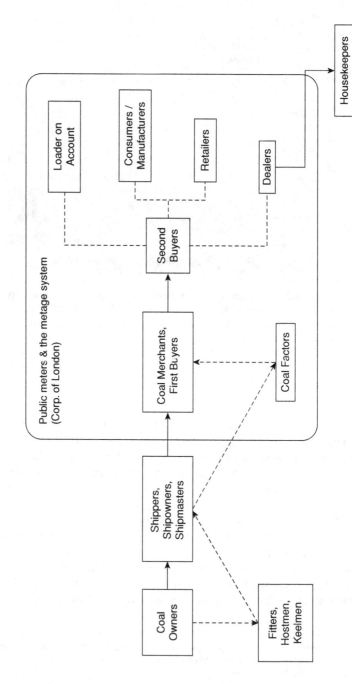

Figure 4.3. Structure of the London coal trade (c. 1830).

being formed at various times throughout the seventeenth century.[17] During the seventeenth and early eighteenth centuries, the Company of Hostmen also came to include a group of middlemen called the *fitters*. At least three principal combinations were formed between 1700 and 1830 in the Northumberland and Durham region – the Grand Alliance, the Limitation of the Vend and the Joint Durham and Northumberland Coal Owners Association.[18] The intent of most of these combinations was twofold: to limit the output of coal and thereby to maintain prices and profits.[19] In addition, the owners were also a politically powerful group, well represented in both the houses of the Parliament. Prominent personalities included Sir Matthew Ridley, MP, Lord Durham and Lord Londonderry, the Marquis of Londonderry.[20]

The role of the fitters was to arrange for the coal to be sold to the shipmasters of seagoing ships or colliers in return for a commission from the pit owner or lessee. The fitter was also responsible for settling all the customs formalities and obtaining a certificate of loading specifying the price and quantity of coal. The coal would be delivered into the colliers by keelmen, who would employ light craft known as *keels* for this purpose. Until the late eighteenth century, the shipmasters would transport the coal to London at their own risk – rarely was coal freighted directly to the London market. However, by the 1790s, some owners had began consigning cargoes to specific commission agents called *coal factors*.[21]

In the early seventeenth century, traffic in coal at the London end increased substantially. In addition, colliers could no longer unload onto the wharves. Consequently, there arose a need for a middleman who could act as a connecting link between the shipper and (1) the market and the buyers, (2) the customs and city offices for payment of duties

---

[17] Sweezy, *Monopoly and competition*, pp. 13–15. F. W. Dendy (ed.), *Records of the company of hostmen of Newcastle-upon-Tyne* (Durham, Surtees Society, 1901). Smith, *History of coal factors*, pp. 2–14.

[18] Flinn, *Coal industry*, pp. 256–67. Sweezy, *Monopoly and competition*, pp. 22–36. Dendy, *Hostmen*. P. Cromar, 'The coal industry on Tyneside 1771–1800: oligopoly and spatial change', *Economic Geography* 53 No 1 (1977). J. A. Jaffe, 'Competition and the size of firms in the north-east coal trade, 1800–1850', *Northern History* 25 (1989).

[19] Jaffe, 'Competition and size', p. 236. Flinn, *Coal industry*, p. 256. Small variations in either costs or prices could make substantial differences to the total profits of coal owners.

[20] Lord Durham was the son-in-law of Earl Grey and the owner of an estate of seventeen thousand acres, with mines connected via a network of private railways. D. Spring, 'The Earls of Durham and the great northern coal field, 1830–1880', *Canadian Historical Review* 33 No 3 (1952). Lord Londonderry was the largest coal owner on the wear. Jaffe, 'Competition and size'.

[21] Smith, *History of coal factors*, pp. 121–22.

and charges and (3) the labour pool who would deliver from the colliers to the wharves. By the 1670s, several intermediaries were fulfilling this role, known variously as *crimps* or *brokers*.[22] Some time during the eighteenth century, the coal factors emerged as an organised group of intermediaries and, by the 1780s, were acting as commission agents in London.[23] Gradually, the factors had become the first point of contact for the shipmasters arriving with their cargoes into the Port of London. Thomas Gillespy, a coal factor and shipowner in London, stated that in 1800, there were nineteen houses (comprising twenty-seven individuals) carrying on the business of coal factors in London.[24] These numbers remained unchanged thirty years later, according to the testimony of another coal factor, James Bentley.[25] On arrival of the ship into London, the ship's papers were transmitted to one of these factors, who in turn would complete the customs formalities and arrange for the sale of the cargo at the Coal Exchange.

The Coal Exchange in 1800 was a closed market conducted from a building in Billingsgate that was built somewhere around 1769.[26] In this exchange, the factors would conduct the sale of coal to a group of merchants known as the coal buyers or *first buyers*. Around 1800, there were about 70–75 of these large merchants operating within the Coal Exchange, and although their numbers appear to have increased to about 150 by 1830, only about 50 or so were considered first houses around this time.[27] Thus the trade was concentrated in the hands of a few individuals who functioned as a conduit for virtually all the coal that entered the London market. Thomas Fletcher, a coal buyer, described the business of the first buyer:

The business of the first buyer [is] to purchase entire cargoes of coal from the factors, and to dispose of them afterwards to his customers, of whom there are five sorts, viz. the loader on account; the dealer; the retailer; the consumer, and the housekeeper. The first is a person who loads Coal in his own craft, but has not capital to buy at Billingsgate, where the practice is to purchase whole cargoes,

---

[22] Ibid., pp. 49–50. J. U. Nef, *The rise of the British coal industry*, Vol. 2 (London, George Routledge, 1932), pp. 85–87.

[23] Flinn, *Coal industry*, pp. 277–78. Smith, *History of coal factors*. Smith reckons that the term *factor* was being used from the early years of the seventeenth century (pp. 66–67).

[24] HC Report Vol. X 1800, *Report from the Committee on Coal Trade*. See Thomas Gillespy's testimony before the committee, p. 553. However, a subsequent report tabled by the committee mentions a figure of fourteen instead of nineteen (*Second Report on Coal Trade, 1800*).

[25] *Report of the select committee on coal trade*, PP Vol. VIII 1830, testimony by James Bentley, coal factor, p. 149.

[26] Smith, *History of coal factors*, p. 85.

[27] *Report on Coal Trade*, 1800, p. 553, Gillespy's testimony. PP Vol. VIII 1830, p. 149, Bentley's testimony.

on an average credit from 28 to 30 days. The dealer buys of us to sell principally to housekeepers. The retailer keeps a shed, and sells them out by the bushel; and the consumer is confined to large manufactories.[28]

The members of this heterogeneous group were sometimes also referred to as *second buyers*. According to one contemporary estimate, the second buyers, excluding the housekeepers, purchased roughly five-sixths of the coal from first buyers.[29] This structure of the supply chain within the London market had remained practically unchanged between the late eighteenth and early nineteenth centuries.[30]

Finally, within this supply chain were the *lightermen* (previously known as woodmongers), who kept and operated barges. In the eighteenth century, the coal factors effectively replaced the lightermen as the middlemen between the seller and the buyer in the London market. By the nineteenth century, the lightermen had turned into a group that would hire out the barges, or *lighters*, for delivering coal from the colliers to the wharf. They were paid by the buyers, who in turn charged their customers with lighterage as the cost of delivery from the colliers to the wharves.[31] Coal was transferred from the colliers onto these barges by *heavers* or *whippers*, who were contracted by an *undertaker* employed by the ship's captain once the colliers entered port.

An important group in the supply chain comprised the *coal meters*, who were first appointed in the fourteenth century to 'ensure fair measure for the consumers'.[32] Most probably, as the traffic into the Port of London increased, and duties on coal and other city dues became an essential part of the customs machinery, the meter became an integral part of that institutional infrastructure. By the late eighteenth century, we perceive two classes of meters: the *sea meters*, those originally employed in the fourteenth century to measure coal being delivered from the colliers to the lighters, and the *land meters*, who were appointed to conduct measurements on the shore.[33] Once the sale of the coal was arranged

[28] *Report on Coal Trade*, 1800, Thomas Fletcher's testimony, p. 548.
[29] Ibid., p. 553, Gillespy's testimony.
[30] PP Vol. VIII 1830, testimony by Joseph Holl to the Select Committee, pp. 117–19. A somewhat different terminology and arrangement is described by Dale, *Woodmongers*. He mentions ten first buyers who took the whole contents of a ship and sold to the second buyers, 'who represented some 60 other firms', and 'beyond these a vast number of brass-plate coal merchants and dealers and retailers who sold by the bushel' (p. 95).
[31] *Report on Coal Trade*, 1800, Gillespy's testimony, pp. 550, 552. See also Smith, *History of coal factors*, pp. 48, 64–66, 146.
[32] Smith, *History of coal factors*, p. 2.
[33] Ibid., p. 52. The land meters were formed around 1767, when a group of coal merchants successfully petitioned Parliament to secure permission to measure coal 'between the Tower and Limehouse Hole [as] the old Coal Meters of 1330 only operated in the City of London on the river'. Dale, *Woodmongers*, p. 82.

on the Coal Exchange, the factor would make an application to the Coal Meters Office for an appointment of a sea meter.[34] The duties of the sea meter on board the collier were to prepare an account of the cargo delivered to the various first buyers on the basis of actual measurements made as the coal was heaved up from the colliers onto the lighters or barges.[35] The land meters were appointed to specific wharves and were expected to 'see all the coal which are sold [was] duly measured, and the due quantity served [and] the whole quantity put into the wagon'.[36]

The meters were employed by the Corporation of London, which charged a metage duty of about one shilling two pence per chaldron for this service.[37] Fifteen principal sea meters were appointed by the City of London to supervise nearly 150 deputy sea meters. Similarly, two principal meters each for London and Westminster and about four for the county of Surrey supervised the work of between thirty and forty land meters in each district. Traditionally, the meters were paid at the discretion of the shipmaster; however, after 1807, the sea meters were paid a fixed amount by the City on the basis of the quantity measured (one penny per chaldron). The land meters were paid a fixed wage per week of up to twenty-eight shillings in London, or less if light work was involved, while those in Surrey were paid between twelve and twenty shillings a week, or less than eight shillings if working occasionally.[38] The metage system effectively performed three vital functions: first, the meters acted as delegated monitors to measure the quantity exchanged between the buyer and the seller; second, these measurements served as a basis for collecting various duties on coal and other dues; and third, the metage duty was a source of revenue for the City.

However, the functioning of this system was not always smooth. The Corporation of London was faced with the problem of monitoring the coal meters. With over 150 sea meters and nearly an equal amount of land meters, the principal meters had trouble supervising their effort and commitment. The sea meters had an incentive to collude with the first buyers to provide short measure as they were paid a fixed fee for every chaldron they measured. As far as the land meters were concerned, their

---

[34] *Second Report on Coal Trade*, 1800.
[35] *Report on Coal Trade*, 1800. See testimonies by James Dixon (coal meter) and Richard Austen (deputy coal meter), p. 558.
[36] PP Vol. VIII 1830. Testimony by John Bumsted (principal land meter), p. 26.
[37] Ibid., pp. 8–9. This comprised eight pence per chaldron for the sea metage and four pence per chaldron for the land metage. The chaldron was the customary unit of measurement used in the trade and is discussed in greater detail in the following pages.
[38] Ibid., appendices 4(i), 8, 11, 16, 20 and 21. Also *Report on Coal Trade*, 1800. See James Dixon's testimony, p. 558.

earnings were not directly based on how much quantity was measured. However, many of them in fact had other occupations as publicans and small shopkeepers, which explains why so many instances of absenteeism were reported among the meters. One internal memo by principal meters lists several offences reported among the meters, including absence from duty, drunkenness, making erroneous returns, giving short measure and so on. Errant meters were disciplined either through prosecution, fines or wage reductions. However, these methods were not always successful, and continuing problems with this system were the source of major indignation within the London coal market.[39]

Measurements used in the London coal trade

In addition to the numerous groups involved in the delivery of coal from the pits in the north to the end user in London, a bewildering array of measurement units were in use well into the nineteenth century. This chapter focuses only on those units employed in the sale and delivery of coal at the London end of the trade route.[40] The cargo of coal bound for London was loaded on the colliers on the rivers Tyne and Wear using a measure called the *Newcastle chaldron* (NCh). This was a weight measure, equivalent to fifty-three hundredweight, eight of which made up a keel load.[41] Once in the Port of London, coal would be sold from the colliers to the first buyers using a local measurement unit known as the *London chaldron* (LCh), which was a volumetric measure.[42] This was the measurement practice that had dominated the trade for over half a millennium. In fact, before the nineteenth century, a majority of the coal transported around England and Wales by the coastwise trade in seagoing

---

[39] [C]orporation of [L]ondon [R]ecords [O]ffice COL/CC/CCN/03/012, *Papers of the Committee on Coal and Corn Meters*, January 1829–July 1830. Letter by principal meters dated 1 October 1829.

[40] Historians such as Pollard have described the changes to the measurement units at the production end of the value chain. Pollard, 'Measurements in coal mining'.

[41] The hundredweight (cwt) is equivalent to 112 pounds (approximately 51 kilograms). The quantity measured by this unit had changed considerably since medieval times, roughly increasing by a factor of 2.5 or 3. See R. A. Mott, 'The London and Newcastle chaldrons for measuring coal', *Archaeologia Aeliana* 40 4th Ser. (1962): pp. 230–35. Also B. Dietz, 'The north-east coal trade, 1550–1750: Measures, markets and the metropolis', *Northern History* 22 (1986): pp. 282–86. Hatcher, *Coal industry*, pp. 561–67. Smith, *History of coal factors*, pp. 361–68, contains a useful glossary of similar customary measurement units.

[42] Throughout this book, the terms *volume* and *volumetric* are used to signify a measure of dimension, i.e. capacity. They generally do not refer to quantities, such as sales volume, without expressly stating so – the term *quantity* is used instead. Often contemporary accounts use the term *measure* to signify a measure of capacity. This is retained in quotations but is treated synonymously with the term *volume*.

Table 4.1. *Quantity of coal shipped coastwise during 1829,*
comparing the quantity sold by weight and volume

Quantity shipped to	Weight (tons)	Volume (chaldrons)
All England and Wales	210,495	2,706,828 (3,451,205[a])
London	265	1,548,170 (1,973,916[a])

[a] Equivalent quantity in tons assuming 1 chaldron = 25.5 hundred-weight and 20 hundredweight = 1 ton.
Source: Customs returns, PP Vol. XXVII 1830, p. 131.

vessels was measured in volumetric units. London alone accounted for more than half of this coastwise trade (Table 4.1).

Coal was physically delivered from the collier to the barge using a measure known as the *vat* (also known as *vatts* or *fatts*). Four vats made up the LCh, and nine bushels in turn made up the vat. There was no physical artefact representing the LCh.[43] In contrast, the vat and the coal bushel were represented by physical standards in the form of metal vessels. The barges were divided into rooms, each holding not more than five chaldrons and one vat (to provide for the ingrain; see later). Merchants purchasing five chaldrons or any multiples thereof would receive the entire quantity of coal in one or more such rooms.[44] The London trade used legal but local measurement units. The coal bushel used in the trade was different from the more generally used Winchester bushel before 1824 and the Imperial bushel that replaced it after 1824. Thus the LCh and coal bushel were evidently in use only in this trade and in a particular geographical area (London) and were a result of peculiar trade practices (Table 4.2).[45]

---

[43] In the north, no physical artefact represented the NCh. Before the mid-eighteenth century, the NCh was estimated using a combination of bolls, wains and cartloads. After the wooden wagon-ways developed, the NCh came to be estimated using wagons each constructed to hold the equivalent of 53 hundredweight. Measurement units such as the boll and hundredweight were legal, as were physical artefacts. PP Vol. VIII 1830. See testimony by Robert Brandling (chairman of the Coal Committee at Newcastle), p. 261. See also testimony by John Buddle (colliery expert and viewer), p. 285. An account of the relationship between the NCh and the various units from which it was derived is discussed by other historians, including Mott, 'London chaldron'; Dietz, 'Coal trade'; Hatcher, *Coal industry*; Taylor, *Coal trade*; G. Bennett et al., *A fighting trade: rail transport in Tyne coal: 1600–1800* (Gateshead, County Durham, Portcullis, 1990).
[44] PP Vol. VIII 1830. John Bumstead's testimony, p. 30.
[45] 47 George III, C. 68, 1807, *Act for regulating the delivery of coals*. This act describes a specific bushel to be used in London for the measurement of coal, which was first defined in 12 Anne Stat. 2 C. 17, 1713, *Act for ascertaining the coal measure*.

Table 4.2. *Measurement units used in the London coal trade (c. 1830)*

		Meterological unit(s) converted	
Seller	Buyer	From	To
Newcastle coal owners	Shippers	Bolls, wain, keels, cartload etc.	NCh
Shippers	First buyers (London)	NCh	LCh
First buyers	Second buyers (dealers, consumers etc.)	LCh	Bushels, vats
Dealers	Housekeepers	Vats	Bushels

Note: Abbreviations are as follows: LCh, London chaldron; NCh, Newcastle chaldron.

How invariable were these measurement standards? Although the LCh was defined as being equivalent to thirty-six bushels, there is almost no consensus in practice on just exactly how much quantity or amount of coal this unit measured.[46] Contemporary experts as well as modern historians have been befuddled by the relationships between the various measurement units used by the trade before the nineteenth century.[47] This issue becomes clearer when we compare the quantity in gallons that the LCh was supposed to contain. Estimates of the LCh have ranged from 288 to 396 gallons, although recent research shows that the LCh was historically estimated to be either 384 or 396 gallons.[48] Such variations in the estimates of the LCh are also evident when we compare the estimates of the weight of coal contained in one chaldron. One estimate concluded that the LCh attained its final level of about 26.5 hundredweight in 1530; another ascribed a weight equivalent of 25.7 hundredweight, while historical sources seem to suggest that the weight estimates existing between 1793 and 1847 ranged from 26.5 hundredweight to 28.46 hundredweight.[49] The following sections discuss the measurement instruments and protocols that potentially had the greatest impact on the measurement of quantities.

[46] 47 George III, C. 68. Para. CIX defines the nominal value of the LCh in terms of the coal bushel.
[47] Hatcher, *Coal industry*. He remarks that contemporary experts in the coal trade were equally 'bewildered by the manifold measures in use, and the relationships which they bore to each other' (p. 557).
[48] Mott, 'London chaldron', pp. 229–30. Dietz, 'Coal trade', p. 284. The 'gauge' used for this estimate was quite clearly the Winchester bushel of eight gallons and not the coal bushel of eight and a half gallons. Hatcher, *Coal industry*, p. 568.
[49] Mott, 'London chaldron', p. 230. Dietz, 'Coal trade', p. 284. Hatcher, *Coal industry*, p. 569. See also Smith, *History of coal factors*, pp. 363–64.

The coal bushel

The coal bushel was equivalent to one Winchester bushel and one quart of water.[50] The Winchester bushel itself was supposed to contain eight gallons or thirty-two quarts. Thus the legal coal bushel was slightly larger than the Winchester bushel, at thirty-three quarts instead of thirty-two, and was generally used in the measurement of dry goods. However, the volume of the Winchester bushel itself varied over the years and at some point may have been less than eight gallons.[51]

There are then two issues here. First, the quantity contained in a single LCh, or its submeasure the vat, would depend upon which bushel measure was used, the legal coal bushel or the equally legal and widely used Winchester bushel. Second, there was a need to monitor that the correct bushel unit was used to measure the required quantity. This monitoring system consisted of delegated monitors such as meters who were supposed to ensure that the appropriate bushel measure was used in each instance. The extent of variation as a result of using the wrong bushel was about 3 per cent: negligible in proportional terms but substantial in absolute terms, given the quantities of coal normally traded in London. Reports of fraud concerning the bushel measure contain references to an inadequate number of bushels used to measure a given quantity rather than the incorrect artefact.[52]

Heaped measures

Another reason for inconsistency in measurements was undoubtedly the practice of heaping. Heaping when measuring dry goods dates back at least to medieval times, particularly for dry, bulky commodities such as grain and coal.[53] The additional quantity in the heap (as compared to the quantity contained within the vessel) apparently increased over the centuries from one-eighth of the quantity contained in the vessel to about one-quarter by the eighteenth century.[54] By the nineteenth century, the thirty-six bushels of coal that nominally constituted the LCh were to be heaped bushels and therefore in actuality equated to about forty-eight

[50] 12 Anne Stat. 2 C. 17.
[51] R. D. Connor, *The weights and measures of England* (London, HMSO, 1987), pp. 164–66.
[52] *Report on coal trade*, 1800, pp. 600–1, appendix 34. This variation due to the different types of bushels may be of relevance to historians attempting to convert historical quantities into modern units. Hatcher, *Coal industry*, appreciated this difference between the two bushels, whereas many earlier historians had overlooked this issue.
[53] Connor, *English measures*, p. 156.
[54] Ibid., pp. 156 and 79. Also Hatcher, *Coal industry*, p. 567.

bushels, if the LCh was equivalent to 396 gallons.[55] Thus the additional quantity in the heap would be about one-third of the quantity contained in a stricken bushel measure. Similarly, the LCh was to contain four heaped vats, each vat comprising nine heaped bushels.[56] As a significant quantity was contained in the heap, the state attempted to regulate the size of the heap. Legislation in 1807 stated that

all coals shall be duly heaped up in such [coal] bushel in the form of a cone, such cone to be of the height of at least six inches, and the outside of the bushel to be the extremity of the base of such a cone; and that each and every chaldron of coals shall consist of thirty-six of such bushels so heaped.[57]

Given the nature and shape of coal, it was not always possible to form identical cones in subsequent measurement instances, which also led to variability in quantity.[58] Consequently, close monitoring was considered necessary to ensure that measurements meted out quantities as close as possible to those intended by both custom and regulation. The metage system, as a monitoring mechanism, was required to use properly stamped or authorised vessels along with triangular gauges to ensure that the size and shape of the cone was as per definition.[59]

The ingrain

Another reason for inconsistencies in measurements was the practice of providing the ingrain, that is, providing about 5 per cent extra quantity for every twenty units of LCh or vats measured. The seller would charge only for twenty units but deliver a score of twenty-one units, in effect providing a discount of 5 per cent on the price.[60] This customary practice had

[55] Forty-eight bushels (not heaped) × 8.5 gallons of the coal bushel = 396 gallons; equally 48 bushels (not heaped) × 8 gallons of Winchester bushel = 384 gallons.
[56] Smith, *History of coal factors*, pp. 367–68. Connor, *English measures*, pp. 180–81.
[57] 47 George III, C. 68. This regulation implied that the quantity contained in the cone of the heap was to be about 30% of that contained within the dimensions of the vessel. This calculation is based on the dimension of the bushel measure along with the cone of the heap shown in the select committee report of 1830 (PP Vol. VIII 1830, plate 3, at the end of the appendix). The inside diameter is assumed to be eighteen and a half inches rather than nineteen and a half inches. See also Smith, *History of coal factors*, p. 363. The volume in the cylindrical bushel measure is assumed to be approximately 1,969 cubic inches, and the volume of the cone of the heap is assumed to be approximately 603 cubic inches. Prior to the 1807 act, there was no way of estimating exactly how much quantity was to be contained within the heap. The Act of 1713 only mentions heaped measures without any dimensions of the heap.
[58] PP Vol. VIII 1830, p. 77.
[59] Ibid., p. 87.
[60] Ibid., p. 361, appendix 4(h), for an example of deliveries made using the ingrain, showing a ship meter's delivery bill.

become a statutory requirement over the years, and by 1807, legislation regulated exactly how the ingrain was supposed to be provided.[61]

This raises a couple of issues. First, it was easy for the merchant seller to withhold the additional quantity and thus deny the quantity discount to the buyer; this practice was called *loading bare*. Furthermore, it was not too difficult for the merchant seller to deliver fewer than twenty chaldrons (or vats) in a score. This could be done easily by adjusting the size of the heap so that even though the measurements were carried out twenty-one times, the effective quantity could be less than the pre-scribed amount. There is plenty of evidence suggesting that this practice was quite common.[62] Second, to alleviate this problem, some effective monitoring system was required. The physical artefacts by themselves were insufficient to ensure that the ingrain was provided. Thus one of the duties of the meters was to ensure that the proper ingrain was given.

Weight–volume conversions

In addition to the method of measuring quantity in London, the variation in the LCh was also the result of converting from a weight measure, the NCh, to a volume measure, the LCh (Table 4.2). One obvious require-ment was to express the relationship between the two different measures as a stable ratio. However, there was no fixed or constant conversion ratio between the NCh and the LCh. Several contemporary estimates put the ratio variously at 8:15, 8:17, 11:21 and 1:2.[63] This implies that the quant-ity estimated by the LCh could vary by about 6 per cent compared to the quantity reported by the NCh. This is a pertinent issue because different types of coal differ in their densities. The density of coal produced from different mines and regions would often vary. Thus coal known as the Northumberland Wallsend would weigh about 78.97 pounds per cubic foot, whereas another type, the Welsh stone coal from Milford, would weigh about 89.38 pounds per cubic foot. On the whole, coals of inferior quality tended to be the heaviest.[64] Consequently, a fixed ratio between the two measures would not have worked unless the density of coal was accounted for in this conversion. Considering the numerous varieties of coal traded in the London market, the general consensus amongst local

[61] 47 George III, C. 68, Para. LXII.
[62] *Report on coal trade*, 1800, pp. 553–54, 56, appendices 34 and 37. Also PP Vol. VIII 1830. P. Linebaugh, *The London hanged: crime and civil society in the eighteenth century* (London, Allen Lane, 1991), p. 307.
[63] Various parliamentary reports. See also R. Edington, *Essay on the coal trade* (London, 1803), p. 51. Taylor, *Coal trade*, p. 24.
[64] PP Vol. VIII 1830, pp. 122 and 305.

Table 4.3. *Specific gravity estimates of coal varieties sold in London*

	Main sample	Subsample of high-quality coals
Observations	77	21
Average specific gravity^a	1,277	1,263
Maximum specific gravity^a	1,432	1,247
Minimum specific gravity^a	1,235	1,278
Standard deviation	37	6.6
Degree of variation (%)	2.9	0.53

Note: From John Buddle's sample.
^{a} Specific gravity is a dimensionless quantity, the number representing the density of the substance compared to that of water, which is assumed to be one unit.
Source: PP Vol. VIII 1830, appendices 24 and 25.

merchants was that 'no two bushels of coal [could] be made to weigh the same'.[65]

Just how large was this variation due to density? John Buddle – a renowned coal expert, consultant and colliery viewer – reported estimates of the variation in density among different types of coal traded in London in the early nineteenth century.[66] His observations of seventy-seven samples 'indiscriminately' collected from different ships shows that the variability was not as considerable as was alleged in contemporary accounts: he found an average variation of 3 per cent (Table 4.3). An analysis of a subset of this sample containing superior-quality coal (Russell's Hetton Wallsend, Lambton's Wallsend, Russell's Wallsend, Northumberland Wallsend, Tanfield Moor, Stewart's Wallsend and Killingsworth) shows that the variance is even less within this subset, with a coefficient of variation of less than 1 per cent.[67]

Thus the variation in quantity, as represented in terms of weight per unit volume, is small enough to have been adjusted within the price mechanism. Coals of different quality, which also differed on the basis of specific gravity, fetched different prices in the London market. The

[65] Ibid.
[66] There are several accounts of the contributions made by John Buddle to the coal industry. For example, he was influential in the adoption of several innovative practices in the northern collieries such as the discounted cash flow method of analysis; see Brackenborough et al., 'Discounted cash flow'.
[67] The selection of this subset is made on the basis of Buddle's own selection, where he uses these seven varieties of coal for further analysis. See Table 4.3 for source.

lightest and best quality of coal was the most expensive, whereas the heaviest and most inferior quality of coal was the cheapest.[68]

Density of coal also tended to change depending upon the size and condition of the individual pieces of coal. Some reports claimed that small coals could be about 10 per cent lighter than larger pieces of merchantable coals, or in other words, small coals occupied 10 per cent more volume than large coals of the same weight. Other experts were doubtful about the extent to which smaller coal was lighter than heavier coal and claimed that this was true only when very large pieces of coal were broken into marginally smaller ones.[69] Nevertheless, this was sufficient inducement to load large coals in the north and to deliver smaller coals in London, coals having been broken, accidentally or deliberately, during the coastwise voyage.[70]

The systematic inconsistencies in the coal measurements were the result of the customary practices in London as well as the measurement artefacts themselves. A detailed analysis of the likely extent of the variation in the nominal measurements is presented in Appendix 4.1. We see that the heaped measures and the ingrain were the major sources of variability surrounding the quantity measured using the LCh, the vat and the bushel. Conversely, the variation resulting from weight to volume conversion was relatively minor. While measurements remained opaque and confounded the trade, consumers complained bitterly about the unreliable measurements meted out by the trade:

I buy all other articles by number, measure or weight, except these coals [is it] too much trouble to obtain satisfaction, that I am supplied with fair measure. I have no faith in the guessing work of the coalmen.[71]

Reforming the coal trade (1800–1830)

The coal trade, and particularly the trade between the north-east and London, had constantly attracted the attention of the state. Since coal was shipped through ports where customs officers were usually present, it became an easily taxable commodity. Also, given that London had no alternative sources of fuel, the demand for coal was fairly inelastic.

---

[68] PP Vol. VIII 1830, testimony of John Buddle.

[69] C. W. Pasley, *Observations on the expediency and practicability of simplifying and improving the measures, weights and money* (London, Egerton's Military Library, 1834), p. 74. T. Y. Hall, 'Remarks on the coal trade', *Transactions of the North of England Institute of Mining and Mechanical Engineers* II (1853–1854): p. 209.

[70] PP Vol. VIII 1830, p. 13. Several witnesses testified to this and claimed that such 'screened' coals resulted in wastage as high as 25%–30% of production.

[71] Letter to *The Times*, dated 13 February 1824.

Table 4.4. *Milestones: review and reform of the London coal trade (1800–1832)*

1800	Parliamentary Committee on Coal Trade appointed to investigate problems in the coal trade, especially • distribution bottlenecks in the Port of London • measurement fraud and the public metage system
1807	Act regulating the sale of coal by volume and reforms to the public metage system
1824	Imperial system of weights and measures introduced by legislation
1829	Parliamentary committee (Lords) appointed to inquire into duties and taxes on coal
1830	Parliamentary committee (Commons) appointed to inquire into the sale of coal by weight Evidence from both committees (Lords and Commons) tabled, and sale by weight is recommended to Parliament
1832	Act regulating the sale of coal by weight introduced; Public metage system abolished; Most duties and taxes on coal in London abolished or reduced

At both ends of the trade route were politically powerful groups who could demand and get the state's attention in appeals against their opponents. By 1830, there were nearly two hundred regulations and acts of Parliament concerning the coal trade.[72] Measurement problems in the London market had become important enough to become the subject of several parliamentary reviews between 1800 and 1830. The review and reform of the London coal trade actually consisted of two phases, the first between 1800 and 1807 and the second between 1828 and 1832 (Table 4.4).[73] On 12 March 1800, a motion was tabled in the House of Commons for an 'inquiry into the present high causes of price in coal'.[74] This followed disruption in the supply of coal to London and an increase in the price of the commodity, both of which excited public comment. A parliamentary committee was appointed to investigate problems in measurement and the distribution bottlenecks within the Port of London, along with other issues such as the alleged monopolistic activities of the coal owners.[75]

[72] Flinn, *Coal industry*, p. 280.
[73] Another parliamentary review was conducted during 1835–1836 that focused almost exclusively on the monopolistic activities of the coal merchants; major concerns regarding measurements were, however, addressed by the 1828–1831 review.
[74] *The Times*, 12 March 1800.
[75] *Report on coal trade*, 1800, p. 538.

The committee's report was tabled after several months of interviews with coal owners and merchants, shipowners, factors, meters, large purchasers, market clerks and city officials.[76] The committee, after reviewing the 'principal evils' affecting the trade, concluded that the practice of loading bare (i.e. withholding the ingrain amount) and improper heaping were the principal causes of the measurement problems. The report stated that such frauds were committed either due to the inattention or with the connivance of the meter. It further stated that payments to the sea meters were 'optional with the ship owner' and that the payment was often related to how satisfactorily the meter measured the quantity.[77]

The committee also reported the inability of the land meters to properly monitor the wharf measures and concluded that sacks were often filled without measuring by the bushel or were deliberately filled short of the proper measure of three bushels. On the whole, the report stated that the meter's office was ineffective in detecting offences and monitoring measurement without additional enforcement. The committee even recommended the abolition of land meters and letting the consumers make the measurements during delivery, that is, self-monitoring instead of delegated monitoring.

The report made no mention of sale of coal by weight, even though the subject of weight measures was raised during the committee hearings. John Nettlefold, a deputy coal meter, when asked about delivering coal by weight, remarked that 'it would be more just that way' but thought that it would be impractical to deliver any more than forty tons a day, given their experience of delivering Scotch coals.[78] John Akenhead, a coal undertaker and shipowner, also thought that 'it would be a more certain method', but he also thought that it was 'not so expeditious or so cheap'.[79] Conversely, George Russell, a manufacturer and ship owner, stated emphatically that weighing coals from 'ship to the lighter [could] be done with as much ease and dispatch, [as] is practised in Ireland'.[80]

Following this review, legislation was introduced in 1807 which intended to iron out the problems of monitoring measurements by specifying the dimensions of the physical artefacts and the rules of custom surrounding their use and by regulating the operation of the metage system, the manner of compensation of the meters and so on.[81] For instance, the units of measurement and the artefacts to be used to measure the

---

[76] Testimonial evidence from thirty-eight individuals was attached to the appendix of the report, along with at least forty pages of documentary and statistical evidence.
[77] *Second report on coal trade*, 1800, p. 642.
[78] *Report on coal trade*, 1800, John Nettlefold's testimony on 23 April.
[79] Ibid. John Akenhead's testimony on 28 March.
[80] Ibid. George Russell's testimony on 28 March.
[81] 47 George III, C. 68.

quantities were specified in paragraphs CVII (dimensions of the sack), CIX (dimensions of the bushel measure) and CX (measurements smaller than the bushel) of the act. The act also stated that coals could be sold either by volume or weight measures (Paragraph CXXIV), and the units used for the measurement by weight were specified in Paragraph CXXII. The legislation also specified the wages and compensation of the meters and regulated the giving of gifts to meters.

Although some historians claim that the legislative review 'marks the end of one epoch and the beginning of another',[82] the measurement infrastructure of the trade remained unchanged. The measurement artefacts in use were the same, the monitoring technology in use remained largely unaltered and the rules and customs that were formalised were mostly based on long usage. Furthermore, as the choice of the measurement standard was left to the market, the London merchants continued to use the volume measures in the bulk of the trades.

Notwithstanding the legislative changes, the problems plaguing the London trade lay simmering below the surface. The quantity of coal shipped into London increased by about 45 per cent in the first quarter of the nineteenth century (Table 4.1).[83] Consequently, the number of ships entering London increased by twenty-five hundred between 1806 and 1824, adding to the congestion in the Port of London.[84] New docking facilities, such as the West India docks (1802), London docks (1805) and East India docks (1806), attempted to reduce congestion by limiting the number of vessels present in the main river channel: a series of bylaws restricted the number of colliers on the Thames to 250 ships at a time. The 1807 act had limited the rate of unloading to forty-two chaldrons a day. The actual rate of unloading, however, depended upon the availability of the meters, the whippers employed to unload the cargo and the lighters (small transport crafts) to transport the cargo from the colliers to the wharves. Factoring this in, the turnaround times ventured into days, if not weeks. Undertakers, who supplied the whippers to unload the colliers, often demanded 'detention money' from the shipmasters, further increasing the turnaround time and cost of securing release.[85] Often meters were assigned to ships that were yet to reach the Port of London. This increased waiting times as a meter had to unload the ship to which he had been assigned before being reassigned to other ships. The merchants and factors constantly complained about the delays caused in deliveries due to the absence of meters. The corporation responded to

[82] Smith, *History of coal factors*, p. 143.
[83] PP Vol. XVIII 1826–1827, *Number of chaldrons imported into London: 1801–1827*, p. 495.
[84] Smith, *History of coal factors*, p. 199. Ville, 'Productivity in shipping', p. 364.
[85] Smith, *History of coal factors*, p. 198.

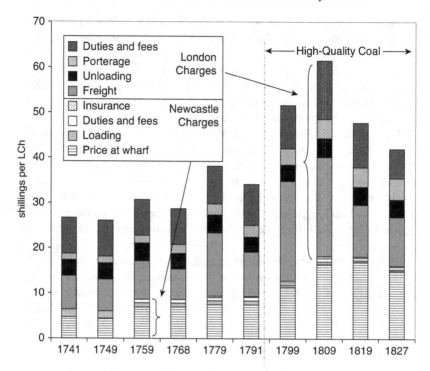

Figure 4.4. Composition of average price paid by Greenwich Hospital for coal in London (1759–1827). Prices in shillings per bare chaldron, i.e. without the ingrain. The averages are reported weighted by quantities. The years are reported in harvest years. After 1791, the prices are for better-quality coal. *Source*: William Beveridge, *Prices and wages in England: from the twelfth to the nineteenth century*, Vol. 1 (London, Longmans, Green, 1939), p. 271.

these complaints by increasing the number of land meters in 1824 but failed to alleviate the situation completely.[86]

Between 1800 and 1824, the retail price of coal also fluctuated considerably. Escalating freight costs as a result of the European war were a primary cause for fluctuating retail prices. The duties, taxes and other charges on coal also increased between 1799 and 1809, before declining to their original levels by 1819 (Figure 4.4).[87] The Greenwich Hospital

[86] Report in *The Times*, dated 28 January 1824, that the Corporation of London had decided to increase the number of sea meters from 118 to 130.
[87] See also A. Velkar, 'Caveat emptor: abolishing public measurements, standardizing quantities, and enhancing market transparency in the London coal trade c1830', *Enterprise and Society* 9 No 2 (2008): figure 4 and table 2.

was paying about ten shillings per LCh as freight cost on coal shipped from Newcastle in 1791, which increased to twenty-two shillings by 1809, before declining to about eleven shillings in 1827. Unloading and porterage charges and the various duties on coal increased from fifteen shillings in 1791 to about twenty-one shillings in 1809, before declining to fifteen shillings in 1827.[88] The real retail price continued to fluctuate even after 1815. Buyers constantly complained of the high price of coal, continuing shortage of stocks and measurement fraud.[89]

In March 1826, a petition was made listing several ways in which the meters themselves perpetuated the problems in the measurement and delivery of coal.[90] This was followed by another petition in 1828 that was on a much broader issue of 'frauds committed against the public under the coal laws'.[91] Around the same time, London merchants began demanding a fresh review of the recurring problems in the trade, particularly of delivery bottlenecks and high duties. The Society of Owners of Coal Craft,[92] together with the London factors, made specific proposals to the corporation seeking the amendment or preferably the abolition of the metage system. They also suggested remedies to solve the recurring measurement problems, including a recommendation to use 'a triangle gauge to determine the cone [of the heap]'.[93] The London merchants did not seek an alternation in the existing measurement artefacts and practices such as a switch to weight measurements.

Meanwhile, coal owners had begun to lobby for the reduction of duties on coal sold in London. Increased competition from other coal-producing regions, such as southern Wales and Lancashire, which had a much lower duty structure compared to the trade from the north-east,

---

[88] W. Beveridge, *Prices and wages in England: from the twelfth to the nineteenth century*, Vol. 1 (London, Longmans, Green, 1939). See also PP Vol. VIII 1830, pp. 9–10. CLRO COL/CC/MIN/01/014 Misc. MSS 241.10 (1/3), *Minute book of the committee on charges upon coals*, 28 May 1828–26 October 1831, entry for 28 May 1828. CLRO COL/CC/04/01/007, *Minutes of the court of common council*, 1826–1828, report dated 8 July 1828. Flinn, *Coal industry*, pp. 279–85.
[89] E.g. see *The Times*, 14 August 1802; 5 November 1804; 17 October 1818; 19 and 20 July 1822; 13 February 1824; 17 February 1824 etc.
[90] CLRO COL/CC/04/01/007, entry for 16 March 1826 referring to the petition by Thomas Bradfield. He appears to have had some interest in a ship called *Jenny*, which sank on the Kentish coast on 14 March 1825. The reason why this petition was made is unclear.
[91] Ibid. Refer to entries for 24 January 1828 and 21 February 1828.
[92] This society effectively comprised the coal merchants of the City of London and is likely to have included most of the first buyers. See Dale, *Woodmongers*, pp. 80 and 96.
[93] CLRO COL/CC/MIN/01/014 Misc. MSS 241.10 (2/3), *Papers of the Committee on Charges upon Coals*, 1828–1831. CLRO COL/CC/04/01/008, *Minutes of the Court of Common Council*, 1829–30, entry for 12 March 1829.

was the reason behind this lobbying. The Richmond shilling, a duty levied exclusively on coal shipped from the north-eastern ports, was amongst the several other duties that the coal owners wanted abolished.[94] In addition, the City of London was evaluating alternative means of bringing coal to London via inland routes such as canals and the various railways proposed from Stockton and Yorkshire.[95]

The coal owners were keen to avoid any anticombination legislation targeting them, although previous attempts to curb their monopolistic activities through legislation had remained ineffective.[96] They engaged in a nineteenth-century version of public relations and media campaigning. One newspaper reported,

Practices in use in the Port of London [will appear] almost incredible to persons not conversant with the coal trade [especially the] method by which the sworn meters on the Thames make a vessel deliver great or short measure, according to the extent of the fee given to them, [coals] can be heaped in such a manner that the measure shall appear just what it may please the will of the meter [the] consequences of [the substitution of weight for volume] cannot be otherwise than beneficial, since not only will the price of coals in the south be much reduced, but the shipping interest of the north will be benefited, in its relief from a system of fraud and delay, of which it was principally the victim.[97]

Another journal commented that 'were coals sold by weight instead of by measure, the change would produce considerable relief to the consumer, and would suffer the coal-owner to lower the price'.[98] Yet another article bemoaned,

That such a system [i.e. sale by volume] should have been long preserved [is truly astonishing], though the attention of honourable gentlemen has been repeatedly called to the easy method of defrauding [it] does not seem ever to have attracted the smallest portion of their concern. They have continued [to] occupy themselves in stopping up the spigot, while the liquor was running out at the bung-hole.[99]

---

[94] Sweezy, *Monopoly and competition*, pp. 52–53. Smith, *History of coal factors*, pp. 158–62. Flinn, *Coal industry*, p. 26.

[95] CLRO COL/CHD/DM/05/04/003 Misc. MSS 207.7, *Minutes of evidence before committees*, 19 November 1829. See evidence on the Clarence railroad and the possibility of increasing supply from Stockton-upon-Tees. CLRO COL/CC/CCN/03/012, entry for December 1829 relating to the proposed railway between Thurlstone and Smeaton in West Riding, Yorkshire.

[96] Sweezy, *Monopoly and competition*. W. J. Hausman, 'Cheap coals or limitation of the vend? London coal trade, 1770–1845', *Journal of Economic History* 44 No 2 (1984).

[97] Extract from the *Newcastle Courant* as appearing in *The Times*, 30 October 1830.

[98] Extract from *The Durham Chronicle* as appearing in *The Times*, 15 February 1830.

[99] 'On the coal trade', *Edinburgh Review* 51 No 101 (1830): pp. 180–81.

The London meter had become the trade's favourite flogging horse. The practice of heaping and measuring by volume also came under ridicule, as did those who continued to use such measures.

Facing an inevitable decline in their share of the London trade and the perceived danger of losing their dominant position to other coal-producing regions spurred the coal owners into action. On 24 March 1829, the Marquis of Londonderry tabled a motion in the House of Lords to appoint a committee 'to take into consideration the whole state of the coal trade, and to ascertain how far the high prices were affected by the taxes [levied] on coals'.[100] Two days later, on 26 March 1829, a select committee was appointed, which met over the course of that year to gather evidence from prominent coal merchants and experts.[101] The significance of this committee's report is that its members extensively discussed the practicality of selling coal by weight.

Robert Brandling, coal owner and chairman of the Coal Committee at Newcastle, stated that the 'way in which [coals] are sold here [i.e. in London], by heaped measure, is a most uncertain mode of ascertaining the quantity of coals sold to the consumer, or the quantity on which government duty is paid; and that the only accurate measure is by weight'.[102] Captain Cochrane, owner of the *Hetton Colliery*, was of the opinion that the heap measure used in London was fallacious and that if coal was sold by the ton, it would also reduce the spurious increase in quantity due to breakage during transportation.[103] During the testimony of John Buddle, colliery viewer, on 8 May 1829, the following exchange took place:

SELECT COMMITTEE (SC): Can you suggest any improvement as to the mode of selling the coals – as to selling them by weight or in any other manner?

JOHN BUDDLE (JB): I have stated it as my opinion that the coal would be sent in a better state to market if it was sold by weight at the place of shipment, rather than by measure, inasmuch as the parties through whose hands the article must pass, between the producer and the consumer, would not be benefited by the breakage of coal.

SC: Do you see any difficulties whatever in establishing the sale of coal by weight; would the revenue suffer in any point?

JB: I should think not. I think in that case the revenue would be better protected than it is at present, [the] duty would be more accurately ascertained by weight than by measure.

[100] *Hansard Parliamentary Debates*, Series 2, Vol. 20, 24 March 1829, 'Debate on coal trade'.
[101] *Journal of the House of Lords* 61 (1829), *Appointment of Select Committee on Coal Trade.*
Journal of the House of Lords 61 (1829), *Report from the Committee on Coal Trade.*
[102] *Report on Coal Trade*, 1800. Robert Brandling's testimony on 1 May 1829.
[103] Ibid. Captain Cochrane's testimony on 4 May 1829.

sc: Would it not, in your opinion, tend to get rid of a great portion of the fraudulent practices now going on at the Coal Exchange and elsewhere?

jb: I should think it would.[104]

Sir Cuthbert Sharp, collector of customs at Sunderland, commented that 'there could be no possible fraud, if [coals] were taken in weight and delivered by weight'.[105] William Dickson, comptroller of coal duties in the Port of London, testified that a majority of the bulk goods arriving in London were charged duties on the basis of weight. This included goods such as sugar, cotton, hemp and wool. He further observed that duties 'taken by weight must of course be taken more accurately than any [duty] taken by heaped measure, as far as accuracy is concerned'.[106]

The state responded to the pressure and began considering several ways to reform the London trade. In early 1828, the Corporation of London was planning to petition the House of Commons to alter and amend the 1807 act. The proposed amendments included provisions regarding measurements used by the trade as well as those provisions regulating the duties of meters.[107] In May 1828, the prime minister, Arthur Wellesley, Duke of Wellington, asked the mayor of London to inquire whether duties on coal brought into the Port of London could be reduced.[108] A committee formed to conduct this inquiry swiftly took the matter ahead and within a week held preliminary meetings with several prominent factors and coal merchants.[109] The committee reached the following conclusion regarding the metage system:

By the abolition of the office of the Land Coal Meter, it had been estimated that a direct saving of about four-pence per chaldron, on the whole quantity imported would be effected, but having the fullest reason to believe, that other payments and allowances than those authorized by the Act of Parliament, are made to the labouring land coal Meter, which greatly enhance the amount paid in respect of

---

[104] Ibid. John Buddle's testimony on 8 May 1829.
[105] Ibid. Sir Cuthbert Sharp's testimony on 4 May 1829.
[106] Ibid. William Dickson's testimony on 20 May 1829.
[107] CLRO COL/CC/04/01/007. See entries for 21 February 1828 and 13 March 1828. A report by the Coal and Corn Committee of the same date (and included in the minute book) states that 'the provisions in the Act relating to coals sold by Pool measure, being inadequate to prevent fraud in the delivery of coals, it is expedient that they should be altered and amended and all coals measured by the Bushel'. There were seventeen other provisions suggested by the report.
[108] Ibid. See entry dated 23 May 1828. The entry suggests that the mayor was met by the Duke of Wellington along with officials from the Treasury.
[109] CLRO COL/CC/MIN/01/014 Misc. MSS 241.10 (1/3). Entry for 28 May 1828. The meeting was attended by several prominent coal factors and merchants, including Thomas Gillespy and William Horne. In their opinion, the coal undertakers system could be done away with, reducing the coal whippers' wages. No comments were recorded on the land metage system apart from confirming the charges paid by the trade as metage.

the said metage, we are convinced that indirectly, a saving of at least six-pence per chaldron would be thereby occasioned.[110]

They were also convinced that

the public do not obtain that security in respect of coals either in regard to quantity or quality which they conceive they do in the appointment of Land Sea Coal Meters and in case the same were abolished the public would be better protected against fraud by looking to their own interests than by placing a reliance upon such uncertain and doubtful security.[111]

Thus it seems that by abolishing the system of land meters, the corporation was hoping to help solve two problems: to seek a reduction in the charges on coal and to solve the continuing problem of monitoring the meters. That monitoring the delegated monitors was an ongoing problem is evident from the various reports of the principal land meters. 'The occurrence of minor offences among the [meters] has of late been so frequent as to produce great inconvenience to the respectable Merchant and not seldom, considerable loss to the Public', complained some city officials.[112] They listed several offences, including absence from duty, drunkenness, making erroneous returns and giving short measure, offences for which, the principals argued, there was no effective remedy. The corporation considered the complete abolition of the land metage system as a serious option and made this recommendation to the Treasury Department.[113]

Having made the decision to abolish the land meters, the corporation began considering options to make the monitoring of measurements more effective by further regulating the existing infrastructure. One of its reports stated,

In order to afford the Public the means of protecting themselves against fraud [the] sacks to be used should be of one size, the dimensions to be defined as at present, and no sack to be allowed to contain less than 3 bushels. [The] purchaser of the coals, if he should be dissatisfied with the appearance of the coals as to their measure, should be allowed to refuse to receive the same or to have them measured by the Carman or other person having the charge of the Cart or Waggon, in the presence of two credible witnesses, one of whom should be a constable or Police Officer, and for that purpose every cart or waggon should

[110] CLRO COL/CC/04/01/007.
[111] CLRO COL/CC/MIN/01/014 Misc. MSS 241.10 (1/3). Entry for 19 June 1828 and the committee resolutions passed for that day.
[112] CLRO COL/CC/CCN/03/012. Entry dated 1 October 1829, which contains the letter to the Sub-committee of Control over Coal and Corn Meters from the two principal land meters, Thomas Reeve and John Bumstead.
[113] CLRO COL/CC/04/01/007. Entry dated 8 July 1829, directing that the committee report tabled on that day be sent to 'the Lord Commissioners of His Majesty's Treasury'.

have in some conspicuous part thereof a perfect legal bushel measure, with a triangle to define the proper height of the cone, and that the penalties as may be imposed for sending coals short of their proper measure should be made recoverable before a magistrate.[114]

However, in early 1830, Thomas Reeve and John Bumstead, the two principal meters of London, claimed that there was 'more fraud in the Pool measure than on the Land [wharf] measure' and that 'the merchants [were] not sending the whole quantity'.[115] On the whole, the wharf-measured coal was more accurately measured than the pool-measured coal, they argued.[116] This implied that all proposals about regulating the bushel measure and remeasurement by consumers would be inadequate remedies if uncertain quantities were being sent from the colliers onto the wharves. They further agreed that 'weight measure could be better than the triangular measure,' even though 'some coals will absorb more water than others', and recommended this as the preferred method of measurement.[117]

The issue of distorting the weight of coal by wetting was a concern voiced by several people at the time. William Russell, the expert engineer appointed by the Corporation of London to evaluate the designs received for weighing machines, personally preferred the volume measure rather than the weight measure for measuring coal. He claimed that no weighing machine could accurately measure quantity by weight or prevent fraud in measurement due to this basic property of coal.[118] On the contrary, William Horne, while testifying in front of the select committee in March 1830, related the results of an experiment he had conducted regarding the increase in the weight of coal when watered. His experiment, which involved samples of different types of coal that were measured when wet at intervals of one hour, three hours, and six hours, showed that the increase in weight was between 1 and 7 per cent.[119] Wetting of coals

---

[114] CLRO COL/CC/04/01/008. See report dated 31 March 1829.

[115] CLRO COL/CC/MIN/01/014 Misc. MSS 241.10 (2/3). Memorandum dated 19 February 1830.

[116] PP Vol. VIII 1830. William Lushington's testimony on 25 March 1830, p. 78.

[117] CLRO COL/CC/MIN/01/014 Misc. MSS 241.10 (2/3).

[118] CLRO COL/CC/CCN/03/013, *Papers of the Committee on Coal and Corn Meters*, September 1830–December 1831. Refer to the report submitted by William Russell dated 9 June 1831.

[119] PP Vol. VIII 1830. See William Horne's testimony on 30 March 1830 and summary of results of the experiment, p. 90. Admittedly, the samples did not control for quality of coal and for the size of coal. Also, we do not know if the weight of the dry coals was with or without the weight of the sack. Ideally, the weight of the wet sack in which the coals were weighed after being watered should have been deducted. Nevertheless, this is a useful report since it provides the extent of variation in weight due to wetting of coals.

was a usual practice by the merchants to keep down dust levels, and most witnesses agreed that detecting wet coals was relatively simple and that only very wet coals would retain a substantial amount of water weight.[120]

The corporation, from this point onwards, became engaged in switching the trade to weight measurements. A parliamentary committee, appointed in 1830 'to see if another method of selling coals by weight instead of measure, might (be) of advantage to the public', concluded that the issue lay not in effective monitoring of measurements but in the customs and rules surrounding the measurement artefacts. The report stated, 'When coal of all sizes is to be placed in the bushel and piled in a conical form on the top, it is not easy to define when a bushel is full'.[121] This problem, the report concluded, could be solved if coal were to be delivered by weight and not by volume. Another select committee of 1829 mirrored this recommendation by stating that 'the selling by weight instead of selling by measure would obviate many of the Temptations to Fraud which at present exist'.[122]

By 1831, the trade in London began preparing itself for the now inevitable switch to the weight standard. Thomas Gillespy, representing the coal factors, stated that they acquiesced with the principle of weighing coals provided it was 'done by quarters as at present'.[123] The merchants, represented by William Horne, delivered a proposition for coals to be weighed into sacks not exceeding two hundredweight at a time in the same vessel that brought them up from the hold and to be lowered into the barge without being emptied. They also submitted a design of a proposed machine for the weighing of coal sacks.[124] Meanwhile, the treasury and the customs offices, anticipating the changes in the coal laws, began reporting monthly coal statistics in tons rather than chaldrons.[125] In August 1831, legislation abolishing most of the duties on coal was introduced. The Act for Regulating the Vend and Delivery of Coal was introduced in October 1831 and abolished the metage system (Paragraphs XXXVIII and LX) and directed that coals had to be sold by weight and not by volume (Paragraph XLIII).[126]

[120] Ibid. Testimonies by William Turquand (p. 68) and William Lushington (p. 81) on 25 March 1830.
[121] Ibid., p. 10.
[122] Ibid.
[123] CLRO COL/CC/MIN/01/014 Misc. MSS 241.10 (1/3). Entry for 21 January 1831.
[124] Ibid.
[125] CLRO COL/CC/CCN/03/013. See letter from Custom House, dated 21 April 1831. See also the monthly coal statistics published for July 1831.
[126] 1 & 2 William IV C. 16, 1831, *Act to discontinue duties upon coals.* 1 & 2 William IV C. 76, 1831, *Act for regulating delivery of coal.*

Significance of the reforms

The review of 1828–1831 resulted in three big changes in the London coal trade: the public metage system was abolished, heaped measures became unlawful and the volumetric metrological units were replaced with the Imperial weight units.[127] In other words, the 1831 reforms made significant changes to the protocols and the standards that had formed part of the measurement practices within the trade.

How can we explain these changes? Historical evidence suggests that the pressure to reform the measurement practices in London came from the market. The trade's desire to reform stemmed primarily from dissatisfaction with the functioning of the metage system and, as far as the northern coal owners were concerned, the highly unreliable practice of heaped measurements in London. The unreliability of measurements was also a concern voiced more generally by London consumers, who had seen wide fluctuations in the retail price of coal. The merchant's commercial concerns coincided with the state's political and economic reasons for reforming the metage system.

Financially, the revenue collected by the sea meters as metage duty was substantial. After deducting payments to the sea meters and other expenses (maintenance, rent, management costs etc.), nearly two-thirds of the duty amount could be transferred to the general account of the Corporation of London as revenue (see Appendix 4.2). In 1829, this surplus sum amounted to more than £17,000 on metage revenues of £26,559. In comparison, the metage charges collected by the land meters just about covered their wages and salaries, and the City was generating very little revenue from this duty. In 1829, the City faced a deficit of £666 on metage revenue of £4,962 collected by the meters within the City of London.[128] Given the problems in monitoring the activities of the meters, and the elaborate infrastructure required to collect the land metage charges, this system was just not worth it from the City's point of view. The City was keen to hold on to the revenue from sea metage, however, and its recommendation to abolish the metage system only included the land meters and the land metage charges.

The political economy of the price and taxes on coal was also an important reason for the abolition of the metage system. There were two opposing perspectives on the perceived high retail price of coal in London. One view, held by most consumers in London, was that the high price of the commodity was a result of combination and

---

[127] Further legislation made heaped measurements unlawful for all dry goods in the country, in addition to coal. 5 & 6 William IV, C. 63, 1835, *Weights and measures (amendment) act*, Para. VII.

[128] PP Vol. VIII 1830. Appendices 8, 10, 11 and 12.

monopolistic practices among the coal owners. The other position, held by the coal owners, was that the high retail price of coal was a result of the numerous duties and charges on the commodity sold in London. Owners also objected to the Richmond shilling, a tax of one shilling per NCh on all coal shipped from the Tyne that 'bore unevenly on coal owners [in Northumberland]'.[129] Institutional buyers, such as the Greenwich Hospital, could expect to pay more than six shillings per LCh as duties and taxes in addition to the eight or nine shillings per LCh as unloading and porterage charges. Although this amount declined almost by half by 1809, it was still considered high for a commodity with a relatively inelastic demand. In contrast, the price of coal in Newcastle had increased from eleven shillings in 1799 to seventeen shillings in 1819 and declined to fifteen shillings in 1827. The coal owners argued that it was the duties and the increase in freight cost that contributed to the rising retail prices rather than any increase in the price of coal in the north.

Historians agree that of the two, the duties and charges on coal were more likely the cause of high retail prices than the monopolistic activities of the coal owners.[130] The coal owners were politically far more powerful than either the London merchants or the consumers. By 1828, they were able to put sufficient pressure on the government to get them to review charges and duties on bringing coal to London. The taxes on coal were fiscally significant, yielding the Exchequer over £1 million of the government's total 1820 revenue of £58.1 million. The London trade contributed almost half of the government's revenue from coal: in 1828, this amounted to more than £440,000.[131] Nevertheless, the Treasury, which was involved throughout the review process, did not block the attempts to reduce the duties on coal. Along with the other duties on coal, metage duties ended in 1832. In the subsequent years, the average amount that the state generated from the London trade between 1833 and 1835 was about £100,000 to £150,000.[132] The government made the political decision to relinquish a substantial portion of the revenue from the coal trade.

The abolition of the metage duties and public measurements for coal was part of this political economy process – not part of any premeditated metrological reform by the government. This profound change to

[129] Sweezy, *Monopoly and competition*, p. 49.
[130] Ashton and Sykes, *Coal industry*, p. 224. Hausman, 'Cheap coals', p. 327. Sweezy, *Monopoly and competition*, pp. 140–45.
[131] Flinn, *Coal industry*, p. 284. CLRO COL/CC/06/01/0357/1, *Papers of the Court of Common Council*, 1830. See petition dated 25 November 1830.
[132] PP Vol. XI 1836, *Report of the Select Committee on Coal Trade*. See Appendices 6, 7, 13, 15 and 18.

the measurement protocols had an impact on the other aspects of the measurement practices within the trade.

The abolition of public measurements left the trade without an effective monitoring mechanism, especially in light of the highly variable measurements that the existing measurement tools provided. To increase monitoring, early proposals suggested reforming the instrument (the bushel) combined with increased regulation of the heaping practices and the method of providing the ingrain.[133] Impractical as some of these suggestions were, they were nevertheless pursued quite seriously. The coal owners, in contrast, had maintained that heaped measures themselves were the main source of unreliable measurements. They argued that the metrological units used in London and the protocols surrounding their use were perpetuating fraud and leading to price increases in the London market. They continued to lobby for a switch in measurement standards to weight units, which they argued were more reliable than the volumetric units. Similar arguments were subsequently taken up within the Corporation of London, where the change of standards was envisioned to solve the problem of unreliable quantities once the public metage was abolished. This cognitive transition, that weight measures were more reliable – and therefore more desirable – compared to volume measures, was an important event in converging towards weight standards. The corporation thus thought that it was replacing one method of monitoring measurements, the public metage system, with a method that reduced the degree of personal judgement required.

But what prevented the London merchants from voluntarily switching to weight measurements, if they were indeed more reliable than volume measures? In other words, what was the source of the inertia associated with switching standards?[134] The first buyers benefited from the variability of the volumetric measures as they could give short measure and withhold the ingrain, particularly as the price of coal fluctuated considerably during the early years of the nineteenth century. Converting from the NCh weight measurement to the LCh volume measurement did not involve significant variations (Appendix 4.1). Thus the metrology worked in their favour as they could arbitrage between the various measurements most effectively. Consequently, they saw no reason to

[133] 47 George III, C. 68. CLRO COL/CC/MIN/01/014 Misc. MSS 241.10 (2/3). *Papers of the Committee to Inquire into All Charges upon Coal for the years 1828 to 1831.* One of the recommendations by the London merchants was that a triangle gauge be used to determine the cone of the heap and that the bushel measure be readily available for inspection by buyers to determine its authenticity.

[134] According to the 1807 act, the choice of using either volume or weight measures was left to the trade. However, only a tiny proportion of coal brought via canals or from Scotland was sold by weight. 47 George III, C. 68.

abolish the existing measurement practices. Although the first buyers may have had no incentive to switch standards, other merchants and consumers certainly had an incentive to alter existing measurement practices. However, switching standards involved overcoming major coordination issues among the merchants. For the switch to be most effective, a significant majority (if not all) of the merchants would have had to have adopted weight standards. This could be interpreted as a failure of collective action, particularly as smaller merchants lacked the cohesiveness and the political power to insist on a change of standard and the first buyers had no incentive to switch by themselves.[135]

Lack of an appropriate technology to weigh a bulky commodity such as coal was also an important source of inertia in switching standards. Numerous methods were used to weigh coal at the origin of the trade route in Newcastle and Sunderland. Apart from outright guessing, weight was ascertained by volume displacement of water at the time of loading the keels on the river. These light river vessels carried nail marks indicating the degree to which the vessel should submerge each time one NCh, notionally equivalent to fifty-three hundredweight, was loaded into it. Alternatively, wagons carrying coal from the pits were weighed using 'average coal' at the pit's mouth, and this weight was marked on the wagon.[136] At the turn of the nineteenth century, and especially after 1830, improvements in port and docking facilities on the Tyne and the Wear meant that coal could be loaded directly onto the colliers without the intervention of the keels. Thus more direct methods of weighing at the production end of the trade route could be adopted in conjunction with the process of loading, either by lowering the tubs or wagons via cranes or by the use of spouts.[137]

In London, there was no parallel technology available for weighing coals on the colliers before being delivered onto the barges. From the hold of the collier, coal was shovelled into baskets, which were then whipped or jerked on the deck. They were measured there using the vat measure, and the basket was emptied into a room within the barges. Each room in the barge was supposed to contain the equivalent of five and a quarter chaldrons of coal.[138] In 1830, city officials met with Richard Trevithick to evaluate his invention of a portable machine that could

---

[135] Unlike the first buyers, who were organised into the Society of Owners of Coal Craft, the smaller merchants and consumers do not appear to have been similarly organized.

[136] PP Vol. VIII 1830. Testimonies by Robert Brandling (p. 261) and John Buddle (p. 285).

[137] Flinn, *Coal industry*, pp. 169–70. Ville, 'Productivity in shipping', p. 363. F. C. Danvers, *On coal – with reference to its screening, transport, etc.* (London, W. H. Allen, 1872), p. 56.

[138] PP Vol. VIII 1830. John Bumstead's testimony, p. 30.

weigh coals and deliver them at the same time. However, this machine, used in some trials conducted in Cornwall, was not in general use at this time.[139] In fact, the corporation advertised a competition in the London newspapers in 1831 promising a reward for a practical design of a portable machine for weighing coals, which elicited an enthusiastic response.[140]

Was it costly to acquire such a technology? What was the scale of investment required? We can estimate the scale of investment required by examining the expenditure on new machinery and equipment incurred after 1832 by the trade. This included expenditure on weights and scales, beams to support them, shoots (chutes) to deliver the coal from the colliers once they were weighed into the barges and so on. Some modifications to the barges were also necessary as a result. The beams and weights appeared to have cost about six pounds and three shillings a set, with an annual maintenance cost of about thirty-five pounds sterling. As far as the shoots were concerned, reports contain varying estimates from tenders submitted by several firms. On an average, larger shoots could cost between three pounds and six shillings and three pounds and fifteen shillings each, whereas smaller shoots could cost approximately two pounds and eighteen shillings each. The annual maintenance costs ranged between twenty-one and thirty-seven pounds sterling, depending upon the number and type of shoots. In February 1833, the total outlay for machinery, new barges and furniture for the previous year amounted to about £2,946, and the expenditures due to wear and tear (depreciation charges provided for) were about £862. By May 1834, the capital stock in terms of barges, shoots, beams, weights, sundry boats and office furniture amounted to £2,312.[141] In comparison, the trade had paid over twenty-six thousand pounds annually as metage duty to the Corporation of London circa 1830.[142] Lumpiness of capital cost of investment

---

[139] CLRO COL/CC/MIN/01/014 Misc. MSS 241.10 (1/3). Entry for 27 February 1830. The committee also met with other engineers as per entry for 15 March 1830. PP Vol. VIII 1830. Richard Trevithick's testimony, p. 202. Smith, *History of coal factors*, p. 288.

[140] CLRO COL/CC/CCN/03/013. See copy of advertisement dated 20 April 1831 and memo dated 26 May 1831. CLRO COL/CC/MIN/01/014 Misc. MSS 241.10 (1/3). Entry for 16 April 1831.

[141] The capital and expenditure estimates are from the papers of the Coal Meters Committee held at the Guildhall Library MS 10162, *Reports of the sub-committees*, Vol. 1, *1831–1834*. See *Report of the Subcommittee for Superintending Weights*, etc., dated 26 January 1832; *Report of Subcommittee on Beams and Scales*, etc., dated 13 December 1831; *Report of the River Committee*, dated 4 September 1832; *Report of the River Committee*, dated 12 February 1833; *Report of the Finance Committee*, dated 13 May 1834; and *Report of the Finance Committee*, dated 7 August, 6 November and 4 December 1832.

[142] *Account of duties charged on coals in London*, PP Vol. XXXIII 1833.

in machinery was unlikely to have been a direct source of inertia. Nevertheless, the merchants in London were unwilling or unable to make the switch to weight measurements unless all or a substantial number of merchants were willing to make the switch. It was only with the reforms of the public metage system and the pressure from the coal owners that the London merchants finally switched from volume to weight measurements.

The first buyers had no incentive to alter either the measurement standards or the instruments. However, they found the mechanism of delegated monitoring useful and in fact elected to retain it, even though the public metage system was abolished. Immediately following the reforms in 1831, the first buyers decided that it was indispensable to appoint private meters whose cost the factors and the first buyers shared equally.[143] The private meters were employed throughout the nineteenth century, although their importance diminished gradually as technological improvements made mechanical or instrumental monitoring easier.[144] This desire for private meters at first seems to contradict the first buyers' appeals to end the public metage system. However, evidently, these merchants valued fashioning a monitoring mechanism that they could control, once the advantages accruing to them from the ambiguous London chaldron were nullified by the switch to weight standards.

Apart from the local trade issues, changes within the maritime trade in general also had an impact on the measurement practices within the London coal trade. Expansion of shipping traffic resulted in increased congestion on the Thames from the end of the eighteenth century onwards. The congestion rendered the turn system – which regulated the unloading of the colliers on the Thames – inefficient. This system was also responsible for some of the peculiarities of the measurement practices within the coal trade. Construction of new docks and harbour facilities, such as the West India docks at the initiative of the West India merchants, addressed this paucity of accommodation.[145] However, delivery bottlenecks could only be resolved by reexamining the turn system and abolishing the inefficient public measurement system.[146]

---

[143] Guildhall Library MS 30679, *Minutes of the Coal Meters Committee*, 1831. Entries for 11 and 15 October 1831 and for meetings between 22 October and 13 December 1831.

[144] Smith, *History of coal factors*, p. 319. Improved methods included automatic weighing during delivery either by derricks or hydraulic cranes.

[145] W. M. Stern, 'The first London dock boom and the growth of the West India docks', *Economica* 19 No 73 (1952): p. 59.

[146] Ville, 'Productivity in shipping', p. 364. PP Vol. VIII 1830. *Report on Coal Trade*, 1800. Similar changes were occurring at the same time at the production end of the trade route in north-eastern England. See A. G. Kenwood, 'Capital investment in docks,

Metage reforms did help to improve overall productivity in the coal trade, although historians contest the extent of productivity improvements and their impact on the maritime industry as a whole.[147] Nevertheless, changes in the coal trade provided a benchmark for other commodity trades in several ways. For instance, the Select Committee on the Sale of Corn turned to the coal merchants in 1834 when they evaluated the possibility of making it compulsory to sell wheat and other grains on the basis of weight measurements (Chapter 6). Thomas Gillespy, a coal factor and shipowner, gave evidence to this committee of how the new system of weighing was 'carried on [completely] to the satisfaction of the trade'. The new machinery installed to deliver coal from the colliers was of particular interest to the corn traders as an example of a cost- and time-efficient system of weighing and unloading bulky yet loose commodities. While this technology did not exist in the early nineteenth century, with the introduction of William Cory's derricks (c. 1860), automatic weighing and delivery of such commodities became generally possible.[148]

Conclusions

This chapter raises some important issues about the universal desirability of invariable measurements. Historically, some groups profited from variable measurements, especially the London merchants and other middlemen. Other groups that equated reliability with invariability or uniform metrological units found it difficult to impose particular practices purely because it was desirable or efficient. The state did not intervene to impose measurement units because it was socially efficient or desirable or because it was the moral – as in the right – thing to do. Conversely, consistency of measurements was an important issue that most merchants and the state cared about. This required more than making measurement instruments and units invariable. It took a major overhaul of the measurement practices and tools – instruments, standards, protocols – to make the quantities exchanged during trade reliable.

The abolition of the public metage system and the heaped measures formed the core of the reforms that altered the measurement practices

---

harbours, and river improvements in north-eastern England 1825–1850', *Journal of Transport History* 1 New Ser. No 2 (1971).

[147] Ville, 'Productivity in shipping'. S. Ville, 'Defending productivity growth in the English coal trade during the eighteenth and nineteenth centuries', *Economic History Review* 40 No 4 (1987). W. J. Hausman, 'The English coastal coal trade, 1691–1910: how rapid was productivity growth?' *Economic History Review* 40 No 4 (1987). See also C. K. Harley, 'Coal exports and British shipping, 1850–1913', *Explorations in Economic History* 26 No 3 (1989).

[148] *Report from Select Committee on the Sale of Corn*, PP Vol. VII 1834. Thomas Gillespy's testimony on 26 June 1834. Smith, *History of coal factors*, pp. 288–93.

within this industry. The protocols that had guided the measurement activity for almost half a millennium were replaced by new protocols. The changes to the measurement protocols were just as important (if not more so) as the switching of metrological units from volume to weight. This switch facilitated the abolition of an institution, the metage system, that had become inefficient over the years. Switching standards made it possible to claim that monitoring quantities did not require public measurements. This was an important change from a political economy perspective, and rhetorically, it helped to demonstrate that the larger problems with the coal trade (its high retail price, distribution bottlenecks etc.) were being addressed.

The increased governance of the distribution end of this vital trade route resulted in less regulation, not more. The state effectively withdrew its considerable participation by dismantling the public measurements infrastructure. Third-party monitoring of measurements was retained as an industry practice, but the liability for this was shifted to the private merchants and buyers. In conjunction with other changes to the measurement practices and measurement tools, this institutional change made it easier to prevent fraud and to detect it. The shift in monitoring was no doubt made easier as the administrative reasons for public measurements – tax revenues from coal – diminished because of the fiscal reforms. The metage system existed for several decades subsequently, but in an altered, more private form – as a delegated monitoring system on behalf of London merchants.

Such changes in governance and regulation reflect the micropolitics of the market. The view that the state intervened to correct market failures does not stand up to scrutiny. The view that the state unilaterally moved to streamline administration by eliminating inefficient functions is also unsustainable, given the evidence. In fact, the intervention of the state was secured by private political interests with strong economic motivations. Even at a local level, the involvement of the bureaucracy was secured by strong lobbying by the merchants. Legislative changes were strategically pursued by politically strong merchants to secure their private interests. This theme connects this case study with that of the wire manufacturers in the following chapter. The wire-producing firms were able to use their political power to secure the state's intervention and consolidate their competitive position vis-à-vis foreign firms. In both cases, reforming measurement practices was of strategic importance to merchants and businesses to maintain their competitiveness.

5 Competition, cooperation and standardisation

Uniform measurements in the British wire industry (c. 1880)

Where there is so much confusion order would be welcome for its own sake, but if it can be secured without any violent disruption of existing rules, it is clearly to the interest of everybody to contribute towards the attainment of the general good.

– *The Ironmonger*, 14 February 1880

The wire industry uses a system of standard numbers to express the thickness of wires that are used in hundreds of applications – wire ropes in suspension bridges, electrical conductors and telecommunication cables; precision scientific instruments such as telescopes, hypodermic needles and so on. Before the wire numbers were standardised in Britain circa 1880, each manufacturer or each wire-producing region used a different system of wire numbers and hence different wire gauges. It was not unusual for these gauges to differ from one another such that wire ostensibly of the same number on any two gauges would actually differ in thickness when measured in inches. At first glance, this appears simply to be a matter of using more precise instruments to minimise measurement errors, but making measurements of wire diameters reliable involved standardising the system of wire numbers (design or technical standards), methods of measuring individual wire sizes (measurement protocols) and the wire gauge itself (measurement instruments).

Theoretically, there are an infinite number of possible wire sizes, each size being different from the next size by an infinitesimal degree and each size capable of being practically and very precisely measured. Problems erupted when, from this infinite set of sizes, a finite number of sizes was to be selected and combined to form a uniform set of sizes. The issue here was which was the most appropriate set of sizes that suited all groups within the industry. The adoption of decimal units, rather than using fractional units, could not and did not make existing sets of sizes more reliable. Standardisation therefore implied synchronising the various sets of desired wire sizes that various groups of buyers and producers were keen on. Abstract, scientific and natural principles could

134

not dominate the practical and economic principles by which the various groups evaluated rival proposals: there was no universally true, accurate or ideal set of wire sizes.

Entrenched interests of various buyer and producer groups resulted in a stalemate circa 1880, with neither group willing to accept any other group's notion of reliable wire sizes. These interests stemmed from different incentives; for instance, the buyers desired sizes that would enable them to use wire products more effectively in their applications, whereas the producers desired sizes that would economise their production costs. The stalemate – between producer associations, chambers of commerce and buyer associations – was overcome once the state was asked to intervene on behalf of the industry: the Board of Trade acted as an arbitrator between the various industry groups.

This case study of the wire industry highlights the struggles between the various business groups – buyers, large producers, small- and medium-scale wire makers and so on – to define a standard one-size-fits-all wire gauge. The industry sought to address two basic issues. First, how to produce wire of a particular specification? Second, could the wire of a particular number be of the same size wherever it was produced? Standardisation in this context implied a rationalisation of wire gauges, that is, from many standards to one uniform standard. The preferences of heterogeneous groups (buyer–producer, producer–producer) were aligned through institutions such as trade associations and chambers of commerce.

The case of uniform wire sizes also highlights how apparently straightforward measurements became strategic issues that threatened the competitiveness of entrenched or dominant producers, how dominant producers preferred to cooperate when faced with the threat of a 'wrong' standard enforced upon the industry, how path dependency significantly affected the choice of the standard and how buyers initiated a convergence towards uniformity. Three broad questions are explored: why was it necessary to standardise wire sizes according to a single uniform wire gauge? Why did the dominant producers consider the wire sizes proposed by the buyers (and the state) to be the wrong standard for the industry? How did institutions reconcile the differing notions of reliability held by various groups of buyers and producers and get the groups to accept one uniform wire gauge?

The case of wire sizes must be considered in the context of the emergence of engineering and manufacturing standards from the late eighteenth century onwards. Historically, a baffling variety of standards were in use before the nineteenth century. Each workshop had its own standard for producing parts such as screws, wires, rivets, bolts and early forms of tools and machine parts.[1] The technological convergence that Rosenberg detected in the engineering industries of the nineteenth century depended upon making things the same. This aspect of product standardisation implied standardising engineering processes such as cutting metal into precise shapes – the result being that machine types and machine tools became standardised.[2] The emergence of engineering standards must be placed in the context of increasing competition between industrialising nations, such as Germany and the United States, and an industrialised Britain. The degree to which British industry adopted manufacturing of standardised parts was a result of the competitive response by British producers to the rise of German and American engineering industries and the manufacturing standards they used.[3]

Nonetheless, engineering firms, and in fact the entire system of interchangeable parts manufacturing, depended not only upon making things the same but ensuring that distinct parts stayed dissimilar. Firms depended upon this scaffolding of sameness–distinctiveness that standardisation brought to interchangeable parts manufacturing. This case study shows how firms struggled to make wire sizes of the same number correspond to the same measurements as well as to ensure that two wires of different numbers remained of different measurements.

The sameness–distinctiveness–quantification tensions were politically charged in several engineering sectors in Britain, especially with the increasing competition from German and American firms. This aspect was not lost on the state, which had set up a separate standards department within the Board of Trade in the United Kingdom circa 1860 and subsequently the British Engineering Standards Association in the early 1900s. As this case shows, the board at times played a pivotal role in the standards debates and in the struggles that British firms went through to remain competitive in a rapidly expanding international market for engineering products.

---

[1] B. Sinclair, 'At the turn of the screw: William Sellers, the Franklin Institute, and a standard American thread', *Technology and Culture* 10 No 1 (1969). J. Whitworth, *Papers on mechanical subjects* (London, E. and F. N. Spon, 1882).

[2] N. Rosenberg, 'Technological change in the machine tool industry, 1840–1910', *Journal of Economic History* 23 No 4 (1963). K. Alder, 'Making things the same: representation, tolerance and the end of the ancien régime in France', *Social Studies of Science* 28 No 4 (1998).

[3] R. C. Allen, 'International competition in iron and steel, 1850–1913', *Journal of Economic History* 39 No 4 (1979). R. C. Floud, 'The adolescence of American engineering competition, 1860–1900', *Economic History Review* 27 No 1 (1974). S. B. Saul, 'The market and the development of the mechanical engineering industries in Britain, 1860–1914', *Economic History Review* 20 No 1 (1967). D. S. Landes, 'Watchmaking: a case study in enterprise and change', *Business History Review* 53 No 1 (1979).

Concomitantly, standardisation in manufacturing implied deskilling of labour when, for instance, limit gauges began to be used for measuring the grinding of machine parts. Gauging had become 'a mechanical affair [not requiring] the same skill or the same knowledge on the part of the workman'.[4] However, machine precision did not entirely replace artisan skills, at least not initially. Instead, mechanical methods depended upon both traditional and newer skills, making this combination the limiting condition determining the nature and extent of standardisation.[5] The objectivity, and the form of nineteenth-century standards, was influenced as much by social factors as it was by technological convergence and competition.

Thus this case study shows how competitive pressures compelled the British wire industry to standardise the product, which depended upon the firms agreeing to a standardised set of wire sizes and identification numbers. This in turn depended upon making changes to the process in which wire was produced, which in turn depended upon fundamental changes in measurement practices. The study shows how the industry overcame inertia in switching standards and adopted a uniform measurement standard. I argue that this crucially depended upon three contingent factors: alliances between large producers, a negotiated settlement between buyers and producers and the involvement of the state as an arbitrator.

Wire manufacturing in England

Standardisation of wire sizes is best understood in the context of the economic geography of wire manufacturing in the late nineteenth century. The origins of metal wire manufacturing in England can be traced to the fourteenth century, with wire drawing technology introduced from Germany. By the early nineteenth century, Lancashire had become an important centre for wire-making activity, encouraged by engineering workshops that became located in this region. For example, Peter Stubs, the Warrington toolmaker, became involved in the wire trade initially as a large buyer of pinion wire, but eventually, the firm he founded became one of the important wire producers in the country.[6] By the 1870s, Yorkshire, the West Midlands and Lancashire had emerged as the

---

[4] Speech by Sir R. T. Glazebrook at a meeting of the Physical Society of London at Imperial College, London, on 28 March 1919.

[5] R. B. Gordon, 'Who turned the mechanical ideal into mechanical reality?' *Technology and Culture* 29 No 4 (1988). Alder, 'Making things the same'.

[6] E. S. Dane, *Peter Stubs and the Lancashire hand tool industry* (Altrincham, John Sherratt, 1973).

major wire-manufacturing centres. The ten largest wire-manufacturing firms were located in and around Birmingham, Warrington, Manchester and Halifax, claiming to produce nearly 80 to 90 per cent of the wire manufactured in Britain. However, a majority of the firms involved in wire drawing were numerous small workshops located in and around these major centres. In Birmingham alone, there were about seventy wire manufacturers and about forty wire weavers in 1875; their numbers had increased from five in 1800 and thirty-five in 1866.[7]

In terms of size and output, some of the larger wire makers had multiple manufacturing locations, specialised in many different kinds of wire, employed large numbers of wire drawers and manufactured other products based upon wire. Richard Johnson and Nephew had works at Manchester and Ambergate, employed about a thousand workers and specialised in telegraph and fencing wire, wire rope, tinned mattress wire and fencing wire. Rylands Brothers and Co. produced about seven hundred to eight hundred tons of wire and wire products per week, employed about seven hundred workers and specialised in telegraph and fencing wire; galvanised, tinned and coppered wire; and roping and netting wire. Similarly, Whitecross Company Ltd. employed between eight hundred and one thousand workers; made puddled bars, iron and steel billets, wire rods, plain and coated telegraph and telephone wires, plain and galvanised fencing wire, rope wire and tinned and copper wire; and was perhaps the largest and most integrated, diversified enterprise. The annual capacity of this firm was thought to be about five thousand tons of rope and five thousand miles of netting and around fifteen hundred tons of nails.[8] On the other end of the scale were the smaller manufacturers of wire with far less capital and machinery and employing fewer people. According to one estimate, wire drawers making jewellery wires in Birmingham employed, on average, fewer than 150 people.[9]

Wire was virtually ubiquitous in its use; one contemporary writer listed no fewer than twenty-five distinct uses, including cable and telegraph wires; wire ropes employed for marine, mining, agricultural and engineering uses; manufacture of pins and needles, nails and rivets and so on.[10] Many of the industries using wire and wire products were located

---

[7] F. White, *Commercial and trades directory of Birmingham*, Vol. 2 (Sheffield, Francis White, 1875). W. C. Aitken, 'Brass and brass manufactures', in S. Timmins (ed.) *The resources, products and industrial history of Birmingham and the Midland hardware district* (London, Robert Hardwicke, 1866), p. 359.

[8] J. B. Smith, *Wire, its manufacture and uses* (London, John Wiley, 1891), pp. 93–98.

[9] F. Carnevali, '"Crooks, thieves and receivers": transaction costs in nineteenth-century industrial Birmingham', *Economic History Review* 57 No 3 (2004): p. 539.

[10] Smith, *Wire*, p. 5.

in the West Midlands, Lancashire and Yorkshire, that is, concentrated in the locations where wire was produced. In Birmingham, there were about thirty-five pin manufacturers, seventy spectacle makers, forty screw manufacturers and twenty musical instrument makers, all using a variety of wire products. Lancashire watchmakers used to purchase pinion wire from wire makers of Warrington and Manchester. Wire netting and wire rope products were also manufactured in the Midlands and around in Birmingham. Jewellers and brass and metal works used fine wire made from gold, silver, nickel, copper and brass. Several pianoforte manufacturers were located in Leeds and other locations in Yorkshire. Finer sizes of Yorkshire iron wire were also used for wool and cotton cards and for sieves.[11]

Apart from these small- and medium-sized buyers of wire products, the large wire buyers included the telegraph companies and consortiums that required wire manufactured to fairly high and exacting specifications. Thomas Bolton and Co., Richard Johnson and Nephew and Webster and Horsfall had supplied large amounts of copper wire to the Atlantic Cable Company. One of the initial orders required 119.5 tons of copper to be drawn into 20,500 miles of wire, which had to be laid into a strand 2,500 miles long.[12] Other large users were engineering companies involved in the construction of bridges and other civil projects. Richard Johnson and Nephew had tendered for an order of thirty-four hundred tons of wire to form the main cables of the Brooklyn Bridge in the late 1860s. Makers of fencing wire were other large users of wire products, while wire ropes were also used in mining operations.[13]

Unsurprisingly, Yorkshire, Lancashire and the West Midlands together employed about three-quarters of the wire drawers in England (Table 5.1). The number of persons engaged in wire drawing or wire making increased during the nineteenth century, indicating growth in wire-making activity in these locations.[14] Wire drawing was a highly skilled activity, and drawers were paid a premium wage compared to other occupations. For instance, in the mid-nineteenth century, a wire drawer's weekly wage could be between three and five pounds sterling in

---

[11] White, *Birmingham trades directory*. Dane, *Peter Stubs*. Landes, 'Watchmaking'. T. Hughes, *The English wire gauge* (London, E. and F. N. Spon, 1879). *Ironmonger and Metal Trades Advertiser* (hereinafter *Ironmonger*), 26 February 1881, p. 261.
[12] Cited in B. C. Blake-Coleman, *Copper wire and electrical conductors – the shaping of a technology* (Reading, Harwood Academic, 1992), p. 157.
[13] M. Seth-Smith, *Two hundred years of Richard Johnson and Nephew* (Manchester, Richard Johnson and Nephew, 1973), p. 75. Smith, *Wire*.
[14] C. Lean, 'Wire drawing and steel wire, and its uses', in S. Timmins (ed.) *The resources, products and industrial history of Birmingham and the Midland hardware district* (London, Robert Hardwicke, 1866).

Table 5.1. *Distribution of wire workers in England and Wales*

	1871		1881		1891	
Total number	7,914		9,243		11,175	
West Midlands	2,138	27%	2,366	26%	2,524	23%
Birmingham	1,031		1,380		1,479	
North-western counties	1,459	18%	2,054	22%	2,690	24%
Warrington[a]					1,027	
Manchester	369		333		685	
Yorkshire	2,112	27%	2,611	28%	3,199	28%
Halifax	408		600		638	
Sheffield	306		535		698	

Note: Percentages represent proportions to total numbers.
[a] No figures were reported separately for Warrington in 1881 and 1871.
Source: Census of England and Wales (1871, 1881 and 1891). Occupation classified as 'Wire Worker and Drawer' in 1871 and as 'Wire Maker, Worker, Weaver, Drawer' in 1881 and 1891.

Sheffield; wire workers' wages were reportedly higher than those of skilled ironworkers in 1873.[15] Nevertheless, wire drawers normally had to pay for the wire to be cleaned before bringing it into the mills, a cost that must be factored into the premium that wire drawers allegedly received.[16] Initially, trade union activity amongst the wire workers was limited as most early workers were self-employed or worked in small-scale shops. By the 1860s, union activity had increased, and in 1868, the Thick Iron and Steel Wire Drawers Trade and Benefit Society was formed. However, union membership decreased during the 1870s, and when the manufacturers began to implement wage reductions after 1878, the union was unable to present an effective resistance. As a result of this, manufacturers were able to negotiate considerable wage reductions in the 1880s.[17]

Contemporary estimates of market size in terms of output are difficult to locate. One tentative estimate stated that about half a million tons a year was the probable domestic production. Another estimate put it between forty thousand and eighty thousand tons, although this may

[15] A. Bullen, *Drawn together: one hundred and fifty years of wire workers' trade unionism* (Wigan, Wire Workers Section of the Iron and Steel Trades Confederation, 1992), pp. 7–8. This varied considerably by location; see Lean, 'Wire drawing'. *Ironmonger*, 11 January 1879, pp. 51–52.
[16] Seth-Smith, *Richard Johnson and Nephew*, p. 81.
[17] Bullen, *Drawn together*, pp. 14–15.

have been an underestimate.[18] The first UK Census of Manufactures estimates the net domestic production of iron and steel wire circa 1907 to have been between 210,000 and 215,000 tons, with brass and copper wires contributing an additional 15,500 tons. The number of persons employed in the wire trade around this time was approximately seventeen thousand.[19] Using these figures, per worker output in 1907 appears to have been about thirteen tons per annum. Later estimates for sales of wire products between 1920 and 1922 suggest that per worker output per annum was between sixteen and twenty tons.[20]

It is very likely that per worker output varied significantly across wire manufacturers, particularly between the larger and smaller firms. At worst, per worker output could have stagnated between the 1880s and the early decades of the twentieth century, but it seems unlikely to have decreased significantly. Making a broad assumption that output per worker between 1870 and 1890 was likely to be 13–15 tons, domestic wire production circa 1881 was very likely to have been between 120,000 and 140,000 tons. Thus the export of wire from the United Kingdom formed around 55–60 per cent of the annual production around this time, whereas this proportion was lower in 1871 and 1891 (Table 5.2). In value terms, exports of wire (iron and steel as well as telegraph wire) amounted to about £2.9 million and £2.3 million in 1881 and 1882, respectively.[21] In comparison, exports of wire from the United Kingdom around 1907 were fifty-five thousand tons, or about 25 per cent of the total domestic production.

The German wire industry – the United Kingdom's closest competitor during this period – had increased production from 179,000 tons in 1878 to 250,000 tons in 1881, and further to 378,000 tons in 1882.[22] The German manufacturers exported around 30 per cent of their production in 1878, which increased to about 60 per cent by 1881–1882. In terms of other iron and steel products, Britain produced about 519,000 tons of

---

[18] L. Thomas, *The development of wire rod production* (Cardiff, Guest, Keen and Nettlefolds, 1949), p. 10. Sir Lowthian Bell, president of the British Iron Trade Association, writing in 1886, declared that 'I have no account to make of [output of wire] in Great Britain, but it looks as if half a million tons a year at least is the total annual production of this article'. L. Bell, *The iron trade of United Kingdom* (London, British Iron Trade Association, 1886), p. 23.

[19] Final Report on the First Census of Production of the United Kingdom (1907), 1912, pp. 113–17.

[20] F. Stones, *The British ferrous wire industry* (Sheffield, J. W. Northend, 1977). See illustrations between pp. 12 and 13.

[21] *Ironmonger*, 13 January 1883, p. 56, extract from Board of Trade Returns.

[22] *Ironmonger*, 9 April 1881, p. 510. Bell, *Iron trade of the United Kingdom*, p. 23. France, Belgium and the United States were also important wire-producing countries during this period.

Table 5.2. *Estimates of domestic production and exports of wire (England and Wales)*

| | No of wire drawers | Annual output | | | UK exports | Exports as % of production |
		Assuming 10 tons per worker	Assuming 13 tons per worker	Assuming 15 tons per worker		
1871	7,914	79,140	102,882	118,710	21,000[a]	20
1881	9,243	92,430	120,159	138,645	75,000	62
1891	11,175	111,750	145,275	167,625	62,000[a]	43

[a] Export figures are for 1870 and 1890.
Sources: Number of wire drawers from Census of 1871, 1881 and 1891. UK exports as reported in L. Thomas, *The development of wire rod production* (1949), appendix VIII.

rails in 1879, which increased to more than 1.2 million tons in 1882. At the same time, Germany produced 481,000 tons of rails in 1880, which increased to 564,000 tons in 1882. In fact, the market for commercial iron products, such as wire, was more important for German heavy industry compared to rails, whereas in Britain, the reverse was true. During the 1880s, the German firms exported more wire products than rails.[23] The major German firms were also larger and more integrated compared to British firms. Eisen-Industrie zu Menden made seventy thousand tons of puddle and rolled bars, wire rods, drawn wire and nails. Westfälische Union, formed from an amalgamation of various older Westphalian firms in 1873, had an output of about one hundred thousand tons annually, employed about three thousand workers and made wire rods, drawn wire, wire strands and roping, nails, rivets and screws, besides large quantities of bar iron, axels, sheet metal and so on.[24]

It was during this period, when German wire producers threatened the dominance of the British wire industry, that measurement problems that resulted from the use of multiple wire gauges became the subject of heated debate within the iron trades. To appreciate the significance and scale of these problems, it is necessary to understand the process of wire drawing and why the wire gauges assumed centre stage in the industry's fight to retain its dominance in international markets.

[23] U. Wengenroth, *Enterprise and technology: the German and British steel industries, 1865–1895*, S. H. Tenison (trans.) (Cambridge, Cambridge University Press, 1994), pp. 139–41; see tables 15 and 17, also p. 186.
[24] Smith, *Wire*, p. 97.

Wire sizes: the source of transactional problems

Wire was produced from wire rods (approximately one-fourth inch in diameter), which were drawn or pulled by wire drawers through perforated surfaces called drawplates. The perforations on the drawplate corresponded with sizes that ranged from Nos 1 through 20 for thicker wires and from Nos 20 through 50 for finer wires – the increasing numbers signified smaller wire diameters.[25] Many of these sizes were further divided into half and quarter sizes. The cost of making wire increased with each successive draw so that finer wire was costlier to manufacture than thicker wire.[26] The primary reason for this was that the wire-drawer's remuneration and other costs, such as annealing (i.e. preparing the metal for drawing), depended directly upon the number of draws made to manufacture wire of a required diameter.[27] A skilled wire drawer knew what intermediate holes could be avoided, and this form of remuneration may actually have encouraged this practice. Conversely, wire reduced more than two sizes in one draw was usually not of good quality, a fact easily assessed by visual inspection. This most likely discouraged the practice of jumping holes.[28] There was a strong economic and technical interrelatedness between the technique of drawing wire, the wire drawer's wage and the overall cost of production.

Wire had to be drawn through a particular sequence of holes to maintain quality. Such sequences were established empirically through long usage. The skill of the wire drawer was to know such sequences. For example, if iron wire No 4 was required,

the drawer [took] annealed wire of No. 1, [gave] it a hole to No. 3 [and another] hole to No. 4. If he had reduced it from size 1 to 4 in one draw, presuming the metal wire were tough enough to withstand the strain, it would be found irregular in thickness, ellipse here, fluted there, and flat further on, instead of being smooth and equal diameter throughout.[29]

The same source gives us another example. Suppose iron wire of No 5 size was required:

The drawer [took] No. 1 annealed rod, [reduced] it, first hole to No. 3, second hole to No. 4, and third hole to No. 5 [making] three draws. Were the wire annealed each draw the reduction to No. 5 could be accomplished in two draws,

---

[25] Sizes greater than No 1 referred to wire rods.
[26] Stones, *British wire industry*. See price list from 1884 between pp. 12 and 13.
[27] 'Annealing' is a process of softening the metal to make the drawing of wire easier.
[28] Smith, *Wire*, pp. 55–56. *Ironmonger*, 26 February 1881, pp. 259–61.
[29] *Ironmonger*, 26 February 1881, pp. 259–61.

but it would not be 'finished' wire fit for the market, and the cost of repeated annealing would ruin the manufacturer.[30]

Also, the wire drawer was required to know the wire sizes and not the actual diameter of the wire being pulled. In other words, it was unimportant for the drawer to know that a No 7 was 3/16th of an inch thick or that a No 10 was 0.14 inches (or 9/64ths of an inch) thick. As long as the drawer was familiar with the sizes and the sequences of holes through which the wire had to pass, he could produce wire of almost any diameter required. Wire drawing involved a considerable degree of tacit knowledge, and a wire drawer could make wire without drawing it through the drawplate. For example, a skilled worker could take six feet of No 22 soft brass wire, fasten one end to a post and pull at the other and thus obtain eight feet of No 24 wire. Or he could take six feet of No 22 soft copper wire and stretch it to seven feet No 22 3/4 wire. The wire drawer knew these metal properties and also that if he got to the 'limits of cohesion', he either 'sucked' or broke the wire; he used the wire sizes as his guide, instead of the drawplates, to do this.[31]

Throughout the nineteenth century, wire-making technology kept pace with developments in wire applications. The move towards machine-made wire meshes and netting in the early nineteenth century led to the shift away from hand-drawn wire to wire drawn by mechanical means. Steam power was used to draw longer pieces of wire by the 1840s. George Bedson, of Richard Johnson and Nephew, introduced a continuous rod-rolling mill in 1862, which effectively enabled longer coils of wire rods to be produced. Around the same time, German manufacturers were also making improvements to rod-rolling technology. By 1878, German wire makers could cut capital and labour costs by making some changes to the manner in which rods were rolled in the rolling mill.[32]

The speed with which wire was drawn and the efficiency of drawing machines improved slowly and insignificantly throughout the nineteenth century. In fact, the techniques for drawing wire in the late nineteenth century had changed little from those used in the eighteenth century. In contrast, the output of rod-rolling mills increased by a factor of almost

---

[30] Ibid. A contrary view held that this was true only of certain sizes and not generally. See Hughes, *Wire gauge*.

[31] *Ironmonger*, 26 February 1881, pp. 259–61.

[32] Seth-Smith, *Richard Johnson and Nephew*. T. Morris, *Four days in the iron wire manufacturing district of Westphalia, Germany*, Warrington Literary and Philosophical Society, as cited in Thomas, *Wire rod production*, pp. 23–24.

fifty.[33] To increase the efficiency of wire drawing, the technique of combining several blocks of wire drawing machines was introduced in the late nineteenth century. In 1871, the Woods brothers from Manchester patented a continuous wire-drawing machine that made it possible to pass wire through four drawplates in a series.[34] Nevertheless, continuous wire drawing technology was relatively new and not generally adopted within the British industry in the 1870s. The exception to this was the Ambergate works of Richard Johnson and Nephew, where, in the early 1870s, engineers from Washburn Co., an American wire manufacturer with whom the Johnsons had had long ties, were brought in to introduce a system that used unskilled labour supervised by craftsmen. This system used cast iron dies in series, similar to Bedson's continuous rod production methods. In fact, the technique was reported as a new innovation even in the 1880s, hinting that the trade was largely unfamiliar with such technology:

An ingenious machine has lately been introduced here for expediting the work, the wire passing through a succession of plates pierced by holes of diminishing gauges, [and] the wire is drawn down three sizes at once, at a great saving of time, labour and cost.[35]

It was only by the late 1880s that wire could practically be drawn from, say, No 34 to No 48 in one continuous operation.[36]

Wire gauges: the source of unreliable measurements

The origin of the slot gauges to measure wire sizes used in nineteenth-century Britain is uncertain. They were likely introduced into England from Germany in the sixteenth century. The sizes were initially divided into vulgar fractions of the English inch. As the number of sizes increased and became cumbersome to denote in terms of fractions, they were collected into a series of identification numbers.[37] The perforations on the drawplate corresponded with the sizes of wire as measured by the wire gauge. The No 1 hole on the drawplate corresponded with the No 1 size

---

[33] Blake-Coleman, *Copper wire*, p. 83. N. K. Laman, 'The development of the wire-drawing industry', *Metallurgist* 3 No 6 (1959): p. 268.
[34] Thomas, *Wire rod production*, p. 15. Laman, 'Wire-drawing', p. 269.
[35] *Ironmonger*, 10 April 1880, p. 494.
[36] Bullen, *Drawn together*, p. 12. Smith, *Wire*, pp. 84–89.
[37] H. W. Dickinson and H. Rogers, 'Origin of gauges for wire, sheets and strip', *Transactions of the Newcomen Society* 21 (1943). Hughes, *Wire gauge*.

Figure 5.1. The Board of Trade standard wire gauge (1884). *Source*: from a private collection.

on the wire gauge used in a workshop, and the No 23 hole on the draw-plate corresponded with the No 23 size on the same gauge (Figure 5.1). The wire gauges in use before circa 1880 were empirically derived, that is, based upon long experience of wire drawing. Some engineers claimed that there was a definite mathematical relationship between the break-ing strength of each wire and the opposition provided by the drawplate while drawing wire.[38] This created a degree of interrelatedness between the drawplates and the gauges. The progressive sequence of holes on the drawplate was empirically derived based on the observation of the breaking strength of wire of different metals.

The original gauges were based upon these sequences of holes, which varied by the metal used to make wire, the workshop, the geographic region and the use-context of a given wire product. In turn, the gauges themselves were used both as a verification tool to ensure that the wire drawn was of the expected diameter and as a template to replicate new drawplates once the older ones became worn out due to repeated use. Historically, virtually every workshop had its own wire gauge, which was devised according to its experience of drawing wire and 'guarded with great care [and] transmitted almost as heirlooms from father to son'.[39]

Minor variations in the sizes of wire inevitably crept into this prac-tice of making wire gauges.[40] Thomas Hughes narrates the following experience:

I saw a set of [some] standard patterns [consisting] of small pieces of iron wire, all sizes from No. 1 to 40; each size was kept in a box for preservation. The owner had had them for about 50 years and made gauges for sale with them.[41]

---

[38] L. Clark, 'On the Birmingham wire gauge (paper presented to the British Association in 1869)', *Journal of the Society of Telegraph Engineers* 7 (1878): p. 338.
[39] Smith, *Wire*, p. 55. Dickinson and Rogers, 'Origin of gauges', p. 88.
[40] Hughes, *Wire gauge*. Clark, 'Birmingham gauge, 1869', pp. 337 and 41.
[41] Hughes, *Wire gauge*.

Very likely this resulted in the profusion of wire gauges as each workshop or region developed its own gauge. In other words, the industry developed multiple technical standards based on the production technologies in use at the time. Many of these different gauges varied marginally in terms of actual dimension. The difference was apparent only when the measurements were expressed using decimal units rather than fractional units of the inch. Nevertheless, there were several distinct gauges where the correspondence between diameters (in fractional inches) and gauge numbers differed significantly.

Consider two different wire gauges used in Warrington and Birmingham around 1879.[42] Comparing these gauges, we discover, for example, that No 30 on the Warrington gauge was 0.0108 inches in diameter, whereas it was 0.014 inches on the Birmingham gauge. Similarly, No 34 was 0.00575 inches on the Warrington gauge as opposed to 0.0106 inches on the Birmingham one. Thus wire drawn to the No 30 hole on the Warrington gauge would be approximately one-third smaller in diameter to that drawn on the No 30 hole on the Birmingham gauge, and wire drawn on the No 34 hole on the Warrington gauge would be almost half as thick as that drawn to the same hole on the Birmingham gauge. The Birmingham No 34 was actually closer to the Warrington No 30 than to the No 34 on that gauge. Admittedly, such differences were more apparent in the finer sizes than in the larger ones (Figure 5.2).

As the number of applications of wire products increased, there was a corresponding increase in the number of wire sizes. Eighteenth-century wire gauges appeared to have used between twelve and sixteen sizes, whereas by 1842, the number of sizes had increased to at least twenty-six. The increasing complexity of sizes also emphasised the need for workmen to remember only the wire numbers rather than the measurements in inches; the gauge numbers functioned as a convenient mnemotechnic.

The most widely known of the gauges was the Birmingham wire gauge (BWG), although no single gauge can be traced which could be termed as *the* authoritative BWG. This gauge was also used in other locations apart from Birmingham such as Manchester and Sheffield. Internationally, the BWG was known in Germany and parts of the United States.[43] The Stubs Lancashire gauge was originally defined by Peter Stubs and was preferred in Warrington, Sheffield, Manchester and Canada. Apart from these, other gauges included the Rylands gauge, the Cocker steel gauge and the South Staffordshire gauge (see Appendix 5.1).

[42] Ibid.
[43] Clark, 'On the Birmingham wire gauge'. *Ironmonger*, 14 February 1880, editorial note.

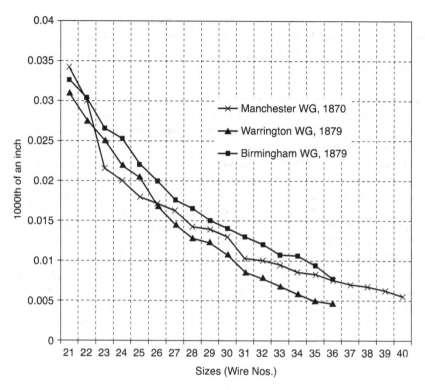

Figure 5.2. Comparison of wire sizes across gauges. *Source*: Thomas Hughes, *The English wire gauge* (London, 1879).

Wire makers did not exclusively use such slot-wire gauges, although they were very widely used in Britain, Germany and the United States, more than any other kind. A micrometer gauge used by some manufacturers in the United States was described in 1877 and was reported to be very precise, and in trials, 'gauge boys [could] very easily be taught to read the thousandth of an inch'.[44] However, the micrometer gauge was not generally used in Britain as its use by workmen was considered to be 'liable to errors of unobserved movement'.[45]

---

[44] 'Report on a standard wire gauge', paper read before the American Institute of Mining Engineers at Amenia, October 1877, repr. in the *Journal of the Society of Telegraph Engineers* 7 (1879): pp. 344–50. Other forms included the old French bent wire gauge, the step gauge used in the eighteenth century, the V gauge used in the United States etc. See Dickinson and Rogers, 'Origin of gauges'.

[45] Smith, *Wire*, p. 117. Hughes, *Wire gauge*. The micrometre gauge was commonly used in the metal sheet and strips trade. See Dickinson and Rogers, 'Origin of gauges'. Also *Ironmonger*, 27 November 1880, p. 621.

In this manner, we can identify various sources of transaction problems arising as a result of the different gauges in use. Different wire numbers on two different gauges could refer to the same diameter of wire (in terms of length units). Or, to put it differently, the same wire number as measured by two different gauges could refer to different diameters of wire. Latimer Clark claimed that he was personally involved in a contract where the use of one gauge instead of another would have made a difference of about eight thousand pounds sterling to the contract value. The solution was to specify both the gauge number as well as the diameter of the wire, which only proved the 'uselessness of the present system'.[46] Thomas Hughes wrote of an order from New York for a No 36 Birmingham gauge wire, where

the [British manufacturers] rightly concluded the gauge intended was Stub's, or Warrington Wire Gauge, that being the 'Birmingham Wire Gauge' commonly [referred to] in the United States. [Had] this order been executed to the Birmingham gauge [the] difference in price [would have been] £28 per ton.[47]

By the 1880s, foreign buyers had become wary of these differences in gauge sizes. Muller, Uhlich and Co. wrote to the *Iron Age*, New York, that 'the diversity in the gauges of wire, sheet iron etc, is the cause of much trouble, especially when orders are sent from the United States'.[48]

Furthermore, wire manufacturers reportedly secured orders through underselling; however, this was the effect of supplying a thicker wire for a given gauge number, which cost less to produce. For example, a No 22 copper wire according to the gauge used in Birmingham could be invoiced as No 21 1/2 in Warrington, Liverpool or Staffordshire, making it cheaper outside Birmingham by four or five pounds sterling per ton. Consumers also took advantage of this asymmetric information to gain a price advantage. Some buyers sought to obtain finer sizes of wire for the lower price of thicker wire by claiming that they could obtain, say, No 36 brass wire at the price of No 33, potentially saving as much as eighty-four pounds sterling per ton.[49] Hughes narrates the following anecdote:

A maker [of wire gauges] told me that when a customer used certain sizes [frequently], the gauge made for him had those sizes made smaller [i.e. a lower size number] than they should be, to enable him to purchase wire cheaper. A case in point shortly after came under my observation. A customer used No. 25 wire largely; notch 24 on his gauge was the same size as No. 25 on any ordinary

46 Clark, 'Birmingham gauge, 1867', p. 226.
47 Hughes, *Wire gauge*.
48 Repr. in *Ironmonger*, 12 March 1881, p. 345.
49 *Ironmonger*, 1 January 1881, pp. 18–20.

gauge; he thereby obtained wire No. 25 at the price of No. 24, saving £4 10s per ton.[50]

In contrast, German wire was drawn to standard sizes by the 1880s. Although the BWG was 'extensively adopted' in Germany, the millimetre gauge was used to measure Westphalian wire by the late 1870s. This gauge was based on the metric measures and expressed wire diameters in millimetres. The system of numbering wire sizes on this gauge easily indicated the actual diameter of the wire; that is, a No 100 wire in this system was 10 millimetres in diameter, a No 55 wire was 5.5 millimetres in diameter and a No 2 wire was 0.2 millimetres in diameter. The wire numbers thus decreased progressively as the wire diameters decreased, in contrast to the English gauges, where the numbers increased as the diameters decreased. German wire makers had earlier used a gauge known as the 'Bergish', with its own unique system of sizes that were expressed in terms of letters such as K, GR, FR, GM or MM. Hughes describes one such gauge dated 1877, which he calls the 'Westphalian Common Wire Gauge'. By 1881, the German wire makers, like the French manufacturers, were using the millimetre gauge to express wire sizes:[51]

Formerly, neither the French nor Germans had a standard wire gauge. A few years ago the French adopted a modification of their old gauge. To facilitate its acceptance they retained the old numbers on one side, and the new numbers indicating the diameters in millimetres, on the reverse. The Germans long discussed a standard wire gauge, ultimately deciding upon one similar to the French.[52]

Buyers purchasing wire in bulk from multiple manufacturers, overseas buyers acquiring wire from British manufacturers, buyers whose gauges did not match the manufacturers' gauges and vice versa faced transaction problems arising from nonuniform wire sizes. There were distinct advantages in making standard sizes uniform. However, some groups could benefit by maintaining an ambiguity between wire sizes and gauge numbers. Theoretically, the industry could reduce transaction costs by specifying the exact dimension of wire required (in length units) for each contract. By the late 1870s, orders for wires had begun to specify diameters in decimal divisions of the inch in addition to the gauge numbers. Wire manufacturers had begun printing lists of wire sizes specifying the

[50] Hughes, *Wire gauge*.
[51] Ibid. See also *Ironmonger*, 14 February 1880, editorial notes, p. 209.
[52] *Ironmonger*, 12 February 1881, pp. 206–11.

diameters (in decimal inches) for each gauge number.[53] Some within the industry felt that a better alternative was to standardise the gauge numbers to signify uniform measurements. Between 1878 and 1883, the several industry associations attempted to define a uniform wire gauge, which they hoped would alleviate problems arising from multiple gauges.

Standardising measurements: a solution for transactional problems

Early attempts

The early attempts at defining an industry standard gauge can be dated back to 1824. However, the first concrete proposal was made by Charles Holtzapffel in 1847.[54] He remarked that 'some irregularity thence exists amongst the gages in common use, notwithstanding that they may be nominally alike'. Consequently, he proposed an

easy and exact system of gages [where] the nomenclature should be so completely associated with the actual measures, as to convey to the mind [a] very close idea of [the] thickness of sizes.[55]

Holtzapffel intended to remove the

arbitrary incongruous system of gages now used [by using the decimal divisions of the inch so that] there could be no more difficulty in constructing the gages of customary forms, with notches made to systematic and *defined* measures, *that may easily be arrived at or tested*, than with their present unsystematical and *arbitrary* measures, *which do not admit of verification.*[56]

Holtzapffel's proposal was published in a textbook on mechanical engineering, in which he outlined his views with reference to the Stubs or Lancashire wire gauge.

A few years earlier, Joseph Whitworth had become involved in the standardisation of the screw threads and cylindrical gauges based on the

---

[53] Hughes, *Wire gauge*. See also [T]he [N]ational [A]rchives, Board of Trade Papers, BT 101/40, copy of advertisement of W & C Wynn & Co.'s gauge, compared to the Stubs gauge, and with diameters in decimal inches.
[54] Dickinson and Rogers, 'Origin of gauges'.
[55] C. Holtzapffel, *Turning and mechanical manipulation*, Vol. 2 (London, Holtzapffel, 1847).
[56] Ibid.; emphasis in original.

decimal subdivisions of the inch.[57] In the 1850s, he claimed that in the wire-making industry,

there [was] no standard of appeal; and the different wire and other gauges differ so considerably that the [customer had] to send a sample of what he wants [to the manufacturer], there being no means of correctly expressing its size.[58]

This prompted him to propose the use of decimal units in the measurement of wire sizes by illustrating the precision with which wire diameters could be measured using the decimal system, a scheme remarkably similar to the one the German manufacturers were to adopt nearly two decades later.[59]

Another engineer who wrote about the standardisation of wire size was Latimer Clark, the telegraph expert. Between 1867 and 1869, Clark presented two papers to the British Association on the need to standardise the BWG. He proposed a scale based on decimal divisions of the inch, where the size of the wire diameters increased by a constant rate of about 11 per cent from the smallest size, or alternatively, the weight of the wire increased by about 25 per cent.[60]

Holtzapffel, Whitworth and Clark were primarily concerned with measuring the wire diameters as *precisely* as possible. They believed that making precise measurements, that is, using decimal units to measure diameters rather than fractional units, would help to eliminate the problems that arose from multiple gauges. Holtzapffel wrote that

when certain objects are required to be so proportional as to constitute a series, the intervals between the decimal measures would be far more easily arranged and appreciated, than those of vulgar fractions.[61]

Similarly, Whitworth wrote that 'there can be no doubt of the beneficial results that would follow the passing of [decimal weights and measures]'. He further wrote that 'small accurate standards of length, of the decimal parts of an inch, would be of much service to some trades [such as wire making]'.[62] Clark stressed that

[57] Whitworth, *Papers on mechanical subjects*. See paper to the Institution of Civil Engineers, 1841.
[58] Ibid. See paper to Institution of Mechanical Engineers, 1856.
[59] Ibid. See proceedings of Institution of Mechanical Engineers, 1857. It is interesting to compare Whitworth's 1857 decimal wire sizes to the German gauge described by Thomas Hughes in 1879, which are remarkably similar in their specifications. Hughes, *Wire gauge*.
[60] Clark, 'Birmingham gauge, 1867', p. 153.
[61] Holtzapffel, *Turning*, Vol. 2.
[62] Whitworth, *Papers on mechanical subjects*. Paper to Institution of Mechanical Engineers, 1856.

for obviating the inconvenience arising from this great confusion among gauges in common use [I] approve of the system of measurement in decimal fraction of an inch.[63]

All these proposals involved replacing existing production methods, either in terms of using decimal measurements or fundamentally changing the relationship between the wire numbers and wire sizes. Whitworth's proposal involved altering the existing system of gauge numbers completely by reversing their order, that is, the smaller sizes had lower wire numbers, and vice versa. Clark's proposed sizes involved a constant decrement in sizes, contrary to many of the existing gauges that had no recognizable or regular pattern in the arrangement of wire sizes. This meant that some of his thicker wire sizes were actually larger than those practically in use. Both Clark's and Holtzapffel's proposals were virtually identical to the gauge known as the Stubs gauge, which was only one of the several gauges in use at the time.

We lack any clear evidence as to how the industry reacted to the early proposals to standardise the wire gauge using decimal divisions of the inch and based on abstract principles of regular or scientifically derived increments in wire sizes. As the use of multiple wire gauges persisted until the 1880s, we can assume that the producers simply disregarded the various suggestions for a uniform series of wire sizes. However, bucking the general trend of resisting metrication and decimalisation of measurements, by the late 1870s, the wire industry had begun to use decimal divisions of the inch to express wire sizes. Hughes wrote,

Of late, wire manufacturers are adopting the plan of sending to their customers [printed] list of sizes of wire [with] diameters of the wire, expressed in decimal parts of an inch, opposite to the number of the gauge.[64]

A trade report from 1881 claimed that 'during the last few months merchants have begun to order wires to decimal fractions of an inch'.[65] A decimal measuring machine was also introduced claiming usefulness to 'manufacturers of wire, copper, brass or charcoal sheets, small arms, sewing machines and others working on the interchangeable system and requiring great accuracy in measuring'.[66] The industry thus did begin using decimal measurements, but did not converge towards a uniform one-size-fits-all standard for wire size.

[63] Clark, 'Birmingham gauge, 1867'.
[64] Hughes, *Wire gauge*.
[65] *Ironmonger*, 1 January 1881, pp. 18–21.
[66] *Ironmonger*, 8 January 1881, p. 43.

Competing proposals and standardisation: 1878–1883

In contrast to this rather lacklustre response to the early standardisation attempts, the decade 1872–1882 witnessed a flurry of activity within the trade, particularly after 1878. During this period, the buyers made several attempts to establish a standard wire gauge. Telegraph cable companies had become large and sophisticated purchasers of wire products, particularly of copper wire. One contract for a submarine cable specified the core to be made of seven No 22 BWG copper wires with a total diameter equal to No 14 BWG, weighing 107 pounds per nautical mile.[67] Other buyers, such as pin manufacturers, demanded greater consistency in wire diameters. Pin making was a large-volume business, where about 50 million pins were being manufactured in Birmingham alone by the late 1880s. These required the equivalent of one hundred thousand pounds sterling worth of wire per annum. The introduction of automatic pin-making machines in the middle of the nineteenth century meant that there was now a greater demand for 'exactitude' in wire diameters. According to Latimer Clark, 'pin makers and others have really to resort to small divisions [and] it is most desirable [that a gauge be defined] so that it can be measured on a machine'.[68] Hughes echoed this by writing,

Much wire is in these days ordered quarter sizes, and even greater divisions, and is worked up by self-acting machines – such as screws, pins, rivets etc. Unless the wire is accurately drawn, the machine either makes an imperfect article or spoils it.[69]

In fact, some contracts required wire makers to manufacture wire to a specified weight per gauge and length in addition to a specified diameter. Many contract specifications included wire diameters expressed in ten-thousandths of an inch or in hundredths of a millimetre. 'The wire manufacturers ingenuity [was] being strained to meet the [specialised] demand for wires of given diameters,' wrote one trade journal.[70] Wire used in fine-woven gauzes also had to be made to fairly exacting and *consistent* standards: some of the gauzes were so finely woven that they contained nearly forty thousand meshes of wire per square inch.[71] The users and retailers of wire were urged to demand an industry standard,

---

[67] Blake-Coleman, *Copper wire*, p. 157.
[68] TNA, BT 101/124, notes on conference dated 27 December 1882.
[69] Hughes, *Wire gauge*.
[70] *Ironmonger*, 1 January 1881, pp. 18–21.
[71] Smith, *Wire*, pp. 6–26. H. I. Dutton and S. R. H. Jones, 'Invention and innovation in the British pin industry, 1790–1850', *Business History Review* 57 No 2 (1983): p. 190. *Ironmonger*, 1 January 1881, p. 18.

with one trade journal writing that 'it is from these classes that the pressure for a standard uniform gauge must come'.[72]

In 1872, telegraph engineers proposed a uniform wire gauge based upon a mass-length standard. They argued that as copper wire was increasingly being purchased either by weight or with diameter specified in thousandths of an inch, this same system could be extended to the purchase of iron wire.[73] Nothing further seems to have occurred on this issue until May 1878, when the Society of Telegraph Engineers (STE) appointed a committee to further consider the issue of the wire gauge. Carl Siemens, brother of Werner and William Siemens, who was involved in the first major transatlantic submarine cable expedition aboard the *Faraday*, was a prime mover in getting the STE committee appointed in May 1878.[74] The committee consisted mainly of telegraph engineers (Latimer Clark, H. Mallock, W. H. Preece, C. V. Walker etc.) but also included J. Thewlis Johnson of Richard Johnson and Nephew, who provided the manufacturer's perspective.[75] The committee's report, published in the society's journal in 1879, acknowledged that any uniform wire gauge 'should not vary materially from the present gauges now in use [as] these gauges have been based on long practice and experience and [are] well adapted to the practical requirements of trade'.[76] Nevertheless, the gauge proposed by the committee as the British standard gauge (BSG) was basically Latimer Clark's geometric gauge of 1867. Although the BSG was to conform closely to the existing gauges, the committee stressed that due to the principle of its construction (geometrically decreasing sizes), it would differ from the existing gauges, sometimes as much as by whole sizes. However, the committee felt that 'the workmen and dealers would gradually become acquainted with it, and would soon begin to prefer it on account of its precision and uniformity, and its authority as a gauge of last appeal'.[77]

In October 1878, the Birmingham Chamber of Commerce (BCC) canvassed the principal dealers in metals and wire and also jewellers to seek their opinion about a uniform gauge.[78] After corresponding with the

---

[72] *Ironmonger*, 18 December 1990, editorial.
[73] H. Mallock and W. H. Preece, 'On a new telegraph wire gauge', *Journal of the Society of Telegraph Engineers* 1 (1872): p. 81.
[74] IET Archives IET/ORG/2/1/2, Society of Telegraph Engineers, Minutes of Council Meetings. See entry for 23 May 1878.
[75] C. V. Walker was a past president of the STE and had presented a paper on the wire gauge in April 1878.
[76] Report on the BWG, STE Journal, 1879, p. 476.
[77] Report on the BWG, STE Journal, 1879, p. 493.
[78] TNA, BT 101/114, Report of the Associated Chambers of Commerce (hereinafter ACC) on Wire Gauge. Birmingham City Archives MS 2299 Acc2000/127 Box 4, Birmingham Chamber of Commerce, Council Minutes Books. See entries for 23 October, 20 November and 18 December 1878.

other chambers of commerce, the BCC council decided to write to Joseph Whitworth, asking for assistance in 'furtherance of a scheme to establish an uniform wire and metal gauge'.[79] Subsequently, in March 1879, at the annual general meeting of the Associated Chambers of Commerce (ACC), the BCC representatives obtained a resolution to establish 'one uniform standard gauge' and demanded that its use be made 'if necessary compulsory by law'. A committee of ACC members first met in October 1879 to discuss the issue of uniform wire gauges and was chaired by T. R. Harding, a pin maker from Leeds. Latimer Clark and Joseph Whitworth both attended his first meeting 'by special invitation'.[80] The committee was unable to report until 1882 as it was difficult to reach a consensus on the form of the standard gauge. The individual members were determined to have their own proposals accepted as the standard gauge:

Certain members of the committee [were] pushing their own ideas, some of the chambers [were] in favour of a metrical gauge ... Birmingham [was] inclined to fight for its own hand, and Warrington [held] to the gauge in general use amongst its manufacturers.[81]

In fact, there were deep divisions within the ACC committee on this issue. The committee itself was composed of both wire makers and buyers of wire products. Each group had its own distinct opinion on what constituted an appropriate standard. In February 1882, several wire manufacturers – Edelsten, Williams and Co., Rylands, Richard Johnson and Nephew, Nettlefolds, Whitecross – met in Birmingham along with W. F. Haydon and T. R. Harding of the BCC. The ACC had recently considered adopting Harding's proposal as its recommended standard gauge. Virtually all the large manufacturers – claiming 70 to 80 per cent share of wire production – were opposed to Harding's proposal, accusing it of being a compromise and 'theoretically imperfect'. Nevertheless, in March 1882, the ACC adopted Harding's proposal as the basis for their standard wire gauge.[82] Harding's proposed gauge differed little from the existing Stubs gauge used in Lancashire, except for finer sizes below No 30.

The ACC subsequently tried to get the industry to accept its proposals. It tried to make the Harding gauge the only legally recognised wire gauge in Britain. In March 1882, the ACC sent a memorial to the Board of Trade (BOT) strongly urging it to consider its proposal 'for

[79] Birmingham City Archives MS 2299. Entry for 18 December 1878.
[80] Guildhall Library Ms 14476/3, ACC, *Executive Council Minutes: Vol 3, Council Papers*, August 1876–August 1883. Entry for 29 October 1878.
[81] *Ironmonger*, 25 February 1882, pp. 268–69.
[82] *Ironmonger*, 25 February 1881, p. 281. Guildhall Library Ms 14476/3. Entry dated 1 March 1882. TNA, BT 101/114.

the purpose of its being legalised [as] the British Standard Wire Gauge'. Immediately thereafter, the BOT invited reactions and opinions from the rest of the industry on the ACC proposal. Several large users of wire products approved the proposal, especially cable wire users such as the General Post Office. Several chambers of commerce also approved the BOT proposal, including the chambers of London, Birmingham, Leeds and Wolverhampton. Also, many small- and medium-sized Birmingham engineering and metalworking firms approved the proposal.[83]

However, the large wire makers, who were opposed to the ACC proposal from the beginning, objected to the BOT proposal forming the *only* legal and uniform gauge. In May 1882, several wire manufacturers formed the Iron and Steel Wire Manufacturers Association (ISWMA) 'to decide upon the course to be taken [in] the matter of a standard wire gauge'. The ISWMA wrote to the BOT stating that the sizes it proposed were arbitrarily specified 'without regard to the method of production' and were different from the sizes 'most generally known to consumers'. The association came up with its proposed list of sizes – the Lancashire wire makers proposing the sizes up to No 20 and the Yorkshire manufacturers proposing the finer sizes from No 21 to No 50.[84] Although the wire sizes in the ACC and ISWMA proposals appear to be virtually identical, the difference between the sizes seemed to be of material importance to the wire manufacturers (Appendix 5.2).

The ISWMA did not represent the opinion of all wire makers. One irate correspondent, presumably a small wire maker from Birmingham, wrote,

Because the major quantity is supposed to be drawn in Warrington all the others must submit to the Warrington wire gauge. [If] iron wire can be drawn to the BWG [in] Birmingham, Yorkshire, Wales, etc., why not in Warrington?[85]

Even within the ISWMA, there was a difference of opinion regarding the response to the BOT's April 1882 proposal. The Yorkshire manufacturers Frederick Smith and Co. and Ramsden Camm and Co. were in favour of the BOT proposal but decided to go along with the majority view of opposing it.[86] As the major wire manufacturers rejected the ACC proposal, the BOT felt that its proposal needed to be modified 'to meet the views of the Warrington district where most of the iron and steel wire [was] made'.

[83] TNA, BT 101/114; BT 101/115; BT 101/116; BT 101/119.
[84] Stones, *British wire industry*, p. 1. TNA, BT 101/116, letter from the ACC to the BOT dated 7 July 1882.
[85] *Ironmonger*, 20 May 1882, letters to the editor, pp. 686–87.
[86] Stones, *British wire industry*, p. 1.

Consequently, the BOT circulated a modified proposal in November 1882, despite the fact that its April 1882 proposal was acceptable to the rest of the industry. The wire makers objected to the November proposal also, and the BOT had to propose a further modified scale in February 1883.[87] Negotiations between the manufacturers, on one hand, and the rest of the industry (including the major buyers), on the other hand, and with the BOT as the facilitator, dragged on for many months. Claude Morris of Rylands, also chairman of the ISWMA, cogently summarised the rivalry between the ACC and the ISWMA:

> On the one hand, [we have] a large & important trade petitioning the BoT against a proposed legislation, and on the other hand, [we have] the ACC [who is] supposed to be representing the trade [but is] actually endeavouring to force the government to establish as legal the sizes which the trade say will be ruin to them![88]

The BOT's February 1883 proposal appears to have met the views of all the major industry groups. Eventually, in August 1883, an Order in Council was passed which introduced the standard wire gauge (SWG), making it a legally recognised standard for wire sizes in Britain. Interestingly, it appears that the BOT had no power to enforce the use of the standard, even though it was a legal standard. We thus have a case here of a legal standard whose adoption was left to the market on a voluntary basis.[89] The ISWMA felt that they could 'congratulate themselves upon having impressed the Board of Trade [with] the weight of their representations [and which] considerably modified the proposal of the Board in favour of the wire trade generally' (see Appendix 5.2 for a comparison of the different proposals).[90]

In comparing the various proposals made by the different groups between March 1882 and February 1883, the following picture emerges. The first BOT scale in April 1882 was virtually identical to the ACC March 1882 proposal, excepting in the sizes finer than No 35. The ISWMA's proposal of July 1882 was considerably different from the BOT's April 1882 proposal, particularly for the finer sizes (below No 27), where the difference in diameters was of the order of two or three numbers on the respective gauges. The BOT's November 1882 proposal incorporated some of the ISWMA's proposed sizes for the larger numbers

---

[87] Ibid., p. 4. TNA, BT 101/119, memo dated 28 July 1882. BT 101/123, letter dated 5 January 1883. BT 101/124.

[88] *Ironmonger*, 24 February 1883, letters to the editor, pp. 249–50; emphasis in original.

[89] TNA, BT 101/943. Letter from the BOT to Stelp & Leighton Ltd.

[90] *Ironmonger*, 17 March 1883, editorial, p. 386. See also letter by Thomas Hughes, p. 392.

but kept the finer sizes unchanged. Although the ISWMA responded to this by modifying its proposal in January 1883, the modifications were very slight, and the diameters remained largely unchanged. The BOT's final proposal in February 1883, which would become the SWG, made significant changes over its 1882 proposals. The size differences between the BOT and ISWMA proposals were decreased considerably by this scale; however, the differences in the finer sizes – especially between No 27 and No 34 – persisted. Appendix 5.2 shows the differences between the SWG and the ACC and ISWMA proposals.

The preceding narrative reveals that there was vociferous, often acrimonious, debate on the issue and that the various groups could not coordinate between themselves to agree on a single industry standard. With the industry unable to resolve the issue by itself, both groups sought an arbitrator. The state, through the BOT, acted as the arbitrator between the rival groups and attempted to solve the coordination problem.

Competition, coordination and negotiation for standard wire sizes

The initiative to establish a standard wire gauge in the 1870s came from the telegraph engineers. Subsequently, there were several different proposals for a uniform gauge under consideration. The STE had its own proposal by 1879; the ACC committee itself considered numerous proposals, including several made by Harding, Hughes and others, before deciding upon Harding's scheme as its preferred wire gauge. It is only after the BOT's decision to introduce the ACC proposal as the legal standard that the dominant wire producers cooperated to suggest their own standard gauge in 1882. Why did the ISWMA oppose the ACC proposal? Why did the dominant manufacturers cooperate in the first place to form the ISWMA? Why did the state intervene to set the industry standard?

Towards the end of the 1870s, the British wire industry was experiencing stiff competition from foreign manufacturers, both in its domestic and its overseas markets. German wire production had nearly doubled between 1878 and 1882, and its exports of wire increased sevenfold during the same period. In contrast, growth in British production and exports was quite modest (Table 5.3). By the 1880s, German wire was outselling British wire in the international markets by a factor of two to one. British firms were losing market share in the North American, Russian, European and Australian markets. US manufacturers, including Washburn and Moen and others, were able to meet domestic demand, particularly telegraph and fencing wire, assisted by tariff protection. US

Table 5.3. *Relative growth of wire exports (United Kingdom and Germany)*

Year	Germany[a] (tons)	United Kingdom (tons)
1877	32,398	51,092
1878	56,644	43,480
1879	76,710	37,259
1880	104,775	59,180
1881	159,416	75,129
1882	227,000	86,686

[a] The figures for Germany also include the export of wire rods.

Source: *Ironmonger*, 5 May 1883.

duties on British iron wire increased from nine shillings and four pence plus 15 per cent ad valorem in 1860 to eighteen shillings and eight pence plus 15 per cent ad valorem in 1880. Similarly, duties on steel wire increased from eleven shillings and eight pence plus 15 per cent ad valorem in 1860 to fourteen shillings plus 20 per cent ad valorem in 1880.[91] 'America drew all the wire wanted for her own use, and supplied Canada, [a] portion of the wire trade has gone, probably never to return. Is the rest to go too?' was a comment heard at a meeting of the Steel Wire Manufacturers in 1878.[92]

German wire was also being imported into Britain during this time: 'the great influx of German wire in England is beginning at last to tell upon the trade.'[93] Even the British government placed an order for one thousand tons of strand wire with a German firm 'due to its cheapness'. Trade reports around this time continually lamented about how domestic demand for German wire was beginning to tell upon the English wire industry. Some British wire makers imported German iron rod to turn it into wire or purchased German wire to make wire products such as screws, needles and piano wire. Rylands was forced to purchase German rods when rod-making firms such as Pearson and Knowles found it difficult to compete with German firms. At least five other wire rod mills closed owing to excessive German competition. Also, pin makers,

[91] *Ironmonger*, 28 January 1882 and 7 September 1878. See also Blake-Coleman, *Copper wire*, p. 212.
[92] Seth-Smith, *Richard Johnson and Nephew*, p. 83.
[93] *Ironmonger*, 3 January 1880, p. 28.

netting weavers, rope makers and others were purchasing German wire in preference over English wire.[94] There were several sources of Germany's competitiveness in wire manufacturing. German heavy industry was protected by tariffs and was dumping iron and steel products, such as wire and rails, onto international markets. German rail prices in their domestic markets exceeded costs by 24 per cent, but export prices were only 92 per cent of costs. The low price of raw materials in Germany contributed to low steel prices. Also, German efficiency in iron and steel manufacturing increased relative to Britain during the latter part of the nineteenth century. The resultant lower steel price in Germany vis-à-vis Britain meant that German firms found this policy of dumping steel and wire products overseas to be sustainable.[95] Additionally, railway freight rates in Britain were more than twice those of Germany, Holland and Belgium. For example, the cost of transporting one ton of packed wire by railway from Birmingham to London was twenty four shillings, while according to German, Belgium and Dutch tariff rates, the same journey would have cost ten or eleven shillings, eight shillings and eleven pence, and eight shillings and two pence respectively. In fact, Belgian wire was available at lower prices in London than wire from the Midlands.[96]

Also, German firms were operating at or near full capacity, compared to English firms, whose domestic capacity had increased faster than demand. In addition, German labour productivity was higher compared to that of British manufacturers. The cost of producing a No 20 iron wire from a No 4 rod was 70 shillings per ton in Germany, compared to more than 130 shillings per ton in England. Lower wages, longer working hours and cheaper raw material were proposed as the primary reasons for the cost differentials.[97] When Thewlis Johnson and George Bedson (of Richard Johnson and Nephew) visited Felten and Guilleaume's wire works in Germany in 1878, Johnson was 'perturbed when he compared the financial structure of Guilleaume's wire production with his own at Bradford'. Another British manufacturer visiting several Westphalian wire works reported that labour costs were about 40 to 50 per cent lower in Germany.[98] The overall picture of the British wire trade that emerges

[94] H. Janes, *Rylands of Warrington: 1805–1955* (London, Harley, 1956), p. 63. *Ironmonger*, 7 September 1878, pp. 929–30; 7 June 1879, p. 763; 3 January 1880, p. 28; 23 October 1880, p. 489; 3 November 1883, p. 651.
[95] Wengenroth, *Enterprise and technology*. Allen, 'Iron and steel', pp. 920, 28–29, and table 8.
[96] Bell, *Iron trade in the United Kingdom*, p. 108. *Ironmonger*, 7 June 1879, p. 763. Cost of Belgian wire is calculated on the river Thames on f.o.b. basis.
[97] *Ironmonger*, 4 October 1878, p. 514; 4 November 1882, p. 635; 5 May 1883, p. 626.
[98] Seth-Smith, *Richard Johnson and Nephew*, p. 78. *Ironmonger*, 27 April 1878, p. 305.

is one of 'slackening demand and increasing competition [and] the wire trade relapsing into [a] state of depression'.[99]

British response to German competition centred on the rationalisation of production costs. Early in 1878, several large wire makers formed the Steel Wire Manufacturers Association with the objective of setting a standard wage scale for wire workers. The association met with the wire workers' union and proposed a reduction in wages. This resulted in industrial action by the wire workers in many firms such as Whitecross, Rylands and others towards the end of 1878. However, the strikes could not be sustained owing to a lack of union funds, and by early 1879, they were called off, with many of the union's members returning to work at reduced wages. A strike of wire drawers at the Bradford works of Richard Johnson and Nephew in December 1878 in protest of wage reductions was soon disbanded, with virtually all wire drawers indicating their desire to return to work. Not all workers could be reinstated, however, and those who did return had to accept reduced wages. As soon as the wage cuts were made, the manufacturers association was disbanded. A second round of wage reductions was attempted in 1883, with the same results: a general strike of wire workers, followed by the workers returning to work in 1884 at substantially reduced wages. Thus the manufacturers 'were fortunate [in reducing wages] without which they [would have had to close their mills on] account of the severity of Westphalian competition'.[100] Wire makers also sought to reduce input costs by substituting cheaper, sometimes lower-quality German wire rods to make wire and wire products. Even so, underselling was reportedly common, creating an intensely competitive domestic market environment.[101]

Apart from cost rationalisation, some firms diversified into related product markets. The firms of Edelston and Williams and Cornforth, makers of iron wire, began manufacturing steel wire for pianofortes – the traditional domain of firms such as Horsfall – in addition to making steel wire for ropes, cables, picture cords and so on.[102] Other firms, such as Nettlefolds, began amalgamating or merging with other, smaller firms producing screws in Smethwick (Birmingham), Stourport (West Midlands), Manchester and so on. This increased concentration, reduced overcapacity and provided Nettlefolds with an assured market for its wire products as well as an assured supply of inputs for its screw-making

---

[99] *Ironmonger*, 31 July 1880.
[100] Seth-Smith, *Richard Johnson and Nephew*, pp. 79–80. Stones, *British wire industry*, p. 5. Bullen, *Drawn together*, pp. 14–16. *Ironmonger*, April 1880; 24 May 1884, p. 711.
[101] *Ironmonger*, 22 January 1881, p. 110.
[102] *Ironmonger*, 7 June 1879, p. 763.

business.[103] Apart from individual firm strategies, cooperative action by manufacturers was actually limited. The wire industry did not form combinations or cartels to tide over this period of stagnant demand and high competition, such as those seen in the German industry or in the US industry in 1894–1895, or even those that were formed in related British industries such as pin manufacturing.[104] There is no evidence of any industry association during this period until the ISWMA was formed in 1882, primarily to deal with the issue of the SWG. There is also little evidence that technological improvement, such as continuous wire drawing, newer methods of cleaning, annealing, and treating wire and so on, helped to improve British competitiveness.[105] Continuous wire drawing, for example, was relatively new and appeared to have been in limited use. Thus British response was to control costs, improve capacity utilisation through diversification or amalgamate and merge to protect domestic markets.

In the context of this competitive environment, we can now evaluate the failure of the ACC and the ISWMA to agree on a single industry standard. The main objection of the ISWMA to the ACC and other proposals was that adopting the new gauges involved altering the wire numbers. For instance, switching from a Lancashire gauge to the ACC gauge implied changing the numbers in thirteen of the fourteen sizes between No 6 and No 18. It is this change in numbers rather than the differences in the length of the diameters per se which increased the cost of producing wire. As a considerable proportion of thick wire was drawn according to the Lancashire gauge, the result of switching to the ACC gauge would have been costly for the manufacturers in a highly competitive environment (Table 5.4).

Production costs for copper and brass wire of finer sizes (smaller than No 30) were also expected to increase anywhere from eighteen to fifty-six pounds sterling per ton. Considering that the price of copper wire was a little more than nine shillings per pound or eighty-four pounds sterling per ton, this was a substantial increase in production costs. However, a switch to the ACC gauge was not expected to affect costs of iron and steel wire finer than No 20 as there was little difference between the

[103] *Ironmonger*, 9 April 1881, p. 511; 3 November 1883, pp. 650–51; 24 May 1884, p. 711.
[104] Seth-Smith, *Richard Johnson and Nephew*, p. 83. S. R. H. Jones, 'Price associations and competition in the British pin industry, 1814–40', *Economic History Review* 26 No 2 (1973). There is mention of an association attempted in the 1860s in Stones, *British wire industry*, p. 1. Bullen, *Drawn together*, p. 14, mentions an industry organisation dealing with export prices around 1867. It is unclear how these associations operated and the purposes for which they were formed.
[105] Seth-Smith, *Richard Johnson and Nephew*, p. 82.

Table 5.4. *Impact of switching from Lancashire wire gauge to Harding's proposed wire gauge*

Lancashire wire gauge no	Harding gauge no	Increase in cost of production (shillings per ton)	Reference price[a] (shillings per ton)
6	7	10	4
7	8	5	4
8	9	10	5
9	10	15	5
10	10	–	5
11	12	10	6
12	13	10	7
13	14	10	8
14	15	15	8
15	16	15	10
16	17	20	13
17	18	25	17
18	19	25	18

Note: The table has been reproduced from estimates reported by Thomas Hughes in *Ironmonger*, 25 March 1882.

[a] The reference prices mentioned here are with reference to the SWG and taken from a price list from 1884 reproduced in Frank Stones, *The British ferrous wire industry* (Sheffield, J. W. Northend, 1977), illustrations between pp. 12 and 13.

existing Yorkshire gauges and the ACC/Harding gauge: finer wire was mostly drawn in Yorkshire.[106]

The dominant wire manufacturers fiercely objected to the ACC gauge becoming the legal industry standard. The ISWMA argued that the ACC gauge would require them to draw the wire to a smaller number just to maintain the same diameter of wire as per existing gauges. This would have increased the number of draws and therefore the cost of the wire. They argued that as the thicker sizes constituted the bulk of the iron wire exported from Britain, the result of legalising the ACC standards would be to 'place the English wire trade at a material disadvantage at a time it is suffering severely from foreign competition'.[107] Furthermore, changes in the wire numbers, as opposed to changes in the diameter sizes, implied 'arranging new prices with the workmen and warehousemen' – a difficult proposition given the extent of wage reductions that had been

[106] Price of copper wire from Blake-Coleman, *Copper wire*, pp. 230–32. *Ironmonger*, 25 March 1882. See letter by Thomas Hughes. See also 5 March 1881, pp. 304–6, for a similar analysis by an anonymous correspondent, most probably Hughes himself.

[107] TNA, BT 101/116. See letter to the Board of Trade dated 7 July 1882.

recently extracted from the workers.[108] Thus the switchover was likely to result in a short-term as well as a long-term impact on the competitiveness of the British manufacturers. Consequently, the ISWMA proposed an alternative gauge, which was different from the ACC gauge. The BOT's February 1883 gauge, which eventually became the legal standard, considerably reduced the differences between those that the ISWMA were demanding and those that the BOT (and the ACC) had originally proposed.

The ISWMA also had to overcome differences between the large manufacturers themselves. In effect, it proposed that all the iron and steel wire and brass and copper wire manufacturers accept Lancashire sizes up to No 20. In return, all the Lancashire manufacturers would accept finer sizes below No 21 that were set by the Birmingham and Yorkshire manufacturers of fine wire.[109] The standard gauge that the ISWMA proposed to the BOT thus aimed to address the production concerns of the manufacturers of different kinds of wire. The standard wire sizes were an amalgamation of sizes from different existing gauges or the ideal sizes desired by the different groups of manufacturers. The production-centred desirable sizes of the ISWMA more or less clashed with the application-centred desirable sizes proposed by the ACC.

But why did the large manufacturers cooperate to form the ISWMA in the first instance? Until 1882, the large manufacturers dominated the industry and remained competitive by reducing wages and rationalising labour. Some, such as Richard Johnson and Nephew, rationalised production techniques to remain competitive. Others, such as Nettlefolds, remained competitive by amalgamating or acquiring smaller firms, eliminating competition and concentrating production facilities. Still others, such as Rylands, decreased input costs by purchasing cheaper German rods to draw wire and wire products. There is no evidence that the German wire makers were able to compete more effectively due to standardised wire sizes. It was their cost structure and productivity that gave them the edge over the British wire makers. Individual wire makers, such as Thewlis Johnson and Thomas Rylands, were involved in discussions with the telegraph engineers regarding standard wire sizes. However, until a legal gauge seemed imminent, there was no evidence of cooperation between the large wire makers regarding a uniform industry standard. The timing suggests that it was formed to prevent the industry from being locked into what the large wire makers considered to be the wrong wire sizes proposed by the ACC. The ISWMA served as a lobby group to

---

[108] *Ironmonger*, 2 December 1882, p. 749.
[109] *Ironmonger*, 25 March 1882. See letter by Thomas Hughes.

oppose the ACC proposals and to influence the BOT to accept the sizes that most suited those manufacturers represented by the ISWMA. The specific objective with which the ISWMA was formed is testified by the fact that as soon as this crisis was over, the organisation was disbanded on 21 June 1884. Thus, before 1882, it suited the manufacturers to use their own separate gauges. But after 1882, they preferred to make wire using a standard *they* had set rather than letting the industry get locked into the so-called wrong ACC standards.

Although the initiative for standardisation had come from engineers, producers and buyers of wire, the state played an important role in arbitration and negotiation between the rival business groups. The motivation for the state's involvement in standard wire sizes dates several decades before the ACC approached the BOT with its proposal in 1882. The interest in standards derives from the state's interest in interchangeable parts manufacturing, for instance, the admiralty's need for gunboats during the Crimean War. The navy's urgent need of engines for these gunboats had been fulfilled by interchangeable manufacturing, in part made possible by Joseph Whitworth's measuring machines and standard gauges.[110] The state had realised the strategic importance of engineering standards, measurement precision and interchangeable manufacturing by the mid-nineteenth century. Whitworth's appointment to the parliamentary commission on the New York Industrial Exhibition, 1851, followed by reports of other parliamentary committees on US manufacturing, testifies to the importance that Parliament and the government attached to engineering standards and practices.[111]

Reflecting this, the BOT, and particularly its Standards Department after circa 1860, maintained an active interest in the engineering standards of the day. In 1877, almost five years before the ACC's proposal, the BOT made its own inquiries regarding the use of wire and plate gauges in Birmingham.[112] By 1880, the Standards Department was in correspondence with Whitworth to have his cylindrical and flat surface gauges – the 'go/no-go' gauges – deposited with the BOT as standards. An internal report described how such gauges were widely used generally by engineers and noted that a similar set of standards for wire sizes

---

[110] A. E. Musson, 'Joseph Whitworth and the growth of mass-production engineering', in R. P. T. Davenport-Hines (ed.) *Capital, entrepreneurs and profits* (London, Frank Cass, 1990), p. 243. Saul, 'British engineering industries', p. 117. M. McCarthy and R. Garcia, 'Screw threads on the SS Xantho Engine: a case of standardization in the 19th century Britain', *International Journal of Nautical Archaeology* 33 No 2 (2004).

[111] *New York Exhibition: General report and special report of Mr. Whitworth*, PP Vol. XXXVI 1854.

[112] TNA, BT 101/14.

was 'highly desirable'.[113] Consequently, when the ACC and ISWMA appealed to the BOT, it encouraged and actively helped to overcome the coordination failure between rival groups.

Apart from the strategic interest, the state, and specifically the BOT, perceived its role to 'act fairly as arbitrators between consumers and companies'.[114] The BOT's position in this regard was expressed strongly in the case of standardisation of measurements and consumption of an invisible commodity such as gas. The BOT felt justified in intervening to overrule the principles of caveat emptor, particularly when it felt that consumers could be disadvantaged due to irreconcilable information asymmetries. The board's position, and actions, in the case of wire sizes was similar, although the grievances in this case were not between consumers and businesses but between different sets of businesses, with conflicting interests.

More directly, however, the BOT's involvement was likely secured due to the personal influence of Joseph Chamberlain, who was president of the BOT between 1880 and 1885. The future secretary of state for the colonies and the leader of the opposition had a more direct interest in the wire industry rather than just upholding the abstract principles of equity and fairness. Chamberlain's father had been an investment partner in Nettlefolds, a large manufacturer of wire, wire ropes and wire products. The firm had been known as Nettlefolds and Chamberlain before becoming Guest, Keen and Nettlefolds. Chamberlain had begun his early business career working with the firm and had maintained close ties with it even subsequent to his retirement in 1874. Additionally, he had been elected the mayor of Birmingham in the early 1870s, a post that had brought him in direct contact with both producers and buyers of wire and wire products. Chamberlain's position at the BOT made him particularly approachable when the ACC decided to recruit the state's help in pushing its proposals for standardisation on the wire industry. In this manner, the economics of competition as well as the politics of the market were key factors in the industry converging towards a one-size-fits-all standard.

Gauges after 1883

Modern wire sizes are expressed using standardised gauges, such as the American wire gauge or the metric wire gauge. Products derived from wire, such as hypodermic needles, use gauges to express sizes rather than

---

[113] TNA, BT 101/76; BT 101/81.
[114] *Report from Select Committee on the Metropolis Gas*, PP VI 1876, p. 12.

measurements such as inches or millimetres.[115] The legalisation of the SWG was intended to remove the confusion surrounding the wire sizes. The industry largely discontinued the use of older gauges such as the BWG. Vestiges of the old gauges survived in the use of the *term* BWG, which was often used interchangeably with the SWG or the Imperial wire gauge (as the SWG also became known). One engineering firm from Birmingham advertised the legal SWG sizes as 'Imperial Standard Wire Gauge, B.W.G.', signifying that many in the trade continued to associate wire gauges with the old BWG, although they used the new legal gauge sizes. When the BOT revisited the subject of gauges in the early twentieth century, it encountered a variety of *terms* in use: BWG, SWG, IWG (Imperial wire gauge), or LSG (legal standard gauge). Notwithstanding this, the legal gauge defined in 1883 was the gauge that was 'generally used in the wire trade'.[116]

Did the adoption of uniform wire sizes assist the British industry in regaining its dominant market position after 1883? British exports of wire remained more or less stable between 1870 and 1906, except for a short increase during 1880–1882 and after 1900. In contrast, exports of German wire after 1880 and that of US wire after 1898 overtook those from Britain. German exports until 1887 comprised primarily drawn wire, whereas the export of rods comprised a major proportion of their exports after this period. US exports continued to be dominated by drawn wire and had a much smaller proportion of wire rods. British exports primarily comprised drawn wire. Uniformity in wire sizes does not appear to have enabled British manufacturers to once again secure the dominance in the export trade that they enjoyed before 1878. However, many of the large wire manufacturers, such as Rylands, Nettlefolds and Richard Johnson, continued to remain dominant wire manufacturers, both internationally and domestically, well into the twentieth century.

Following the standardisation of wire gauges, other trades attempted to standardise gauges. For instance, in 1893, the Needle and Fish Hooks Trade Association unsuccessfully tried to standardise a gauge for needles.[117] In a move to standardise an international gauge for 'flats and rounds', the American Society of Mechanical Engineers proposed a collaborative association with the BOT in 1894; no such gauge is known to

---

[115] J. S. Pöll, 'The story of the gauge', *Anaesthesia* 54 No 6 (1999).
[116] TNA, BT 101/537; BT 101/538; BT 101/943, letter from the deputy warden of standards.
[117] TNA, BT 101/346.

have emerged from this.[118] The American industry, in fact, continued to use a variety of wire gauges until the early decades of the twentieth century.[119]

Conclusions

The case study of standardisation of wire sizes addresses several inter-related issues. The study traces how intense international competition exacerbated endemic transactional issues. Whereas prior to the rise of German wire manufacturing circa 1875, producers and buyers of British wire and wire products were able to internalise many of the agency issues arising from nonstandardised wire sizes, this situation became untenable for British producers after 1875. Product standardisation became imperative for firms to remain competitive, for firms to retain market share and perhaps even for the very survival of many British wire producers.

Product standardisation hinged upon the state of the measurement technology that the industry used. This in turn was embedded within the measurement practices on which wire drawing depended. The degree of interrelatedness between production and measurements became the limiting factor for changes in the technology and standards. Measurement instruments (gauges, decimal units etc.) as well as protocols (e.g. a single wire gauge to be used for wires of all metals) had to be altered to align the measurement practices with the demands of product standardisation.

Altering the local measurement practices involved coordinating be-tween the conflicting positions of different businesses groups. Overcom-ing economic inertia required political coordination. Negotiation, arbit-ration and compromise were necessary to achieve a coordinated switch to common standards. Standardisation was secured with the state's involve-ment, reflecting the political–economic trade-offs that producers and buyers of wire faced.

The standard that emerged was not a de jure standard, although it had legal sanction. The SWG was a consensus standard, privately set with the industry groups and voluntarily adopted by producers, which ensured a high degree of compatibility between products. Individual firms retained the flexibility for nonuse, but as a consensus standard, it went a long way in mitigating the persistent problems in market exchanges caused by the confusing array of various standard wire sizes. Buyers and sellers

---

[118] TNA, BT 101/ 386.
[119] C. A. Adams, 'Industrial standardization', *Annals of the American Academy of Political and Social Science* 82 No 1 (1919): p. 292.

needed a way of distinguishing between different qualities and types of wire, even as they needed a way of ensuring consistent measurements. This is reflected in the following chapter on measurement standards and quality grades within the international grain markets. The solution to the various economic issues was a socio-politico-technical one, born within the microcontext of the British wire industry.

6   Globalisation, commodity grading and quality measurements in nineteenth-century wheat markets

> In purchasing wheat and choosing the description necessary to secure a uniform brand of flour, millers must often feel the want of a reliable test to guide them. It requires a very long and constant experience to judge the quality of even those wheat appearing daily in our markets; but we are left with the most unpleasant uncertainty when new descriptions are introduced to our notice.
>
> – *Miller*, 4 October 1875

Following the repeal of the Corn Laws, an increasing quantum of wheat was imported into the United Kingdom in the latter half of the nineteenth century. By circa 1880, imported wheat varieties were outselling home-grown varieties by eight to one. Most economic historians accept the fact that, coinciding with this trend, price spreads between transatlantic grain markets converged as a result of political, institutional and technological changes. These changes included declining freight, distribution and other transportation costs; reduction in restrictions on international trade such as tariffs and customs duties; stable monetary regimes, particularly under the gold standard; and decline in other transaction and coordination costs. Such changes greatly aided price convergence and directly contributed to the globalisation of British wheat markets.[1]

One implication of such globalising markets was the proliferation of wheat varieties that became available in British markets of the period: from sixteen to over sixty-five varieties within twenty years. The business groups involved in the production, intermediation and purchase of wheat varieties had to develop ways of managing this proliferation, in addition to managing the organisational and technological changes that

---

[1] I use the term *globalisation* rather than *internationalisation* to indicate that the late-nineteenth-century international trade in wheat was occurring in markets that exhibited price integration. International trade, to mean cross-border trade, predates price integration of the late-nineteenth-century transatlantic markets. This point was forcefully argued by O'Rourke and Williamson, although other historians argue that this is rather a narrow way of defining globalisation. K. H. O'Rourke and J. G. Williamson, 'When did globalisation begin?' *European Review of Economic History* 6 No 1 (2002). However, I do not engage with this debate in this volume.

171

globalisation implied. A crucial issue that these business groups faced was the standardisation of the set of product attributes that would capture ex ante the differences in wheat varieties, that is, a standard set of search attributes. The institutional limitation, in contrast to the technical one, was that businesses had to find a way to minimise the number of search attributes such that they were internationally acceptable along a long and complex value chain. This case study traces the emergence of these attribute sets as quality grades during the latter half of the nineteenth century. It demonstrates how reforms to measurement practices were central to the development of the grading system. It also explores the complex reasons underlying the fact that it took nearly fifty years for an internationally accepted grading system for wheat and other grains to emerge.

Quality grading for heterogeneous commodities is generally complicated by the fact that it is not practical to delineate all search attributes of the product to make meaningful comparisons possible. This is very closely related to the other measurement problem where complete information about any economic good is costly because it is based upon multiple measurement criteria (Chapter 1).[2] One of the main aims of this case study is to explore how business groups solved this particular measurement problem by standardising a limited set of search attributes that could be effectively measured, whilst at the same time seeking to reduce the measurement costs along a globalising value chain.

The increasing heterogeneity of wheat attributes, compounded by the increasing proliferation of varieties, combined with the heterogeneous preferences of different economic groups (producers, merchants, millers and bakers) to make quality grading a highly complex process. Quality is a relative concept rather than an absolute one: it can have different meanings depending upon who is conducting the measurement. There is quality 'in the eyes of producers', but there is also quality 'in the eyes of the consumers'.[3] To someone responsible for producing or inspecting a product, quality can be defined narrowly or absolutely. In contrast, to the user, product quality is a relative concept, to be compared with other similar or substitute products. Theoretically, this implies that quality will be measured, by any given economic group, on the basis of 'summary criteria', that is, on a set of product attributes that a particular group will

---

[2] Y. Barzel, 'Measurement cost and the organization of markets', *Journal of Law and Economics* 25 No 1 (1982): pp. 28–29. S. C. Pirrong, 'The efficient scope of private transactions-cost-reducing institutions: the successes and failures of commodity exchanges', *Journal of Legal Studies* 24 No 1 (1995).

[3] P. Bowbrick, *The economics of quality, grades and brands* (London, Routledge, 1992), pp. 2–11.

choose to proxy for the product's quality. This set of attributes is most likely to differ amongst groups if each group has a different notion of product quality.[4]

Grading of wheat varieties sought to standardise the summary criteria used by the different groups such that information about the commodity could be readily shared between groups who would otherwise have only partial access to such information. In other words, grading sought to ensure that important facts about wheat varieties travelled well between groups along a value chain.[5] Travel of facts between groups depended upon all groups using the same summary criteria, the same measurement tools and consistent practices. The case study investigates how international commodity grading developed when merchants and other business groups standardised the attributes for measuring quality, developed standards to compare observations of selected attributes, established rules to sort products into different categories based on quality measurements and developed institutional rules and organisational structures to monitor the process. The development of commodity grading in globalising markets was indelibly linked to the development of international institutions that fundamentally altered the measurement practices along a global value chain.

The case traces how different groups had historically developed their own individual criteria for evaluating the quality of produce. Assessing samples of wheat required a high degree of tacit knowledge and reliance on tactile senses (touch, smell, taste etc.). The advent of formal grading methods replaced these older forms of assessment, centralising the process and becoming the dominant form of measuring quality within the trading commodity. Downstream industries, such as milling, continued to rely upon different quality measurements, even though they began using the new vocabulary of the commodity grades.

The centralisation of grading implied development of new quality assurance mechanisms, in addition to centralising measurements. The

---

[4] Barzel, 'Measurement cost', pp. 28–32, for a discussion of how buyers and sellers sort commodities into multiple classes. S. Ponte and P. Gibbon, 'Quality standards, conventions and the governance of global value chains', *Economy and Society* 34 No 1 (2005): p. 7, for a discussion of quality from the perspective of convention theory. The authors stress that there is no universal understanding of quality and that quality is cognitively evaluated in different ways. See also B. Daviron, 'Small farm production and the standardization of tropical products', *Journal of Agrarian Change* 2 No 2 (2002).

[5] Facts do not travel well between different groups because they are immutable. They travel well if they have the right vehicles and are packaged well for travel. They may even need good travelling companions. As a result, 'false' facts could travel just as well. Grades are examples of packaging that help facts about quality travel well between business groups. See M. S. Morgan and P. Howlett (eds), *How well do facts travel? The dissemination of reliable knowledge* (Cambridge, Cambridge University Press, 2010).

new assurance mechanisms were shaped by institutional as well as technological changes. Traditional quality assessment techniques depended upon visual inspection, sampling and pricing of wheat produce. The techniques used in traditional wheat markets were similar to the hog-round marketing followed in US cotton markets and, indeed, in the wholesale cotton markets of Liverpool and Manchester.[6] In contrast, the development of commodity grading centralised the procedures for classing and sorting the produce into different grades in addition to centralising the process of describing the grades in the first instance. This implied that new methods of inspection and sampling, certification of quality grades and dispute resolution mechanisms had to be instituted.

The case traces how these institutions and mechanisms developed independently in the United Kingdom and United States – at both ends of the value chain – and explores the reasons why this occurred. The focus remains upon the UK markets, however, and the case analysis shows how the involvement of the British state in the grading process was minimal. Industry organisations and commercial institutions drove the centralisation of the grading process at a meso-level, in contrast to the United States, where state involvement was necessary in the quality certification of graded wheat exported from that country.[7]

The grading of wheat grains by the commodity exchanges also greatly aided the alienation of the commodity from the producer's identity by delinking residual rights in the commodity from its physical possession or origin. Tradability no longer depended upon the ability to deliver the physical product. The globalising trade was able to reduce risk by hedging and futures trading. Instruments of futures trading in the commodity in fact required such alienation and did not have to account for the vagaries of the physical cargo or at least shifted the immediate risk of quality dissipation. Such essential elements of global markets – alienation and managing risk through futures trading – depended upon fundamental changes to measurement practices. In this context, centralised measurements contributed significantly to the increasing efficiency of international grain markets in the late nineteenth century.

The case also examines relevant technological changes accompanying the globalisation of wheat markets. Changes in transportation and

---

[6] A. L. Olmstead and P. W. Rhode, 'Hog-round marketing, seed quality, and government policy: institutional change in US cotton production, 1920–1960', *Journal of Economic History* 63 No 2 (2003).

[7] L. D. Hill, *Grain, grades and standards: historical issues shaping the future* (Urbana, University of Illinois Press, 1990). Hill explores the involvement of the US state in solving coordination issues between the numerous grading systems developed by the commodity exchanges in the major wheat-growing states and the powerful farm lobby.

distribution technologies (e.g. grain silos for storage or pneumatic elevators for unloading) enabled the trade to separate the delivery process from the quality assessment process. In addition, technological changes in the downstream milling industry also significantly impacted the demand for new wheat varieties and, in consequence, the demand for commodity grading and quality assurance. Advances in the understanding of grain chemistry shaped the development of summary criteria as finer attributes, that is, those not apparent through visual inspection, could be reliably measured by industrial buyers.

British wheat markets in the nineteenth century

An overview of the wheat trade in the nineteenth century presents unmistakeable evidence of the globalisation of the value chain. The composition of the trade altered in terms of the sources of grain (domestic vs foreign), the different groups involved in the trade and their specialisation, the enormous heterogeneity of wheat varieties available in British markets and the internationalisation of some of the institutions. This in turn influenced the measurement of quality in terms of who measured it, at what stage of the value chain it was measured and how it was measured after circa 1860.

In the first half of the nineteenth century, domestic wheat sales showed a slow steady growth, growing roughly fives times in quantity between 1815 and 1850. With the repeal of the Corn Laws, which had restricted the import of foreign wheat between 1815 and 1846, imports increased nearly tenfold between 1830 and 1885. By the 1860s, more wheat was imported than was being sold in the domestic markets. The commodity was imported from several sources, the main sources being the United States and Russia in the late nineteenth century. However, wheat was also imported from Argentina, Australia, India and several other locations in Europe. In addition to wheat, these markets supplied the United Kingdom with other grain and cereals such as barley, malt and rye. The US imports became the single most important overseas source of grain for the United Kingdom in the last two decades of the nineteenth century. On an average, imports of wheat from the United States accounted for nearly half of the annual wheat imported into the United Kingdom between 1875 and 1885 (see Figures 6.1 and 6.2).[8]

---

[8] *Return of total quantity of various kinds of grain and flour imported into the UK in each year from 1828*, PP Vol. LX 1886, p. 405. *Quantities and average price of wheat as sold in the towns of England and Wales between 1815 and 1888*, PP Vol. LXIII 1889, p. 423. Statistical Abstracts, UK, No 37 and No 38.

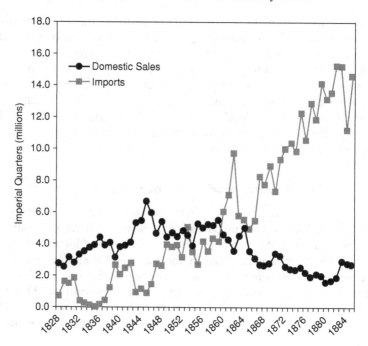

Figure 6.1. Trends in domestic sales and imports of wheat into Britain. *Source:* data on domestic sales from PP Vol. LX 1889, p. 23; data on imports from PP Vol. LX 1886, p. 405.

The proportion of British population consuming wheat (and wheaten bread) increased throughout the nineteenth century compared to consumption of other cereals. Whereas in 1800, about two-thirds of the population of Great Britain was estimated to have been consuming wheat, by 1900, wheat consumption had become nearly universal, while the consumption of oats and barley declined. These shifts were a result of several factors such as the decreasing price differentials of the various cereals, the high cross-price-income elasticity of wheat, the degree of urbanisation, the emergence of professional bakers and millers, technological improvements in milling and changing eating habits. Thus per capita consumption of wheat is estimated to have increased during the mid-nineteenth century from 5.1 bushels to 5.5 bushels.[9]

---

[9] E. J. T. Collins, 'Dietary change and cereal consumption in Britain in the nineteenth century', *Agricultural History Review* 23 (1975): pp. 114–15.

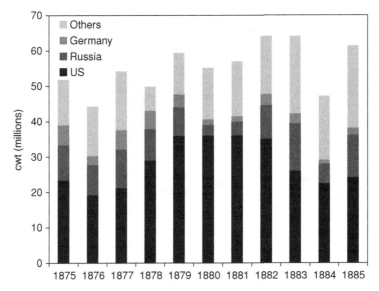

Figure 6.2. Composition of wheat imports. *Source:* UK Statistical Abstracts Nos 37 and 38.

The structure of the trade had evolved since the eighteenth century and by the end of the nineteenth century involved a fairly complex organisational structure, characterised by layers of interrelated firms and organised commodity markets (Figures 6.3 and 6.4).[10] Historically, mealmen purchased grain from other up-country middlemen, then milled the grain (or got it milled from millers) and subsequently sold the flour directly to the bakers or on the open market.[11] Some time during the eighteenth century, the functions of the miller and the mealman began to merge, as the millers integrated several related activities: corn buying, grinding, dealing in meal and flour and so on. Up until then, the mealmen had been responsible for mealing, or mixing of flour, a function taken over by the millers. Some bakers had begun to integrate backwards, combining the functions of the baker, miller and mealmen. Nevertheless, not all bakers had integrated backwards, and we find the millers and bakers as distinct groups in the nineteenth century.[12]

---

[10] M. Rothstein, 'Multinationals in the grain trade, 1850–1914', *Business and Economic History* 12 2nd Ser. (1983).

[11] F. J. Fisher, 'The development of the London food market, 1540–1640', *Economic History Review* 5 No 2 (1935): p. 61.

[12] D. Baker, 'The marketing of corn in the first half of the eighteenth century: North-east Kent', *Agricultural History Review* 18 No 2 (1970): pp. 142–43.

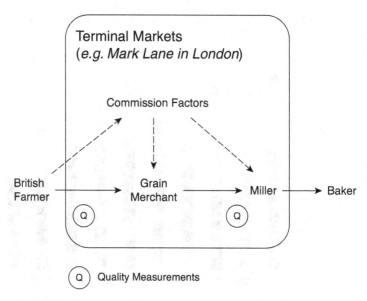

Figure 6.3. Structure of the domestic wheat trade in Britain (c. 1830).

Concomitantly, a powerful group of corn factors, known as *hoymen*, had emerged by the early eighteenth century. They sold corn in London markets, such as the one at Bear Key, on commission basis on behalf of the farmers. In these markets, wheat was mainly sold to the miller, while other grain was purchased by 'a galaxy of corn dealers [and other middlemen], many of whom were engaged in "dealings" or speculative activities alongside their basic trades'.[13] Initially, private bargaining had characterised the trade, with open or regulated market trades being insignificant. By the mid-eighteenth century, the Corn Exchange was set up in Mark Lane in London, signalling the beginnings of an organised or terminal market for wheat and other grains. Supplies to this market came from the home counties of Kent, Essex and Suffolk as well as from foreign destinations. Very few farmers sold directly at Mark Lane, and wheat was sold through the factors to millers or to shipping factors for reshipment. Wheat that was not sent to London was sold to country millers, although it was not unusual for country millers to obtain wheat from London-based factors.[14]

---

[13] Ibid., p. 136.
[14] C. R. Fay, 'The London corn market at the beginning of the nineteenth century', *American Economic Review* 15 No 1 (1925): pp. 72–73. Baker, 'Corn marketing', p. 138.

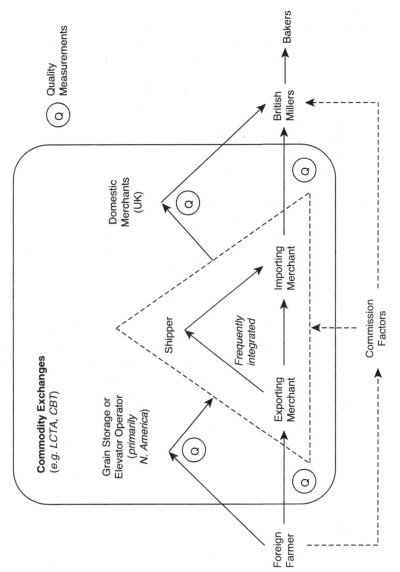

Figure 6.4. Structure of the international wheat trade (c. 1880).

Commodity Exchanges
(*e.g. LCTA, CBT*)

Grain Storage or
Elevator Operator
(*primarily
N. America*)

Domestic
Merchants
(UK)

Ⓠ Quality
Measurements

Shipper

Exporting
Merchant

*Frequently
integrated*

Importing
Merchant

Commission
Factors

Foreign
Farmer

British
Millers

Bakers

By the end of the eighteenth century, a parallel structure had emerged as increasing amounts of imported wheat began reaching British markets such as supplies of Irish grain sold in Liverpool. The *importing merchant* became an important member in this chain, although it was the factor that remained a conduit for the trade buyers of wheat, that is, the millers. The Baltic Exchange, which had its origins in the Virginia and Baltick Coffee House of Threadneedle Street in London, was primarily a place where merchants involved in the international trade would meet. Later it would serve as the headquarters of the London Corn Trade Association; practically all London grain dealers were members of both the Baltic Exchange and the Corn Association.[15] The members included importing merchants as well as foreign merchants and shippers. In the auction room, oil and tallow were offered for sale initially, and after the repeal of the corn laws, wheat and other grain were auctioned.[16]

As imports of wheat grew dramatically after circa 1860, the structure of the trade at the exporting country became significant. Broadly speaking, wheat sold by the farmer to the *exporting merchant* for reshipment to Britain would normally arrive in sacks at the importing port, which could be identified with the original seller. If grain was mixed, it was done by the importing merchant at the port of import. The most important exception to this was North American wheat, which was sold to the operators of the grain elevators. Here the grain would be mixed with other grain of similar quality, the farmer receiving the price according to the quality. The operators would sell this mixed grain of standard quality either at the trade exchanges or to the exporting or commission merchants at the large primary markets such as Milwaukee or Chicago.[17] In the United States, grain barons emerged during the latter half of the nineteenth century, who ultimately dominated various parts of the value chain, including milling, warehousing, storage and transportation. Many of the storage facilities and grain elevators were owned and operated by dominant merchants such as Issac Friedlander, Washburns, Pillsburys, William Cargill and Frank Peavey.[18] Exporting countries, particularly the United States and Canada, also developed dedicated institutions

---

[15] R. B. Forrester, 'Commodity exchanges in England', *Annals of the American Academy of Political and Social Science* 155 No 1 (1931): p. 200. J. G. Smith, *Organised produce markets* (New York, Longmans, Green, 1922), p. 30.

[16] H. Barty-King, *The Baltic story: Baltic coffee house to Baltic Exchange, 1744–1994* (London, Quiller Press, 1994). Forrester, 'Commodity exchanges', pp. 200–1.

[17] *Miller*, 5 April 1880, p. 99. Rothstein, 'Multinationals in grain trade'. Such practices were similar to the organised 'hog-round marketing' practices in the cotton trading markets in the United States.

[18] D. Morgan, *Merchants of grain* (New York, Viking Press, 1979).

and organistions that coordinated the marketing, distribution, storage and quality control along the commodity chain (e.g. Chicago Board of Trade, Board of Railroad and Warehouse Commissions). Wheat markets in the United Kingdom dealt with numerous varieties of wheat grains, based upon botanical distinction as well as distinct characteristics of each botanical variety. By 1840, several new wheat varieties were added to the existing Red Lammas type of low-yielding British varieties. At least sixteen different domestic wheat types were available for sale in English grain markets in the 1850s, each differing not only in gluten content – the chemical substance which determines the bread-making ability of wheat – but also in terms of yield (i.e. the quantity of grain per acre).[19] In addition to the domestic varieties, wheat imports greatly increased the total number of varieties available for sale in British markets. An analysis of English and foreign wheat available in 1884 listed more than twenty-five domestic varieties (including distinct grain types as well as grains of different quality) and about forty foreign ones. The foreign varieties were used mainly in the manufacture of flour, particularly in southern England.[20]

The heterogeneity of varieties, in nonbotanical terms, was not unique to wheat or grain. The variety and quality of imported cotton differed according to the region from which they were sourced. For example, in the eighteenth century, 'fine varieties' of West Indian cotton, such as Cayenne, Surinam, Issequibo, Demerara, Tobago, Guadeloupe, Grenada and Martinico, were available with other 'dirty' varieties such as Barbados, Tortola, St. Vincents, St. Kitts, Montserrat, Anguilla, Nevis and Antigua.[21] By the early twentieth century, American cotton, although limited to one botanical variety, the upland cotton, was further divided into distinct classes, which in turn could be further divided into sub-classes. Thus, on the basis of 'grade' (i.e. presence of foreign material and the physical condition of the fibres), its colour and the staple length, American cotton could be classed into more than twelve hundred possible varieties.[22] Agricultural products could not be standardised by simple

---

[19] J. R. Walton, 'Varietal innovation and the competitiveness of the British cereals sector, 1760–1930', *Agricultural History Review* 47 No 1 (1999): pp. 45–48.

[20] W. Jago and W. C. Jago, *The technology of bread-making* (London, Kent, 1911), pp. 272–79.

[21] John Slack, *Remarks on cotton* (Liverpool, 1817), cited in S. Dumbell, 'Early Liverpool cotton imports and the organization of the cotton market in the eighteenth century', *Economic Journal* 33 No 131 (1923): p. 370.

[22] A. B. Cox, 'Relation of the price and quality of cotton', *Journal of Farm Economics* 11 No 4 (1929): p. 543. A. H. Garside, *Cotton goes to market: a graphic description of a great industry* (New York, Frederick A. Stokes, 1935), pp. 46–67.

and controllable processes. They were affected by several natural factors, and quality variations within the same variety or breed could occur in an unpredictable fashion. This made assessing their quality a particularly difficult process.[23]

An important issue here is at what stage in a long value chain was the quality of wheat measured, and who measured it? Figures 6.3 and 6.4 indicate the different nodes at which quality was measured as the structure of the trade changed during the eighteenth and nineteenth centuries. Traditionally, it was in the interest of the mealman, who mixed different grades of wheat, to assess the quality of grain he bought, as there was often a substantial price differential between the best and inferior quality wheat.[24] When the millers integrated the functions of the mealman by the eighteenth century, the mixing of different grain quality, and therefore the assessment of quality, was done by them. With the establishment of the organised markets, such as Mark Lane or other regional markets, the assessment of quality was done at these nodes. This coincided with the rise in the practice of selling by sample. The buyer and the seller would agree on a price upon inspection of the sample, and the delivery by the seller would have to conform to the quality of the assessed sample.[25] When foreign grain was imported in large quantities after circa 1860, the inspection and sampling issues became particularly important to assess the quality of grain being imported, although their significance in earlier periods, especially for Irish imports, should not be underestimated.[26] After circa 1860, grain imported from North America, especially from the Midwest area of the United States, was shipped according to distinct quality grades. The grain elevator operators did the grading, particularly since grain from different producers was being mixed during storage and prior to transportation. Broadly speaking, the nodes at which quality was measured changed and varied as the structure of the trade changed between the eighteenth and nineteenth centuries. Measurements were made some of the time at the exporting end and at other times at the importing end of the trade.

---

[23] W. A. Sherman, 'Standardizing production – what has been done and what can be done', *Annals of the American Academy of Political and Social Science* 142 (1929): p. 419.

[24] C. Petersen, *Bread and the British economy, c1770–1870* (Aldershot, Solar Press, 1995), pp. 158–59. *Report of Select Committee on Import and Export of Corn*, PP Vol. III 1805, p. 195. See evidence of Peter Giles to the select committee stating that the price of good-quality wheat could be double that of wheat of inferior quality.

[25] Baker, 'Corn marketing', p. 138. PP Vol. XLIX 1834, p. 259.

[26] S. Dumbell, 'The sale of corn in the nineteenth century', *Economic Journal* 35 No 137 (1925).

Measuring quality: a supply-side perspective

Historically, buyers developed their own individual criteria for evaluating the quality of produce and the degree to which it matched their requirements. Varieties were identified according to their geographical origin. However, quality according to this criterion varied considerably and was not always consistent.[27] Samples of wheat sold in important markets such as London or Liverpool were submitted for inspection, and the natural weight of the grain (i.e. its weight per cubic capacity), its colour, its dryness, presence of impurities and other physical characteristics were important attributes on which quality was assessed. The extent to which tacit knowledge was used to assess quality was high as 'the eye, nose and hand were necessary [in] judging the value of grain and dealers could determine its specific gravity by "merely taking up and poising a small quantity of it in their hands"'.[28] Grain quality was assessed on the basis of such attributes before the advent of systematic grading by commodity exchanges after circa 1860. Prime, medium and inferior reds and whites existed alongside English, French, Chicago, Milwaukee and New Orleans varieties of grain, and most millers made their selection of grain with 'care and deliberation'.[29]

While the distinction between different wheat qualities was important to the buyers and the trade, British wheat farmers were mainly concerned with the 'harvest index' of the crop. This index referred to the proportion of total shoot weight accounted for by the grain, the balance being the weight of the stalk (Figure 6.5). To the farmer, both the grain and the stalk were of value, particularly in the high farming systems, where the stalk provided valuable livestock fodder. In addition, there was an inverse relationship between the quantity of grain produced (yield) as opposed to its natural weight or density. Generally, varieties that had higher yields, in terms of volume per acre, had lower densities. Also, there was no single variety available that could produce heavy stalk yield and a large volume of grain at the high densities preferred by the baking trade.[30]

Grain yield was a multifaceted concept to the British farmer, who had to balance all three aspects of the harvest, that is, the weight of the

---

[27] Daviron, 'Small farm production', p. 169.
[28] Dumbell, 'Corn sales', p. 144. It is important to consider the difference between *specific gravity* and *natural weight* in this context. Specific gravity measurements usually refer to the density of individual wheat grains. However, as will become clear later in the chapter, due to the manner in which natural weight measurements were made, they included the density of empty spaces (or air) in addition to the density of the individual grain.
[29] Ibid.
[30] Walton, 'British cereals sector', pp. 39–40.

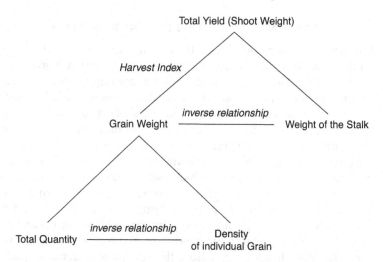

Figure 6.5. Determinants of the yield of British wheat crops. *Source:* adapted from Walton, 'British cereals', pp. 39–40 and 48, figure 1.

stalk, the weight of the grain and the total amount of grain produced. The application of high fertilizer doses in the nineteenth century, while increasing the overall yield of the crop, changed the character of the crop in one of two ways. If the harvest index was reduced, that is, the proportion of stalk to grain went up, this increased the density of the individual grains, while reducing its yield in terms of the total quantity of grain produced. But if the overall quantity of the grain increased, that is, the harvest index increased, it resulted in decreased density of the grains.[31] This quest for greater yield gradually resulted in a varietal shift of wheat available in domestic markets, as farmers preferred the high volumetric yielding varieties but with lower density. Such soft wheat varieties began to replace the harder, lower volumetric, higher density yielding varieties previously grown.[32]

For example, Talavera (originally introduced from Spain), a variety that offered a high flour extraction percentage and good-quality flour, had a comparatively lower volumetric yield than another variety, such as Spalding, which had lower bushel weight and higher volume yields. By the 1860s, Talavera was largely abandoned by farmers, whereas Spalding, 'a farmer's wheat than a miller's', was extensively grown.[33] Thus we see a

---

[31] Ibid., pp. 39–40 and 48.
[32] Ibid., pp. 48–50.
[33] Ibid., pp. 48–51.

dissonance between the preference of the British farmers and large buyers of wheat: millers complained that they could no longer find suitable domestic wheat for bread making. This varietal shift implied that the softer high yielding wheat increasingly grown in Britain after circa 1860 was unsuited to the rolling mill technology introduced in the 1880s, and millers had to import hard wheat that was more suited for this new technology, as we shall see later.

In several domestic markets, selling on the basis of natural weight or density emerged as a common method of assessing the quality of produce. This method guaranteed that the contracted volume of grain, say, one bushel measure, would weigh a specified amount, say, sixty pounds. If the actual weight was more or less than the guaranteed weight per volume, the contract price was adjusted proportionately.[34] For example, a contract for wheat from circa 1830, guaranteeing delivery weight to be eighteen stone per quarter, specified price and terms as fifty four shillings and six pence 'pay or be paid'; that is, the farmer was to make a 'proportionate allowance' to the merchant in case the net weight on delivery was under eighteen stone four pounds, and conversely, the farmer was to receive an allowance from the merchant in case the net weight on delivery was found to exceed eighteen stone four pounds.[35] In another example from Sheffield, weight per load was mentioned by the seller as confirmation of quality and could vary from twelve stone nineteen pounds to thirteen stone ten pounds, according to the quality of wheat. Also, wheat brought into this market from Gainsborough and Lynn was sold by the quarter weighing 504 pounds, whereas wheat from Hull was to be delivered at 480 pounds per quarter.[36] In the market town of Lewes, if the wheat purchased did not weigh the quantity stated by the seller per cubic capacity, 'a diminution in price agreed upon [was] made', and when the grain exceeded the weight stated, 'the price [was] advanced'.[37] There are similar examples from other market towns such as Lincoln, Stamford, York, Leeds, Wakefield, Hull, Whitby, Malton, Durham, Stockton, Darlington, Newcastle-upon-Tyne and Whitehaven.

Returns from corn inspectors suggest that a majority of wheat markets in the United Kingdom were selling wheat on the basis of their density, or at least on the basis of volume measurements, in 1834; this proportion

---

[34] The other methods of selling grain in domestic markets were on the basis of volume–only or weight-only measures. *Report from Select Committee on the Sale of Corn*, PP Vol. VII 1834. *Summary of returns by corn inspectors*, PP Vol. LXV 1878–1879.

[35] *Returns from corn inspectors*, PP Vol. XLIX 1834, p. 259. One stone equals fourteen pounds and 6.35 kilograms.

[36] Ibid., p. 262.

[37] Ibid. See letter by John Bartlett, dated 27 August 1833.

remained more or less constant until the last quarter of the nineteenth century. Few markets sold on the basis of weight only, and of the top twenty towns accounting for about 60 per cent of the wheat sold in domestic markets in 1880, eleven markets were reported to be using density measurements. These included towns such as Norwich (10%), London (4%), Boston (3.5%) and Northampton (3%).[38]

The use of natural weights to assess the quality of wheat was not unique to Britain. French bakers regularly used this method to distinguish between a setier of good wheat and average-quality wheat. Although 'artful and meticulous bakers' could assess quality of grain through sensory examination, by itself this was not considered to be a sufficient guarantee of quality; the most reliable test of goodness was the density of the grain.[39] As the density of wheat brought into Paris would vary sharply from year to year, a 'three-quality-range' had emerged in the mid-eighteenth century. The setier, the Parisian measure of volume, was equated to either 240, 230 or 220 livre, the French measure of weight, for a normal year, the highest weight representing the best-quality wheat. In an exceptionally good year, the weight of the setier could be set as high as 250 livre. The three-quality-range could vary: in 1769, the range was set at 241, 236 and 233 pounds in Etampes, whereas in Pontoise, it was set at 229, 223 and 220 livre.

Such natural weight measurements did not capture information about the *condition* of the grain such as the presence of impurities, dryness or moisture content, texture and so on – attributes that were equally important to the miller and the baker in addition to the density of the grain. Historically, information about the condition of the grain could be verified through sampling and visual inspection. However, even inspecting samples could prove to be problematic. Samples could hide the extent of variation in the quality of a given stock. They were also liable to damage due to exposure or handling and therefore could not represent the actual quality of the entire stock. For example, after selling on the basis of samples became common practice in the mid-eighteenth century, there were complaints against corn factors that they exposed only a selection of their samples so that the buyers did not get a complete picture of the actual quality of stock they represented. Similarly, American grain inspectors sampling wheat from railway wagons faced similar problems

---

[38] PP Vol. XLIX 1834, p. 256. *Return showing total quantity for wheat in 1880*, PP Vol. LXXXIII 1881. The figures in parentheses represent the proportion of grain sold in that market town compared to the total grain reported as sold for that year.

[39] S. L. Kaplan, *Provisioning Paris: merchants and millers in the grain and flour trade during the eighteenth century* (Ithaca, Cornell University Press, 1984), pp. 52–53.

in the early twentieth century. Sampling from fully loaded wagons, particularly those loaded to the roof, was fraught with difficulties in terms of the reliability of the samples extracted. Sampling was also problematic in other commodity trades. Cotton sellers in Liverpool often accused brokers of carelessly handling samples, which 'prejudiced the sale of the whole lot and often put the seller to the expense of re-sampling'.[40]

From the mid-nineteenth century onwards, commodity exchanges, such as the London Corn Trade Association (LCTA) or the Chicago Board of Trade (CBT), began to develop detailed mechanisms to measure and grade these complex goods.[41] Developing grades involved selecting a finite set of characteristics, or 'summary criteria', such that the commodity could be graded into a manageable number of classes. This was important given the plethora of wheat varieties available and the incredibly large number of ways in which it could be classified. Criteria used to determine the commercial grade of grain from the samples submitted for inspection included moisture content, natural weight, freedom from foreign material (cleanliness), condition and texture of the kernels, general condition (whether the grain is cool and sweet or musty, sour, heating or hot) and so on.[42] Previously, grain traders had adopted a distinct vocabulary to describe quality characteristics. This included several terms such as sound, bright, common, extra, choice, merchantable, clean, fair, hot and unsound.[43] Many of these terms were used to describe the grades that the commodity exchanges developed.

The British exchanges were primarily concerned with grading imported wheat, not domestic wheat: there is no evidence that either of these exchanges developed formal grades for the domestic trade. This is perhaps not surprising, as by the time these exchanges began developing formal grades circa 1880 or thereabouts, the quantum of foreign imports was roughly eight times that of domestic sales (Figure 6.1).[44] By the end of the nineteenth century, guaranteeing quality of imported wheat traded in the London market involved four distinct grading

---

[40] Daviron, 'Small farm production', p. 169. Hill, *Grain, grades and standards*, p. 6. Fay, 'Corn market', p. 73. J. C. F. Merrill, 'Classification of grain into grades', *Annals of the American Academy of Political and Social Science* 38 No 2 (1911): p. 63. T. Ellison, *The cotton trade of Great Britain: including a history of the Liverpool cotton market and of the Liverpool cotton brokers' association* (London, E. Wilson, 1886), p. 177.

[41] Pirrong, 'Commodity exchanges', p. 234.

[42] L. S. Tenny, 'Standardization of farm products', *Annals of the American Academy of Political and Social Science* 137 (1928): p. 209.

[43] Hill, *Grain, grades and standards*, pp. 13–14.

[44] In 1880, foreign wheat imports amounted to 55 million tons, as opposed to 6.7 million tons reported in domestic returns. *Statistical tables of corn averages*, PP Vol. LX 1889, p. 423. PP Vol. LX 1886, p. 405.

methods: certificate final, sealed sample, fair average and fair average quality (FAQ).

Certificate final referred to grades that were certified by an authority in the originating country such as by the CBT in the United States. These grades functioned as classes or standards, ranking the quality of the produce based on descriptions of certain attributes, which British merchants could accept as guarantee of quality. In the fair average method, a standard was issued by an authority in the producing country based upon samples from the produce in a given period from the growing regions in that country. These standards could change depending upon the quality of produce in a given year. In contrast, sealed sample and FAQ methods involved inspection of samples once the produce had reached the UK ports. These differed according to the methods of sampling and the basis on which the samples were used, either for sorting the grain into grades or for resolving disputes relating to the quality of the product.

The FAQ method was the one that was most commonly adopted in London. Under this method, samples of all grain imported into the United Kingdom, including several ports in Europe, were periodically collected by the LCTA, who would then arrive at the grades for any given year. The actual mechanism or methods used to describe the grades could not be determined from the archival records. Since the FAQ grades were developed on a responsive basis, that is, based on annual samples collected, they functioned as ranked categories into which the different samples could be sorted.

When the LCTA began grading grain on the FAQ basis, the description of quality depended upon the source of the produce. For instance, when Indian grain was graded on FAQ terms, allowance was made for dirt and other impurities (such as nonfarinaceous seeds). While drawing up the standards for Indian wheat for the 1889 season, the East India Grain Committee of the LCTA defined the standard for No 1 Club Bombay Wheat as containing

[not over] 3% of impurities of which 1(1/2)% may be dirt for shipments to the 30th June, and 3(1/2)% [impurities], of which 2% may be dirt, for the remainder of the seasons shipments.[45]

Similarly, standards for New Zealand wheat were made separately for round-berried and long-berried wheat.[46] North American grain was

---

[45] *Minutes of East India grain committee: Vol. 1 (1888–96)*, London Corn Trade Association, Guildhall Library MS 23186/1. See entry for 8 August 1889.

[46] *Minutes of American and Australian grain committee: Vol. 1 (1882–96)*, London Corn Trade Association, Guildhall Library MS 23177. See entry for 9 April 1891. Smith, *Organised produce markets*, pp. 24–25.

gradually accepted on the basis of 'official certificate of inspection to be final as to quality', that is, according to the quality guaranteed by the official inspection certificates issued in the United States. Even so, the LCTA would sometimes inspect the samples prior to accepting the grades.[47]

While making the FAQ grades, the LCTA would take into account the differences in the natural weight of the grain from Argentina, Australia, California or other locations. For example, while fixing the standard for Australian wheat in 1894, the LCTA fixed an average weight of sixty-three pounds per bushel for the season's wheat. Conversely, the average weight of Californian White was assumed to be sixty and a half pounds per bushel while fixing the standards for 1895. Similarly, for grain imported from the Black Sea ports, the committee had developed rules to account for the natural weight, especially for rye and barley.[48] In Liverpool, natural weight was used to grade American milling wheat specified as spring wheat (weighing sixty pounds per bushel), soft winter (sixty-one pounds per bushel) and hard winter (sixty and a half pounds per bushel). The North and South Argentine wheats, too, were graded according to their natural weight at fifty-nine and a half and sixty and a half pounds per bushel, respectively, and the Australian wheat was specified at sixty and a half pounds per bushel. No wheat weighing more than one pound per bushel 'under basis' was accepted within these grades.[49]

The LCTA had to periodically review the samples on FAQ basis to determine the acceptable average natural weights of the different varieties and did not use a defined, unchanging numerical standard. The association also used other criteria, such as cleanliness, colour or proportion of impurities, to establish its grades.

In contrast, the CBT in 1858 began classifying grades according to fixed descriptions of colour, quality and general condition and at the same time certifying those grades.[50] Four basic grades for spring wheat, for instance, were established: Club, No 1 Spring, No 2 Spring, and Rejected.[51] When this system of grading attracted opposition, because

47 MS 23177. Entry for 1 January 1891. Pirrong, 'Commodity exchanges', p. 236. *Subcommittee to examine rules of arbitration*, London Corn Trade Association, Guildhall Library MS 23175. See suggested alteration to Contract Forms 1898 proposed by the Liverpool Corn Trade Association on 8 November 1897.
48 MS 23177. Entries for 24 September 1895, 20 February 1894 etc. See also *Minutes of Black Sea Grain Committee: Vol. 1 (1890–1901)*, London Corn Trade Association, Guildhall Library MS 23183, esp. the comparative table for the regulation of the natural weight of rye. Also Forrester, 'Commodity exchanges', p. 202.
49 Forrester, 'Commodity exchanges', p. 204.
50 Merrill, 'Grain grades', p. 58.
51 Hill, *Grain, grades and standards*, p. 15.

it lacked uniformity and 'responsible inspectors', the CBT continued to refine these grades; there were allegations that inspectors had too much discretion based upon their 'own judgement of quality and grade'.[52] In 1859, the CBT added 'test weight', that is, natural weight, as a grading factor for wheat. The following minimum test weights (pounds per bushel) were introduced: Club, sixty pounds; No 1, fifty-six pounds; Standard, fifty pounds; and Rejected, forty pounds. These did not always work, as in 1859, when grain less than forty-five pounds per bushel but of Standard grade or better was delivered. As a result, the CBT revised the grades and the minimum test weights as follows: No 1, fifty-six pounds; Standard, fifty pounds; No 2, forty-five pounds; and Rejected, forty pounds. Even these standardised natural weights failed to gain approval by the trade. The CBT consequently left the specification of the test weight to the discretion of the grain inspectors when ascertaining grade.[53]

By the turn of the century, a numerical system of grading the various varieties of red, white, winter and spring wheat had emerged. For instance, No 1 white winter wheat was defined as that which was pure white, sound, plump and well cleaned. No 3 was defined as not clean and plump enough for No 2 but weighed not less than fifty-four pounds to the measured bushel. The Board of Railroad and Warehouse Commissioners had developed this system of rules for inspection to 'establish a proper number and standard of grades for inspection of grain'.[54] These rules took into account the natural weight of grains such as wheat, barley and oats to define certain grades in addition to other attributes.

Nevertheless, the numerical grades in the United States were not entirely based upon *quantitative* measurements of quality. Quantification of quality attributes continued to remain problematic and elusive. When the US Grain Dealers National Association adopted inspection rules in 1908, their Grade 1 specified moisture content to be 15 per cent, impurities (dirt, broken grains etc.) to be 1 per cent. Yet, circa 1914, numerical grades continued to be based upon descriptions such as sound, dry, reasonably clean, sweet, mature and plump.[55] Studies conducted by the US Department of Agriculture (USDA) after 1909 to identify 'tangible factors' influencing the 'intrinsic value' of corn considered weight per bushel as an important factor (apart from moisture,

---

[52] Ibid.
[53] Ibid., pp. 13–16.
[54] *The forty-seventh annual report of the trade and commerce of Chicago*, Chicago Board of Trade 1905, pp. 30–33.
[55] Hill, *Grain, grades and standards*, p. 76. See table 3 comparing grades specified by the USDA and those used in the three major grain markets of New York, Chicago and Minneapolis.

breakage and cleanliness). When the USDA promulgated official grades for commercial corn in 1914, six distinct numerical grades were defined on the basis of moisture, damage to the kernels (due to heat or presence of broken corn) and presence of foreign material.[56] Natural weight continued to remain an important test factor for quality, but it was not one of the attributes that defined the numerical grades.

Commodity grading thus developed independently in the United Kingdom and United States. The grading systems were quite distinct and employed very different summary criteria to describe and grade wheat varieties. Broadly speaking, the density of wheat was considered as an important measure of the bread-making ability of a given variety of wheat, as it had in traditional markets. Other search attributes were just as important in assessing the condition of the grain. There was no standardised set of attributes used to measure quality, and the summary criteria differed according to the trade route and sources of imported wheat. Exchanges, particularly in the United States, found it difficult to arrive at numerical standards of quality. The LCTA in the United Kingdom did not develop numerical standards, but rather, its grades functioned as ranked categories into which the samples of imported grain were sorted. Quality measurements for most (not all) American wheat were made prior to exporting, whereas measurements for grain from other international sources were made at the time of importation into the United Kingdom. Evidence suggests that initially, the grading systems were developed for the cash market rather than with the express intention of developing a futures trading market. This corresponds to the evidence provided by Pirrong and Hill for the US exchanges.[57] The futures trading may have benefited from the grading systems, but there is no evidence that they were developed with such trading instruments in mind. Grading systems were also accompanied by systematic dispute resolution or arbitration mechanisms developed by the commodity exchanges. In this regard, commodity exchanges therefore functioned as quality assurance centres, in addition to coordinating the measurement and grading activity.

Measuring quality: a demand-side perspective

While important changes were occurring upstream along the trade and distribution end of the value chain, there were corresponding and equally significant changes in the downstream milling industry around the same

[56] Ibid., pp. 18–19 and 71–73.
[57] Pirrong, 'Commodity exchanges'. Hill, *Grain, grades and standards*.

time. After circa 1870, we discern a professionalisation of the industry as the process of milling became highly specialised and technically sophisticated. This is evidenced by at least two developments that have direct relevance to this case study. First, in this period, we witness some radical changes in the methods, locations and reorganisation of the milling industry that stem primarily from revolutionary technological advances made after circa 1870. Second, we also see the emergence of some institutions in this period that further engineered the professionalisation of the trade. These institutions included technical and trade journals and industry associations that sought to overcome the knowledge and skills deficit within the industry. The structural reorganisation and institutions helped to modernise the milling industry.[58]

The milling technology in use circa 1870 had remained unchanged since the late eighteenth century, when steam milling had reduced the industry's dependence on wind and water. Millstones continued to be used for grinding wheat, the replacement of wooden gear wheels with iron ones being the only improvement of note in the intervening period.[59] This sudden-death grinding method ensured that the wheat grains were ground thoroughly and as quickly as possible. The consequence of this method was that the flour obtained contained a significant proportion of bran, although the extraction rate of flour from the wheat grain was as high as 80 per cent.[60] New developments in milling technology, particularly in Hungary and the United States, involved the improvement and perfection of roller milling techniques.[61] Rolling produced whiter flour, although the extraction rate decreased to about 72 per cent of the wheat grain.[62] The main advantage of this new technology was that it improved the quality and the whiteness of flour obtained for the same proportion of grains used to produce the coarse household-grade flour using the older grinding technology.[63]

The speed and extent of adoption of roller milling was shaped by at least three important factors: increases in the domestic demand for white

---

[58] H. Macrosty, 'The grainmilling industry: A study in organization', *Economic Journal* 13 No 51 (1903). G. Jones, *The millers: A story of technological endeavour and industrial success, 1870–2001* (Lancaster, Carnegie, 2001), esp. chapter 1. R. Perren, 'Structural change and market growth in the food industry: Flour milling in Britain, Europe and America, 1850–1914', *Economic History Review* 43 No 3 (1990). J. Tann and G. Jones, 'Technology and transformation: the diffusion of the roller mill in the British flour milling industry, 1870–1907', *Technology and Culture* 37 No 1 (1996).

[59] Perren, 'Flour milling', p. 424.

[60] Jones, *Millers*, p. 22. Tann and Jones, 'Roller milling', p. 60.

[61] Tann and Jones, 'Roller milling', pp. 41–43.

[62] Jones, *Millers*, pp. 23–25.

[63] Perren, 'Flour milling', p. 423.

flour, unsuitability of softer domestic wheat varieties to the technology and increases in the imports of foreign flour and hard wheat varieties. The causal links between all these factors is not entirely clear. Very likely the increasing demand for white flour had to be satisfied either by importing better-quality foreign flour or by increasing the domestic production of white flour using the new technology. The increased imports of foreign wheat varieties, which gradually nudged out the domestic varieties in the UK markets, were directly related to the gradual adoption of roller milling in the United Kingdom. The roller milling technology was more effective with the harder wheat, which had been edged out of domestic markets when domestic wheat varieties gradually shifted towards the softer 'farmer's wheat' of the high-yielding varieties, as we have seen earlier.[64]

The import of foreign hard wheat after circa 1860 certainly aided the diffusion of the new technology. Imports of milled flour, too, increased during this period. Within a decade from 1875, the quantum of flour imports had nearly trebled, and most of it was sourced from the United States. The imported flour constituted nearly one-fifth of the national consumption by the end of the 1880s, almost double compared to the previous decade.[65] The impact on domestic wheat and flour prices, and profitability, concerned not only the millers but also the corn trade in general.[66]

The take-up of roller milling technology was slow and uneven. Similarly, the industry structure and demand profile displayed uneven contours. There was a polarisation of the industry into a few large firms, serving regional and national markets and hundreds of small country mills serving mainly local demand. The small firms formed about 95 per cent of the mills in the United Kingdom in the late 1880s but produced about 35 per cent of the domestic flour. By 1910, five of the largest roller milling firms (from a total of more than eight hundred firms) accounted for about one-fifth of the total output; this concentration increased to nearly two-thirds by 1930.[67] The large firms were concentrated around the major port areas, which were a source of both raw materials and demand and were characterised by significantly higher throughput rates due to the adoption of roller milling.

After 1870, several industry associations were set up, which at first sought to regulate the conditions for sale of flour but later became a forum

[64] Tann and Jones, 'Roller milling'. Perren, 'Flour milling'.
[65] Perren, 'Flour milling', p. 425.
[66] *First Report of Royal Commission on Depression of Trade and Industry*, PP Vol. XXI 1886, p. 93. See memo from Liverpool Corn Trade Association.
[67] Perren, 'Flour milling', pp. 432–33. Tann and Jones, 'Roller milling', pp. 62–66.

to establish procedures and governance mechanisms as well as serving as nodes to disseminate knowledge and information. The Regional associations included the Sheffield Association (founded 1873), the London Association (founded 1878) and the Liverpool and Manchester District Association (active c. 1878).[68] However, the association that undoubtedly had the greatest impact on the industry was the National Association of British and Irish Millers (NABIM), formed in 1878. Its general aim included the collection of information regarding the trade involving various technical, practical and commercial aspects.[69]

In terms of NABIM's membership, it received strong support from millers in London, Liverpool, Sheffield, Leeds, the Bristol Channel and South Wales area, Northamptonshire and other locations where large milling firms were established; in-country and small milling firms failed initially to see the benefit of this association.[70] The association functioned as a clearing house for knowledge and information. For instance, a series of annual conventions was organised by NABIM between 1884 and 1890 on topics such as 'Bookkeeping for Millers', 'Gradual Reduction Milling', 'The Carter and Zimmer Sorting System' and 'The World's Wheat Crop and Wheat Values'.[71] It also acted as an educator and a promoter of milling as a 'science' beyond its obvious industrial origins. The association complemented the various efforts that were under way to establish some sort of organisational structure for technical education in general; for the milling industry, NABIM and the individuals associated with it, such as William Voller and William Dunham, provided the general structure and supervision of technical education.[72]

However, the association mainly acted as a pressure or lobby group on behalf of its members and the milling industry more generally. For instance, NABIM lobbied the Board of Trade in 1878, expressing the opinion of the milling trade regarding the metrological units to be used in the sale of wheat and other grain. It had canvassed the regional and local millers' associations, corn merchants and agriculturists through a series of more than twenty meetings held across the country throughout 1878. The issue at stake was whether to make it mandatory to sell wheat using weight-only measurements and not by volume or density measurements in domestic markets. NAIBM had managed to garner the support of millers throughout the United Kingdom for mandatory use

---

[68] Macrosty, 'Grainmilling industry', p. 331.
[69] Jones, *Millers*, p. 139.
[70] Ibid., pp. 141–44.
[71] Ibid., p. 148.
[72] Ibid., pp. 150–56. Voller was one of the pioneers of technical education in Britain. Dunham was the founder of the trade journal *Miller* (London).

of weight-only measurements for the sale of wheat. This testifies to the organisational ability and the overall influence that NABIM had within the milling and wheat marketing trades.[73] NABIM was also involved in the quality standardisation and grading process for wheat. For example, it proposed various amendments to the LCTA standard contract forms in 1896. One particular amendment it suggested regarded the proportion of dirt and foreign matter that should be allowed in the grain imported from India. This suggestion was, however, rejected by the LCTA on the basis that the limits suggested by NABIM were 'impracticable'.[74]

Another institution that had a similar impact on the professionalisation of the milling industry was the rise of various technical and trade journals that were exclusively devoted to the miller. The journal *Miller* was started in 1875 by William Dunham, and G. J. S. Broomhall started the journal *Milling* in 1891.[75] Publications such as these served as forums to exchange information, knowledge, opinions and developments that directly affected the millers and how they conducted their trade. In it one would find information about new developments in the milling process pioneered by milling engineers such as Herbert Simon, or about the state of the wheat crop in Britain or its foreign sources, or letters seeking opinions about the best method of mixing grain to get the ideal flour, or news articles on developments affecting the wheat, milling and baking trades. The editorial, technical and commercial content was supplemented by the growing amount of advertising as well as by opinions voiced by individual millers. Such journals provided much of the basis of news, ideas and discussion for both formal and informal networks of communication throughout the industry.[76]

Consequent to the radical changes occurring in the milling industry, the manner in which grain quality was considered, the quality attributes of grain that were important for making flour of a given quality and the manner in which they were measured were reexamined and refined. It was generally acknowledged within the trade that wheat of higher density had greater bread-making qualities. An article in *Miller* in 1879 stated that 'the value to the miller of a certain variety of wheat depends upon the quantity of fine flour it will yield'.[77] Wheat of least specific gravity was known to yield a lower quality of flour, and vice versa. The proportion

---

[73] The National Archives, Board of Trade papers, BT 101/43, letter by William Chatterton, president of NABIM, dated 7 November 1878.
[74] MS 23175. See entry for 1896.
[75] Jones, *Millers*, pp. 18–21. Broomhall had started another publication covering the corn trade called the *Liverpool Corn Trade News* (1888).
[76] Ibid., pp. 20–21.
[77] *Miller*, 5 May 1879, Technical Issue, p. 193.

of albuminoids or flesh formers was thought to determine the quality or fineness of flour. It was found to increase as the density of grain increased and was one of the principal reasons why denser grains were considered to have better bread-making ability. 'More flour is produced from corn of higher specific gravity, and more bread from such flour, than from inferior corn or inferior flour', a report from 1834 had claimed.[78] Although lighter, coarser grains could yield a larger proportion of flour, this was achieved by including coarse bran and thereby reducing the quality of the flour obtained.[79] Generally, the millers and bakers preferred wheat varieties with high natural weights to the softer wheat varieties with lower densities.[80]

But it was not only the density of the grain that was important to the miller: the strength of the grain or flour was crucial to the miller (and the baker) as well. The strength was initially defined as the ability to absorb and retain moisture, which later was modified to indicate the quantity and quality of gluten the grain contained.[81] Stronger flour was preferred because the number of loaves obtained from a given weight of flour was more than the number obtained from weaker flour.[82] Hard wheat of the low-yielding (and conversely high-density) variety was considered stronger wheat, whereas softer wheat was considered to be of the weaker kind. British wheat, on the whole, was considered to be of the weaker kind.[83] The miller basically had to balance both the density and the moisture characteristics of the grain, as those varieties with the highest bushel weight with low moisture content usually gave the greatest amount of flour.[84]

Apart from these, other differences were also of importance to the miller. Before the introduction of the rolling mills, when wheat was ground between millstones, the colour of the grain was important to the miller, as invariably some of the bran or coat of the grain was also ground along with the fleshy part. Flour from red-grained wheat was never as white as that obtained from white-skinned wheat; white flour commanded a higher price in the market. In any case, white wheat was known to yield a slightly higher proportion of flour than red wheat. This difference in the colour of wheat became less important once the roller system of milling was adopted after circa 1880, as with this new

[78] PP Vol. VII 1834.
[79] Miller, 5 May 1879, Technical Issue, p. 193; 3 November 1879, p. 682.
[80] Walton, 'British cereals sector', pp. 39–40.
[81] Jago and Jago, Breadmaking, p. 291. Jones, Millers, p. 60.
[82] J. Percival, Wheat in Great Britain (Reading, 1934), p. 69.
[83] Ibid., p. 71.
[84] Ibid., p. 72. Jago and Jago, Breadmaking, p. 369. Jones, Millers, pp. 59–60.

technology, very little of the bran was mixed with the rest of the flour, and flour from red-grained wheat could be as white as that from white-skinned wheat.[85]

One of the greatest skills that a miller had to possess was to know which varieties of wheat to process and mix together as grist, that is, flour that the bakers would accept as consistent and which suited their trade. Flour itself could be graded into different types: whites, firsts (or best households), seconds (or second households or standard wheaten), thirds (third households or fine middlings), fourths (or coarse middlings or sharps), and wholemeal.[86] Millers scarcely recognised a consistent system of grading flour, however, each flour grade required a different quality of grain.[87] Mixing of different wheat qualities also allowed the widest possible use of inferior grades of wheat, which by themselves would have been unsuitable for making baking flour, particularly in London and other larger towns. Mixing also eked out the supply of expensive best-quality wheat and enabled the miller to enhance his margin by mixing expensive and inexpensive wheat and still sell the mixed flour at a price higher than that of inferior-quality flour.[88]

A typical mixture recommended in the eighteenth century included one part best-quality wheat to one part second-best-quality wheat to two parts inferior-quality wheat.[89] Such a mixture implied a price ratio of about 100:91:81 for best-, second-best- and inferior-quality wheat, respectively.[90] As the availability of foreign wheat increased, best-quality imported wheat was mixed with lower-quality domestic varieties.[91] This, and the eventual abolition of the assize in 1836, greatly increased the choice of wheat available for the miller to mix in various proportions, vastly increasing the complexity of the mealing process. By the latter half of the nineteenth century, millers required knowledge about the varieties available, their sources and their quality; the millers craft now required a great deal of experimentation and risk. Millers had to consider, for each variety of wheat, whether it would contribute to one or more aspect of

[85] Percival, *Wheat*, p. 72.

[86] Petersen, *Bread*, pp. 53–54.

[87] J. Kirkland, 'The relative prices of wheat and bread', *Economic Journal* 6 No 23 (1896): p. 479.

[88] PP Vol. V 1814–1815, p. 1353. See evidence by E. G. Smith. Petersen, *Bread*, pp. 158–59.

[89] Petersen, *Bread*, p. 159. Historically, wheat had been divided into 'best', 'second' and 'third' quality categories according to some quality attributes for the purpose of setting the Assize of Bread, 12 Henry VII cited in PP Vol. V 1814–1815, p. 1344.

[90] Petersen, *Bread*, table 6.2 on 160. The average prices in the table have been calculated from evidence provided to the Select Committee on Sale of Corn by Richard Page, PP Vol. VII 1834, p. 356.

[91] Petersen, *Bread*. PP Vol. VII 1834. PP Vol. V 1814–1815, various testimonies.

flour quality: strength, colour, taste or general appearance. Consequently, wheat buying was governed by experience, general principles and a considerable degree of detailed knowledge, and no two millers agreed on what constituted ideal grist.

Consider, for instance, this exchange between two millers in 1878. One miller, with thirty years of milling experience, describes an 'ideal milling process [for] making the best and greatest quantity of flour from a given quantity of wheat', For this he uses an ideal grist composed of twenty bolls each of No 1 American, Canada Club, Saxonska, Californian or Oregon and British wheat (each boll being equivalent to 240 pounds). These one hundred bolls, according to this miller, could yield sixty sacks of fine flour, an additional five sacks of 'overheads' (a lower grade of flour), fifteen hundredweight of 'feeding' seconds and about thirty hundredweight of bran. The gross margin in this case would be about twelve pounds five shillings. In response to this, another miller claimed that using a different configuration of machinery, for the same grist combination, he could obtain twenty-three sacks of new process flour, forty-four sacks of first-grade flour, eight hundredweight of thirds and thirty-two and a half hundredweight of bran at a gross margin of twenty-two pounds eighteen shillings.[92]

In another instance, one miller invited comment on whether the following mixture 'ought to make a good sack of bakers flour': three sacks red winter; two sacks Michigan; two sacks No 2 spring and five sacks English white.[93] He received at least five suggestions from other millers, all different. One correspondent suggested that the proportion of English wheat was too high and instead recommended that three sacks of Michigan be used instead of two and that English white be limited to two sacks. Another correspondent suggested that the original mixture would result in 'lack of strength and colour' and suggested eliminating English white altogether and adding an extra sack of No 2 spring to the mixture; alternatively, the red winter, No 2 spring and English white could be mixed in equal proportions. A third correspondent suggested leaving the English white out altogether, grinding the remaining mixture separately, and then letting the meal sit in the sack for a few days before mixing. The fourth correspondent suggested that if this was milled in the country, then six parts each of No 1 American spring with 'sound' new English white wheat, mixed well in a bin a week before grinding, could give the desired results. The fifth correspondent recommended one sack each of Dantzic and American spring, three sacks each of American white and

[92] *Miller*, letters on 'Milling Reform', 1 April and 6 May 1878.
[93] *Miller*, 2 February 1880, letter 669, p. 922.

American winter and four sacks of English white (part new and part old).[94] Thus milling was not an exact science; it remained an acquired skill based upon experience and experimentation.

Mixing was important since a direct volumetric relationship existed between grain inputs and flour output. Consider this example from more recent times. The Chicago CBT specified that No 2 soft red winter wheat (SRW) uses fifty-eight pound per bushel test weight as a criterion. A miller usually based grain price to flour ratios on the assumption of a 73 per cent flour extraction rate, implying that 2.36 bushels would be required to produce one hundred pounds of flour. A reduction of test weight from fifty-eight pounds to fifty-seven pounds per bushel had two implications. First, at the same extraction rate, the miller now required 2.40 bushels of wheat to produce one hundred pounds of flour. Second, a reduction of test weight, and hence quality of the grain, was likely accompanied by a reduction of extraction rate to, say, 70 per cent, which further increased the quantity of grain required, 2.50 bushels, to produce the same quantity of flour. The resulting cost differential of wheat to flour was not always reflected in the price discounts for the different wheat qualities.[95]

To the British miller in the late nineteenth century, therefore, it was not only the price of individual variety of wheat that was of ultimate importance but the relative cost differentials between the individual varieties. The miller had to balance his margins according to the price of bread and the price of wheat. The relative cost of wheat to the miller thus depended upon the price of wheat grains that were mixed, which in turn determined the cost of producing the flour from that mix. At times, millers were forced by competition to sell flour at prices that were lower than its cost as compared to a given mix of wheat grains.[96] The pricing of wheat and flour, on one hand, and the quality of the grains in the mix, on the other, suggest a complex relationship that the millers struggled to manage.

As the milling process became more specialised and sophisticated, the differences in quality between varieties as well as the consistency of quality in a given variety became crucially important. Measuring quality was necessary to achieve the desired quality of flour and to enable the millers to remain profitable. How did the millers measure the quality of grain?

[94] *Miller*, letters: reply to 669, 1 March 1880, pp. 45–46; 5 April 1880, p. 119. See also Kirkland, 'Bread prices', p. 481.
[95] E. Jones, 'The role of information in US grain and oilseed markets', *Review of Agricultural Economics* 21 No 1 (1999): pp. 250–51.
[96] Kirkland, 'Bread prices', pp. 481–82.

Throughout most of the nineteenth century, millers relied upon the visual inspection of samples to purchase grain, the attributes of relevance being the density, colour, texture and extent of cleanliness. When the volume of imported grain increased and the number of varieties available multiplied, the millers, like the merchants, began to rely upon the grades and standards set by the various commodity associations such as the LCTA or the Liverpool Corn Trade Association. The correspondence between millers presented earlier regarding the different varieties and grades of wheat is indicative of this shift. We discern a trend of shifting reliance from visual inspection and assessment of quality to a gradual acceptance of the grading and standards developed by the various commodity associations. Millers purchasing domestic grain continued to do so based on older techniques of visual inspection and natural weights, although the importance of domestic wheat had diminished by the twentieth century; only about 19 per cent of home-grown wheat was used for bread making by 1914, down from 60 per cent circa 1860.[97]

Notwithstanding this shifting reliance on grades, assessing the quality of grain still depended upon the 'empiricism of the practical miller'.[98] By the last quarter of the nineteenth century, techniques for assessing the quality of wheat were still fairly uncertain. One expert wrote in 1890 that 'it will be well for mixing purposes to consider wheat as coming under one of three heads – strong, coloury or neutral'.[99] He further pointed out that wheat buying was governed by experience, general principles and by what varieties of wheat happened to be available in supply. After 1880, changes in milling technology were accompanied by development and improvements in testing and measuring the different quality attributes. The increased understanding of the chemical composition and properties of gluten, the substance in grain that lends strength to the flour, aided these developments. Various testing methods and instruments were made available for assessing the quality of flour: Pekar's method of assessing whiteness of flour, Boland's aleurometer to test the strength of gluten and Robine's method for estimating quantity and likely bread output are some examples.[100] Even so, each miller had to discover for himself the strength of any given flour as there was 'no satisfactory method of numerically registering strength except through a baking test'.[101]

To summarise, the milling industry, towards the end of the nineteenth century, required more sophisticated ways of assessing the quality of

[97] Perren, 'Flour milling', p. 425, table 1. Jones, *Millers*, p. 59. Percival, *Wheat*, p. 71.
[98] Jones, *Millers*, p. 61.
[99] W. R. Voller, *Modern flour milling*, Gloucester, 1889, as cited in Jones, *Millers*, p. 59.
[100] Jones, *Millers*, pp. 59–61.
[101] Jago and Jago, *Breadmaking*, p. 291.

wheat compared to the relatively crude test of natural weight measurements. The millers sought to capture the grain composition in more explicit terms of gluten and protein content rather than the simplistic notion of density. The millers were beginning to rely upon the grades established by the LCTA to assess the condition of grain reaching Britain. This was an iterative process with the grading of quality helping the milling industry to become more professional, which in turn, and in conjunction with other changes in the industry, required further refinement of the quality grades themselves. The grades served as labels as far as the millers were concerned and could not guarantee quality as the millers defined it. The millers increasingly relied upon baking tests and other measurements to ascertain quality ex post, in contrast to relying upon the historical methods of testing quality ex ante using natural weight measurements and visual inspection.

The case of natural weight measurements

The declining importance of natural weight measurements illustrates the changes in measurement practices evident in the globalising value chain. These de facto, decentralised measurements diminished in importance and were gradually replaced by alternative, more centralised ways of measuring quality. Whilst it was difficult to fix numerical grades of quality using natural weights or other criteria, changing practices involved changes to both measurement instruments and protocols.

Natural weight measurements were historically used to approximate the density of wheat, distinguish between different varieties of grain and serve as de facto quality standards. The differences in the natural weight measurements functioned as numerical grades signifying the relative differences in wheat quality in terms of flour-making ability: the higher the density, the better the quality of flour obtained. This was a decentralised, de facto grading system that emerged long before commodity exchanges began establishing formal or numerical grades. It was also a practical system that the trade relied upon to make a rapid and straightforward assessment of quality.[102] There was a wide range of natural weight standards in use for the sale of wheat in domestic UK markets. The standard weights ranged from 470 to 512 pounds per quarter, that is, fifty-eight to sixty-four pounds per bushel. Imported wheat showed a similar variation in terms of natural weight standards as compared to the domestic varieties grown in England. A comparison of thirty-five distinct varieties of foreign wheat sold in Britain with twenty-five domestic varieties suggests

---

[102] PP Vol. VII 1834, p. 87. See testimony by Patrick Stead, a corn merchant.

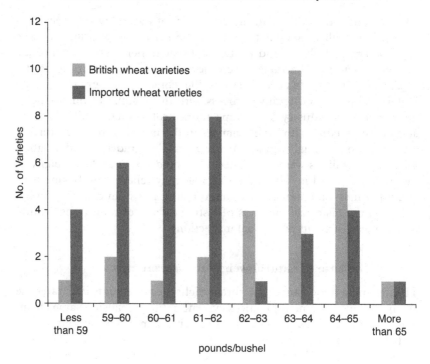

Figure 6.6. Comparison of densities of British and imported wheat grains (c. 1884). *Source:* based upon analysis reported in Jago and Jago, 'Breadmaking', pp. 273–79.

that on an average, the natural weight of foreign wheat was somewhat lower than that of the domestic varieties (see Figure 6.6).[103]

The density of a particular variety of wheat was notoriously difficult to maintain, as it was sensitive to climatic and other conditions.[104] Even under controlled conditions, variation in the natural weight of a specific wheat variety on the same plot could vary over time. Thus variation in natural weight occurred not only across different varieties of wheat but also across years and different conditions for the same variety. The degree of control that producers had on this particular attribute was limited by a variety of factors, many of which were beyond their control. This was exactly what the natural weight system was designed to capture: variations

---

[103] Jago and Jago, *Breadmaking*, pp. 273–79.
[104] *Miller*, 1 March 1880, p. 109, 'Chemistry of breadmaking – Part III: Lectures by Prof. Graham'. Refer to table by Lawes and Gilbert showing influence of seasons on the character of wheat crops.

in quality from one season to another for the same variety or between two stocks of the same variety. However, variation in natural weights could also arise due to the very act of making such measurements. British grains with the highest densities did not always register the highest natural weights. This was due to the shape of the grain itself, which left empty spaces – or large volumes of air in between the grains – when the bushel measure was filled. Also, the reliability of this estimator of quality was greater when relatively uniform varieties of wheat were involved, as in the case of American spring and winter wheat. The intrinsically problematic nature of British wheat meant that high grain density did not always translate into high bushel density, that is, natural weights.[105]

This disadvantage could be overcome by packing the grain in a more compact manner into the bushel measure. Closely filled grain would increase the natural weight estimate compared to loosely filled grain in the same volume. The height from which grain was poured into the measure determined whether grain was loosely or closely packed: the greater the height, the closer the grain was packed, and hence the greater the weight per volume when measured.[106] In addition, the practice of heaping increased the amount of grain that could be packed into a bushel measure by as much as one-eighth to one-quarter. The extent of the heap in turn was dependent upon the physical shape of the vessel. The flatter the vessel, the greater the volume of the heap would be, and vice versa.[107] Even when the bushel measure was not heaped, the method used for striking the grain, that is, ensuring that the grain was filled only to the brim of the measuring vessel and no more, could make a difference. Experiments conducted circa 1830 confirmed that when the same variety of wheat was stricken using a round cylindrical roller as opposed to a flat ruler, the difference in natural weight could be as much as 6 pounds per bushel (fifty-six pounds instead of sixty-two pounds, respectively).[108]

---

[105] Walton, 'British cereals sector', p. 51. A. S. Wilson, *A bushel of corn* (Edinburgh, David Douglas, 1883), p. 21.

[106] Isaac Roberts, 'Determination of the vertical and lateral pressures of granular substances', *Proceedings of the Royal Society of London* 36 (1883–1884), p. 240. W. Kula, *Measures and men*, R. Szreter (trans.) (Princeton, Princeton University Press, 1986), pp. 47–49. A. D. C. Simpson, 'Grain packing in early standard capacity measures: evidence from the Scottish dry capacity standards', *Annals of Science* 49 No 4 (1992): pp. 342–44. Also PP Vol. VII 1834, appendix 12. R. T. Balmer, 'The operation of sand clocks and their medieval development', *Technology and Culture* 19 No 4 (1978): pp. 615–32.

[107] R. D. Connor, *The weights and measures of England* (London, HMSO, 1987). Kula, *Measures and men*, pp. 49–51. See also Chapter 4 in this volume for a detailed discussion on variability due to the use of heaped measures.

[108] PP Vol. VII 1834, appendix 12.

204 Markets and Measurements in Nineteenth-Century Britain

As the quantity of grain measured varied due to differences in measurement practices, this affected the natural weight estimates, irrespective of
the quality of the grain.

Thus variation in natural weight estimates was a result of the variation in the density of individual ears of wheat as well as the variability
of measurement practices.[109] Without understanding the measurement
practices, or indeed standardising them, it was difficult to separate the
effect of changing quality of wheat on its natural weight measurements.
This unpredictability or inconsistency of natural weights was commonly
known circa 1880, if not earlier, and trade journals were cautioning
millers about the potential problems.[110]

The use of natural weights as a basis for setting contract terms during the nineteenth century was further complicated by the multiplicity
of units used to make such measurements. Some markets used load per
quarter, or stone per quarter, or pounds per quarter; other markets measured in bushels, and still others used gallons, coombs, bags, bolls, sacks
and centals.[111] Even the configuration of the volumetric units themselves
differed across markets. The smaller Winchester bushel, preferred by
the state before the nineteenth century, was not acceptable to the merchants and growers in the south-west, where a larger bushel measure was
used.[112] In Cumberland, the bushel used was the Carlisle bushel, which

---

[109] This can be represented as follows:

$$w_n = f(d, m),$$
$$d = f(v_w, E, T, S),$$
$$m = f\left(p_{(l,c)}, h, s_{(r,f)}\right),$$

where w_n captures the variation in natural weight, d captures the changes in density of grain and m captures changes due to the local measurement practices. The
density estimate was dependent upon the particular variety of grain v_w, the environ-
mental conditions E (such as quality of soil, climatic and other geographical conditions
etc.), the method of cultivation or the level of technology T and other social factors
S (e.g. civil disturbances, political instability). The variation due to measurement
practices (m) was dependent upon whether the grain was loosely or closely packed
($p_{(l,c)}$), the extent to which heaped measures were provided (h) and the method of
striking grain if the measure was not heaped ($s_{(r,f)}$). See also a report by Professor
Graham appearing in *Miller*, 1 March 1880, p. 109, 'Chemistry of breadmaking –
part III'.

[110] *Miller*, 1880 (Vol. 6), p. 109.

[111] C. R. Fay, 'The sale of corn in the nineteenth century', *Economic Journal* 34 No 134
(1924). PP Vol. XLIX 1834. PP Vol. LXV 1878–1879.

[112] R. Sheldon et al., 'Popular protest and the persistence of customary corn measures: resistance to the Winchester bushel in the English west', in A. Randall and
A. Charlesworth (eds) *Markets, market culture and popular protest in eighteenth-century
Britain and Ireland* (Liverpool, Liverpool University Press, 1996). Fay, 'Corn sales',
p. 212.

was three times the size of the 'ordinary one'.[113] Similarly, the definitions of *stone* and *load* differed across the markets.

Given that natural weight measurements could vary unpredictably, or were inconsistent across market towns, there were numerous (unsuccessful) attempts made to standardise the sale of wheat, on the basis of either weight-only or volume-only measurements, throughout the nineteenth century. In the House of Commons, proponents of volume-only measurements resisted attempts by other politicians to make it compulsory to sell wheat by weight-only measurements. Evidence of advantages of selling by volume was countered by evidence of selling by weight in several parts of the country.[114] In 1864, the chancellor of the Exchequer pointed out to the House the 'intolerable injustice of the double process of weighing for purpose of the corn duty and measuring [by volume] for the municipal tax [in London]'.[115] A parliamentary select committee of 1834 had concluded that the standard measure to be used throughout all markets for the sale of grain should be a combination of weight and volume measurements as 'the combination may be used for the purpose of identification [of quality, as well as] employed as the standard of quantity'.[116] Disagreements as to the significance of measuring by natural weight continued within the trade. Some groups claimed that natural weight measurements were actually weight measurements, whereas others countered this by claiming that they were actually volume measures qualified by their weight equivalents.[117] Merchants from the south preferred the sale of corn by volume-only measurements, whereas merchants in the north preferred the sale by weight-only measurements, especially in markets such as Liverpool.[118]

Also, the question of how much a bushel of wheat should weigh continued to dodge the trade and the state throughout the nineteenth century. The state dealt with the multiplicity of customary measures by requiring the corn returns to be expressed in terms of Imperial bushels, even if grain contracts were made using local measures. In fact, early-nineteenth-century legislation specified fixed-weight equivalents of grain for both

---

[113] Fay, 'Corn sales', p. 216.
[114] *Hansard Parliamentary Debates*, Series 3: Vol. 149, 27 April 1858, cc1839–41; Vol. 150, 18 May 1858, cc913–8; Vol. 155, 20 July 1859, cc122–30. *Bill to establish uniform measurement in the sale of corn*, PP Vol. II 1868–1869, p. 5. *Bill to ensure uniformity of weight in the sale of corn*, PP Vol. II 1883, p. 193. See also other bills included in PP Vol. I 1890–1891, p. 427, and PP Vol. I 1898, p. 381.
[115] *Hansard Parliamentary Debates*, Series 3, Vol. 176, 23 June 1864, cc163–76.
[116] PP Vol. VII 1834, p. xxvi.
[117] *Hansard Parliamentary Debates*, Series 3, Vol. 149, 27 April 1858, cc1839–41.
[118] *Hansard Parliamentary Debates*, Series 3, Vol. 150, 18 May 1858, cc913–18; Vol. 155, 20 July 1859, cc122–30.

Table 6.1. *Weight per bushel of different cereals charged with duty as specified in the corn returns*

	Wheat	Barley	Oats	Rye	Beans	Peas
Winchester bushel	57	49	38	55	–	–
Imperial bushel	59	51	39	57	63	64

Note: All weights are in pounds.
Source: corn returns, 10 March 1834, *Returns from corn inspectors*, PP Vol. XLIX 1834, p. 253.

the Imperial and the Winchester bushels, whereas in later legislation, the weight equivalents are specified only for the Imperial bushel.[119] As far as the corn returns were concerned, circa 1820, the natural weight of wheat was assumed to be fifty-nine pounds per bushel, that of barley was fifty-one pounds, oats were thirty-seven and rye was fifty-seven pounds per Imperial bushel (Table 6.1).[120] Throughout most of the nineteenth century, the state interest in standardising grain measurements reflected its endeavours to accumulate, as consistently as possible, the average price of grain in domestic markets through the corn returns. As long as these returns were seen to be capturing fluctuations in grain prices, the use of local measures as well as measurement practices was left undisturbed. This is confirmed by the following extract from a memorandum from the comptroller of corn returns:

> The maximum error which may arise through sales being made by weight instead of by measure, or by weight and measure combined, and the improper return of such sales is very inconsiderable, apparently less than one per cent [and] even the existence of so much error is not proved. It is also an error of a kind that would be compensated in good seasons in consequence of the Imperial [bushel] weighing more than the customary [measures] by which sales with weight and measure combined are made.[121]

By requiring that all grain measurements be reported in standard measurement units, the issue of 'how much quantity did a bushel of corn contain' was resolved rhetorically, as far as the state was concerned.

By the late 1870s, several merchant groups had come to prefer weight-only measurements. There were some debates within the trade circa

---

[119] PP Vol. XLIX 1834. Order in Council under Corn Returns Act, 1882, reproduced in *Report of Select Committee on Corn*, PP Vol. X 1888, pp. 134ff.

[120] PP Vol. XLIX 1834.

[121] *Memorandum by comptroller of corn returns*, PP Vol. LXV 1878–1879, p. 134. See memo to the Board of Trade in 1879.

1878 as to which metrological unit – the hundredweight of 112 pounds or the cental of 100 pounds – should be regarded as the standard unit of measurement.[122] The cental became popular around Liverpool and was briefly used on the United States–Liverpool trade routes. However, its use diminished towards the end of the century, and the trade mostly used the Imperial weight units such as the bushel, pound and hundredweight. In fact, the bushel came to be used primarily as a unit of weight and not of capacity in the wheat trade. Sale of grain by the bushel assuming a weight equivalent was thought to be 'nominally by measure of capacity, but in reality by weight'.[123] By circa 1890, most within the trade had come to prefer the weight-only measurements for the sale of grain in general.[124] The Corn Sales Act of 1921 eventually made it mandatory to sell grain by weight-only measurements. This mirrored the shift in measurement practices that had already occurred some time in the late nineteenth century and the declining importance of the natural weight measurements within the trade in general.

In summary, before the advent of commodity grading, natural weight measurements were crude but practical and relatively straightforward indicators of grain quality. They were both numerical and quantitative and served as de facto grading attributes. They were used in conjunction with inspection of several other attributes that revealed the condition of grain. Such measurements were inherently unreliable primarily because the variation in natural weight could be the result of factors influencing the measurement methods. Such effects were difficult to isolate from the production-related factors without knowing the manner in which meas-urements were made in a specific context. Even where measurement techniques could be standardised (pouring grain into the measuring ves-sel from a standard height or using a uniform striking method), the multiplicity of measurement units in use could result in the observed differences in natural weight.

The use of natural weights as a basis of contract terms continued in British markets for the sale of domestic wheat. With the globalisation of the value chain, and the demand for more sophisticated quality assess-ment methods, the use of natural weights in quality testing diminished by the end of the nineteenth century. Both the LCTA and CBT used several other criteria apart from natural weights to describe the quality of wheat. When the USDA was able to establish numerical grades in the

---

[122] TNA, BT 101/43, extract from J. E. Beerbohm's *Evening Corn Trade List*, dated 5 November 1878, p. 7. BT 101/49. BT 101/127.
[123] *Report of Select Committee on Corn Sales*, PP Vol. XI 1893–1894, pp. vii and xiii.
[124] Ibid.

early twentieth century, it did so without reference to natural weights. Natural weights declined in use as an ex ante quality assessment criterion, although they continued to remain an important test factor ex post.[125]

Measurements, grading and institutions

The globalisation of wheat markets in the nineteenth century was thus characterised by several interrelated developments, including the emergence of commodity exchanges and the grading systems introduced by them, the various monitoring and dispute resolution mechanisms that the exchanges introduced, the changes in the composition and varieties of the wheat grains available in the UK markets, the introduction of roller milling in the United Kingdom, the development of instruments and techniques to analyse the chemistry of the wheat grain, the centralisation of quality measurements, the decline of traditional practices such as selling by natural weight measurements and other changes described in the preceding sections. Globalisation of the sources of wheat grain depended primarily upon the ability of commodity exchanges to develop effective and internationally acceptable grading systems. This in turn hinged upon two crucial changes. First, changes to 'who measures' for quality – the centralisation of measurements – were crucial in making the grading system a quality assurance system. Second, the 'how measured' changes – the relative standardisation of summary criteria – were also crucial in the development of grading systems by making complex measurements possible. Both the who measures and how measured aspects helped to shape the globalisation of the value chain.

Previous sections showed how the British farmers and millers favoured different quality attributes of the wheat grain. To the farmers, the composition of the grain was important in terms of its density; the lower the density of the individual grain, the higher the quantum of the yield obtained by the farmers. The composition of the grain was also important to the millers. However, they preferred the density of the grain to be higher, as it increased its bread-making ability. In addition, the millers were also concerned about other compositional attributes, such as colour, shape, and texture, as well as the condition of the grain. Practically, grain

---

[125] E.g., standard contracts developed for use in the late twentieth century by FOSFA International (Federation of Oils, Seeds and Fats Associations Limited) or GAFTA (Grain and Feed Trade Association) include 'test weight' (or grain density) as one of the specifications in international grain contracts, along with several other attributes such as protein content, moisture, oil content (for oilseeds such as soya beans), presence of foreign material and damage to kernels.

with certain undesirable attributes, for example, high moisture content or high impurities, could be corrected and re-sorted into higher grades. But grain with undesirable compositional attributes could not be corrected. In such a scenario, the buyer (i.e. the millers) would be the one to measure for quality.[126] The primary logic here is that there was little incentive for the seller (e.g. farmers, traders) to sort the commodity, as the quantity – not quality – of the grain was of importance to the seller. If required, the seller would prefer to sort using as few attributes as possible. The buyer, conversely, preferred to sort it as finely as possible, on more attributes or at least different attributes from those chosen by the seller. These considerations shaped the contract terms, buying practices and quality assessment in domestic wheat markets. With the increase in the import of foreign wheat, this situation altered dramatically. The LCTA enabled the standardisation of both product grades and contract terms.

Why did commodity exchanges standardise quality grades and commercial terms? The measurement-cost argument suggests that because primary commodities are effectively heterogeneous, absence of standards or grades resulted in costly and duplicative examination by buyers and sellers.[127] Another view is the transaction cost argument, which suggests that standardised contract terms helped to institutionalise arbitration mechanisms and helped the clearing house system within commodity exchanges.[128] The internationalisation-of-farms argument suggests that commodity exchanges were instrumental in developing quality grades on the basis of which futures trading could develop, which could transfer the price risk to a specialised group of speculators (the broker-merchants) and link local farms to the international markets.[129] Finally, the creation-of-trust argument suggests that third-party or official grades are better able to guarantee quality than individual inspection or certification.[130] It is likely that a combination of factors influenced the emergence of standardisation by commodity exchanges.

The LCTA wheat grades were based on several attributes, including natural weight, moisture content, cleanliness and other descriptors

---

[126] Barzel, 'Measurement cost', pp. 29–32.
[127] Pirrong, 'Commodity exchanges', pp. 232–33.
[128] R. B. Ferguson, 'The adjudication of commercial disputes and the legal system in modern England', *British Journal of Law and Society* 7 No 2 (1980): pp. 144–45. C. Chattaway, 'Arbitration in the foreign corn trade in London', *Economic Journal* 17 No 67 (1907): p. 428. Forrester, 'Commodity exchanges', pp. 201–3. The 'clearing house system' refers to the exchange of shipping and other commercial documents between traders, settlement of contracts, clearing of differences etc.
[129] Daviron, 'Small farm production', p. 163.
[130] Merrill, 'Grain grades', p. 61.

(such as long or round berried for New Zealand corn). Other corn associations, such as the Liverpool Corn Trade Association (LvCTA), also
developed such grading methods.[131] The LvCTA began establishing contract grades of wheat after circa 1855, which differed somewhat from the
LCTA. However, by the end of the nineteenth century, Liverpool merchants were content to use the grades established by the LCTA.[132] The
grades so developed were primarily for wheat imports from East Europe,
Australia, South America or India. Imports from the United States, with
the exception of California, were graded at source and were accompanied
by certificates of quality by institutions such as the CBT.

Pirrong argues that the differences in the storage and distribution
methods in the United States compared to other producer nations
determined why wheat from the United States was graded at source compared to wheat imported from other locations, which was graded in the
United Kingdom.[133] The elevator-based storage system that developed
in America in the latter half of the nineteenth century enabled systematic
grading and, in fact, required it. The grain (wheat) was graded at the
point when the farmer brought it for storage at the shipping point. The
elevator agent, upon examining the quality of the grain, settled with the
farmer both the grade of the grain and its value. This grain was stored
in the elevator along with grain of similar quality, thus segregating the
identity of the grain parcels from that of the individual sellers. The seller
(farmer) received value according to the lowest quality that the grain
could be graded into. This strengthened the incentives of those shipping
the grain to elevators to maintain quality before storage.[134] Once the
graded grain was loaded onto ships or railway cars for transport, it was
nearly impossible to mix grain of varying qualities. Such opportunism
problems and malpractice were possible prior to storage. The only dissipation of quality could occur due to damage caused by moisture and
poor storage conditions. The incentives to maintain quality prior to shipment were high, but not during the transportation of the already graded
grain. This problem was alleviated somewhat when the US government
began supplying moisture content certificates, which could then be used
to compare with the actual condition of the grain when it arrived at its
destination.[135]

---

[131] Forrester, 'Commodity exchanges', p. 203.
[132] Minute books of the LCTA, Guildhall Library.
[133] Pirrong, 'Commodity exchanges'. J. Stewart, 'Marketing wheat', *Annals of the American
Academy of Political and Social Science* 107 (1923): pp. 187–88. Merrill, 'Grain grades',
p. 66.
[134] Pirrong, 'Commodity exchanges', p. 237. Stewart, 'Marketing wheat', pp. 187–88.
[135] Pirrong, 'Commodity exchanges', p. 237. Merrill, 'Grain grades', p. 66.

In contrast, handling facilities for grain imported from other countries such as Argentina and Australia were extremely crude. Crude handling methods exposed the grain to varying weather and insect conditions, and the absence of elevators meant that it was most efficient to ship grain in bags. This made it virtually impossible to create parcels of grain of standardised grades by combining grain from individual growers prior to shipment, as was possible in the elevator-based storage of North America. Furthermore, with individual shipments retaining their identity, inspecting quality at the importing country economised on the number of measurements necessary along such a trade route. There were few incentives to prevent dissipation of quality prior to bagging and storage. But all things being equal, this system would have given the shipper an incentive to take care of the cargo at sea.[136] In such practices, quality could not be guaranteed prior to shipment. The FAQ system, an ex post method of grading, was particularly suited in these instances. It adjusted standards to reflect systematic factors affecting the quality of grain from a particular location (level of quality due to grain composition as well as condition due to storage, transport, handling etc.) and made fewer quality distinctions between different shipments. The method minimised the number of potential disputes regarding product quality.[137] In effect, the market developed different measurement protocols for different trade routes.

The LCTA and US (primarily CBT) grades were fundamentally different. The FAQ method that the LCTA used effectively produced ranked categories. The description of quality tended to change according to the season, the year and the actual cargoes of grain. This was very different from the grading systems that emerged in the United States, pioneered by the CBT in Illinois and emulated by other wheat-growing states. The US grades were intended to be fixed standards, with descriptions of grain attributes that were unvarying. On this basis, the grain inspectors could issue an official certificate of inspection, guaranteeing the quality of a particular cargo.

For a long time, UK (London) buyers resisted and challenged the practice of US exporters to dispatch US wheat on the basis that inspection certificates were 'final as to quality'. A major objection was that inspection prior to shipment did not account for dissipation of quality due to moisture and poor storage conditions during shipment. Indeed, this was a major problem with transatlantic imports into the United Kingdom in

---

[136] This would also have depended upon the contract and shipping terms, i.e. who had the residual property rights on the cargo and who paid for insurance, freight etc.
[137] Pirrong, 'Commodity exchanges', pp. 238–39.

particular and European ports in general.[138] Consequently, the LCTA
would inspect and confirm US wheat grade quality, along with imports
of wheat from other foreign sources. Californian wheat, which was not
certified by inspection, was naturally graded by the LCTA, a practice still
common in the 1890s. Eventually, in 1898, the London and Liverpool
associations decided to accept the inspection certificates to be 'final as
to quality' and inserted clauses to that effect in the standard American
Cargo and Parcel Forms used by the LCTA members.[139] This acceptance was the result of continuing negotiations between the LCTA and the
US commodity exchanges. The moisture content certificates that were
issued also helped to make the inspection certificates acceptable to the
UK and European buyers.

 Also, dispute resolution by arbitration became widespread in the latter half of the nineteenth century, as the corn trade associations set up
transparent resolution mechanisms. Merchants preferred arbitration to
adjudication to settle the several disputes, mostly regarding the quality
and condition of grain.[140] Often the arbitrators appointed by the LCTA
in case of disputes would include millers in addition to merchants and
corn factors, ensuring that buyers as well as sellers were represented in
the process. At times, NABIM was also involved in the process for setting
grades and often made suggestions to the LCTA on quality standards.[141]
In this way, the exchanges functioned as quality assurance and dispute
resolution centres apart from aiding in the assessment and measurement
of quality. The centralising authority of the LCTA, the governance structures it instituted and the dispute resolution mechanisms it developed
were crucial in coordinating the vastly increased trade volumes and the
greater heterogeneity of wheat varieties reaching UK markets by the end
of the nineteenth century.

 Grading definitely enabled the alienation of the produce from the
producer's identity. Indeed, futures trading of wheat and other grain
developed on the basis of systematic and centralised grading. It mattered
less for futures trading that US grades were not universally accepted by
the British trade as 'final as to quality'. Similarly, it mattered less that
LCTA grades, based on the FAQ method, could change slightly from

---

[138] Merrill, 'Grain grades', pp. 65–66. Merrill was president of the CBT at the time he
wrote this article. See also Hill, *Grain, grades and standards*, pp. 25–27. M. Rothstein,
'Centralizing firms and spreading markets: the world of international grain traders,
1846–1914', *Business and Economic History* 17 (1988): p. 107.
[139] MS23177, 1 January 1891. Also MS23175. See suggested alteration of Contract Forms
1898 proposed by the Liverpool Corn Trade Association on 8 November 1897.
[140] Ferguson, 'Commercial disputes', p. 145. Chattaway, 'Arbitration'.
[141] MS 23175. See entry for 1896.

year to year. Any potential increase in the measurement and monitoring costs was balanced by the trade's ability to reduce risk by hedging. Thus grading of wheat grains, and the changes in the measurement practices that it required, enabled alienation by delinking residual rights in the commodity from its physical possession or origin and in turn made it possible for markets to limit transactions costs by developing futures trading and managing risk.

Apart from institutions, technological changes too made alienation of the commodity possible by delinking the delivery and unloading processes (at the ports) from the quality measurement process. This made centralisation of quality measurements and grading technically feasible. Consider the method of measuring the natural weight of wheat to ascertain grain quality. Determining the natural weight required measuring the same stock of grain twice, once in terms of volumetric units and again in terms of its weight. For a bulky commodity like wheat, this implied a considerable increase of effort and time at the importing ports where grain from coastwise routes as well as foreign grain was unloaded. Towards the beginning of the nineteenth century, grain transported on ships would usually be put into sacks to ease its removal from the ship's hold and also during delivery on the wharves. This process involved using the bushel (or some other volumetric) measure, as each sack was expected to hold a specific capacity; for example, the sacks in Liverpool would usually contain four *bushels* each.[142] If grain had to be weighed, it was done once it was sacked and hoisted onto the deck. Each sack, or a sample of sacks, would then be weighed using scales to arrive at natural weight measurements.[143]

Changes in the transport and discharging technology in the latter half of the nineteenth century altered this unloading process. The sacking process in UK ports could partly be eliminated when foreign grain began arriving in sacks. Grain from India and Australia would be packed in twill bags and could support repeated handling and did not require rebagging at British ports. But grain arriving from Argentina and the Pacific coast of North America often had to be rebagged.[144] The introduction of pneumatic elevators in the 1890s further made the sacking process redundant.

<hr />

[142] Once Liverpool switched to weight-only measurements c. 1860, sacks would normally be the equivalent of 280 pounds each, a unit preferred by the baking trade; Dumbell, 'Corn sales', p. 142. G. J. S. Broomhall and J. H. Hubback, *Corn trade memories: recent and remote* (Liverpool, Northern, 1930), p. 24.

[143] PP Vol. VII 1834, pp. xix–xx.

[144] B. Cunningham, *Cargo handling at ports: a survey of the various systems in vogue, with a consideration of their respective merits* (London, Chapman and Hall, 1923), pp. 4–5.

Grain could be vacuumed from the ship's hold and poured onto scales for weighing, from where it would eventually be discharged out of the ship.[145] At the end of the nineteenth century, foreign grain was mostly sold using weight-only measurements.[146]

Another important technical development that helped to separate the delivery–unloading and quality testing processes was the introduction of instruments that could measure the density of grain directly such as the chondrometer or *grain tester*. This portable mechanical device helped to reduce measurement costs by directly measuring the specific gravity of grain using a steelyard of unequal arms and a copper or brass container of known density.[147] The appeal of such an instrument was that the density of grain could be estimated without measuring grain twice – at first its volume and then its weight. The major drawback of such an instrument was that it could only determine the specific gravity of small samples of 'not more than half a pint'. However, when these instruments were used in conjunction with grain hoppers, this drawback of testing small quantities could be overcome.[148] In this manner, in the latter half of the nineteenth century, it became possible to separate the process of grain delivery–unloading from the process of quality assessment.

In this way, measurements of the wheat's compositional quality, that is, its density, were no longer technically interrelated with measurements of quantity, that is, the amount of grain exchanged. Quality measurements used in the grades did not have to be physically made during the time of delivery and unloading. This made the FAQ system of grading practically feasible and resulted in less overall costs of measurement and unloading. Diminution of the interrelatedness thus influenced significant changes in the measurement activity: it changed the protocols in terms of who measured what and at what stage of the commercial process.

The professionalisation of the milling industry also influenced the measurement activity to a great extent. Changes in milling technology, science (primarily in chemistry) and education also influenced quality measurement practices. Scientific study of the wheat grain and the nutritive value of its different parts focused on understanding the

---

[145] H. V. Driel and J. Schot, 'Radical innovation as a multilevel process: introducing floating grain elevators in the Port of Rotterdam', *Technology and Culture* 46 (2005): p. 63. Prior to the use of such pneumatic elevators, bucket elevators were used in places such as Glasgow. Cunningham, *Cargo handling*. PP Vol. VII 1834, p. xx. However, only once the pneumatic elevators became widespread could large volumes of grain be discharged effectively in much less time.

[146] PP Vol. XI 1893–1894, p. iii.

[147] PP Vol. XII 1890–1891, *Report of Select Committee on Corn Sales*, pp. 53–54.

[148] PP Vol. XII 1890–1891, pp. 54–56.

chemical and physical properties of its proteins, especially gluten.[149] An increased understanding of the chemistry of wheat and advances in testing increased the sophistication of quality assessment techniques in comparison with the relatively crude and unreliable estimation of quality using natural weight measurements. This was accompanied by an increased effort to educate millers in the science of milling. The NABIM organised meetings, presentations, symposia, technical classes and so on to increase the awareness of these methods and further the practical requirements of retraining mill staff.[150] The millers had begun to use the terminology of the grades. Nevertheless, they could independently test for quality, guided both by experience as well as the new science of milling and bread making.

The development of third-party grades, separation of handling and quality measurement processes and the sophistication of quality testing by buyers were significant changes. The complexities involved in the quality assessment and control were managed through the involvement of third-party organisations. This was a form of coordination that the market adopted to make the monitoring and guaranteeing of quality more manageable and effective. Third-party coordination of measurements of multiple product attributes involved changes to many different aspects of the measurement activity: instruments, standards, protocols and so on. Also, different groups developed methods to capture different aspects of the product's quality, be it compositional, conditional or functional aspects. There was no *single or uniform* way of capturing information about the product's quality, and this was reflected in the different measurement practices by the millers (buyers) and the trade (sellers). There were differences in practices between different groups of traders: US sellers versus other grain-exporting countries, domestic versus importing merchants and so on. The British markets did not use standardised practices as far as quality measurements were concerned. The attributes measured, the standards used, the measuring instruments and the measurement protocols all varied according to the trade routes. This is not to imply that standardisation was unsuccessful. On the contrary, we detect an increase in the use of many different kinds of standards (product grades, instruments, metrological units etc.). The institutional development of international commodity grading made it possible to employ several standards suited for highly specialised purposes, according to the specific context.

---

[149] H. Chick, 'Wheat and bread: a historical introduction', *Proceedings of the Nutrition Society* (1957): p. 3. Jago and Jago, *Breadmaking*, pp. 272–73 and 369–70.
[150] Jones, *Millers*, pp. 150–56. Tann and Jones, 'Roller milling', p. 68.

Conclusions

This case study shows that the quest for a standardised and internationally acceptable set of search attributes resulted in the centralisation of quality measurements in the form of commodity grades developed by trade exchanges. The centralised form of quality measurement and assurance replaced the traditional, decentralised and de facto market standards employed in the domestic UK trade. It is tempting to interpret this example of standardisation as the provision of public goods. There is no compelling evidence that grading in the United Kingdom was motivated by the failure by markets to set standards. However, grading did prevent costly and duplicative measurements along a globalising value chain. The state was involved at various stages during the nineteenth century in regulating various standards used in the sale of wheat (e.g. the sale by weight or volume, the legislation of the cental as a unit of measure). Ultimately, meso-level institutions, such as the industry associations and commodity exchanges developed privately set public goods in the form of standards and measurement practices. The standards (commodity grades) did not have the force of legislation to enforce them in the United Kingdom and were only voluntarily adopted.

The second important point that the case study raises is the role that measurements play in ensuring the *fungibility* of a commodity, that is, the characteristic of being mutually interchangeable. Fungibility ensures that a sample (of wheat or any other commodity) is held to be identical to another sample (of the same variety) and is therefore mutually interchangeable. This case shows that fungibility was an institutional construct rather than a technical attribute of the commodity. The commodity had to be made easily describable so that it became fungible and tradable; it was not universally or easily describable to begin with. To contemporary neo-classical economists, such as Marshall, the extent to which a commodity could be traded depended upon the ability to describe it completely and in known terms.[151] The analysis of quality measurements and grading shows that the fungibility of various varieties of wheat depended upon its alienation (from the producer's identity) rather than its homogeneity – that is, a high degree of sameness of the produce. Centralised grading made alienation possible by delinking residual rights from their physical possession. Changing measurement practices

---

[151] Marshall had argued that commodities such as wheat could be traded over large distances because they could be easily and exactly described. A. Marshall, *Principles of economics* (London, Macmillan, 1891), book V, chapter 1, p. 285.

made centralised grading feasible by delinking quality assessment from physical possession.

The third important point that emerges from the case study is how different groups along the value chain develop different summary criteria to make measurements. The merchants in the United States developed their own summary criteria to reflect the measurement issues typical to that context. The UK trade developed a similar but different set of criteria, which varied according to the trade route. Each set of criteria reflected the vagaries and measurement issues in different trading contexts. The downstream millers and upstream farmers (in the United Kingdom) had their own different summary criteria that they preferred to measure. Measurement according to different criteria required different measurement tools (instruments, protocols and standards) as well as different rules to contextualise those measurements. In short, the various business groups were using different measurement practices. Institutions made it possible to coordinate the measurements made using different summary criteria. This aspect may be one of the ties that bind such global value chains in the absense of direct ownership. Adoption of similar practices and the acceptance of measurements made using different practices was very likely one of the key conditions for the globalisation of this value chain.[152]

---

[152] G. Gereffi, 'The organization of buyer-driven global commodity chains: how US retailers shape overseas production networks', in G. Gereffi and M. Korzeniewicz (eds) *Commodity chains and global capitalism* (Westport, Praeger, 1994). G. Gereffi et al., 'The governance of global value chains', *Review of International Political Economy* 12 No 1 (2005).

7   'Man is the measure of all things'

Conclusions and Implications

> Do the things differ as the names differ? And are they relative to individuals, as Protagoras tells us? For he says that man is the measure of all things, and that things are to me as they appear to me, and that they are to you as they appear to you. Do you agree with him, or would you say that things have a permanent essence of their own?
>
> – Plato, *Cratylus*

The kaleidoscopic measurement practices explored here illustrate how measurements in the nineteenth century continued to be *anthropocentric*, even as measurement units became devoid of human form, activities and occupations. Practices and conventions continued to be based on human relations, values and ideals. Ironically, this made them natural in one sense, although metrological realism of the post-Enlightenment period equated naturalness with the absence of human values, ideals and relations. The case studies illuminate the tensions between the persistence of various human conventions and the values of precision championed by abstract metrological systems. They show why markets and businesses continued to encounter fundamental issues of measurements throughout the nineteenth century, despite metrological standardisation. They reveal how solutions to these issues were sought at the microlevel.

Britain's particular model of industrialisation meant that many businesses in the nineteenth century grappled with the problems of making things the same as values of interchangeability and fungibility (to mean substitutability) became important in trade and industry. Standardisation was necessary to achieve sameness, be it defined in terms of consistency across samples of the same product over time and space (e.g. coal or wheat) or in terms of uniformity within a given sample (e.g. wire of a given size). The sameness of a product had to be reconciled with its distinctiveness from other similar products. Buyers and sellers sought the ability to establish what a commodity *was* and *was not*; they had to be sure that a No 33 size wire was not a No 35 size wire. The sameness–distinctiveness tensions amplified as transactions and the sheer number of products offered in the market grew exponentially – in terms of both *scale* and *scope*.

Commodity exchanges, industry associations and other economic institutions helped businesses to describe tens or hundreds of physically similar – and yet economically distinct – products.[1] The sameness–distinctiveness tensions were alleviated not entirely through abstract or scientific methods of classification but also through material politics of the commodity and market relations. The reconfiguration of the local measurement practices was not driven exclusively by ideals of metrological realism – by advances in precision instrumentation and technology, error reduction sampling methods and so on. Such ideals, encapsulated in the centralisation of metrology and the emergence of metrological centres, did indeed have an important role in making measurements of coal, wire and grain considerably more reliable. However, the sociopolitical solutions to many of the sameness–distinctiveness tensions suggest that a large degree of conventional realism was also driving the reconfiguration of local practices. Merchants, traders, buyers, consumers, business firms and so on rarely subscribed to a universal true value of measurements to classify commodities such as wire or wheat. Alongside precise measurements, groups jostled with one another to have their version of the true value accepted as the standard. Accuracy in such cases, as Marcel Boumans has suggested, had a qualitative (i.e. subjective) origin and not a quantitative (i.e. objective) one.[2]

Whatever its pedigree may be, accuracy of measurements for complex commodities, such as wheat or coal, was often dependent upon the measurement of summary criteria.[3] Selection of summary criteria was itself the product of conventions and institutions (Chapter 6). In such cases,

---

[1] The Railway Clearing House understood the magnitude of the sameness–distinctiveness issue as it revised its General Classification of Goods in 1880s. It had to distinguish and describe over four thousand items in a two-hundred-page document. P. S. Bagwell, *The Railway Clearing House in the British economy 1842–1922* (London, Allen and Unwin, 1968). J. Mavor, 'The English railway rate question', *Quarterly Journal of Economics* 8 No 3 (1894). Utility companies had to distinguish between different levels of consumption (and consumers) for an intangible product – a distinction that was highly sensitive to the measurement practices. M. J. Daunton, 'The material politics of natural monopoly: consuming gas in Victorian Britain', in M. J. Daunton and M. Hilton (eds) *The politics of consumption: material culture and citizenship in Europe and America* (Oxford, Berg, 2001). Presently, telecom companies and broadband service providers face similar problems of distinguishing between different levels of consumption based upon measurements of usage.

[2] M. Boumans (ed.), *Measurement in economics: a handbook* (London, Elsevier, 2007), p. 15.

[3] S. Ponte and P. Gibbon, 'Quality standards, conventions and the governance of global value chains', *Economy and Society* 34 No 1 (2005). B. Daviron, 'Small farm production and the standardization of tropical products', *Journal of Agrarian Change* 2 No 2 (2002).

reliability of measurements – and consequently, the reliability of the classification schemes promoted by the exchanges, associations and so on – was dependent upon the entire package of measurement practices, not only the precision of individual measurements. Accurate classification of products was a lubricant that drove the engine of market integration, value-chain internationalisation and the interchangeable system of manufacturing in nineteenth-century Britain. One cannot overemphasise the importance of local measurement practices in this context.

Naturally, businesses and merchants did not have the lofty goals of market integration when they sought to reconfigure measurement practices. They had more practical motivations such as improving coordination of exchanges and transactions and preventing opportunism by others. The constant manoeuvring by each group to have its preferred measurement methods adopted as standardised practice was intended to detect and defend the group from fraud and bad bargains, while securing maximum economic benefit from transactions. Metrological standardisation and the entire gamut of the weights and measures legislation certainly made it easier to detect fraud. Nevertheless, merchants and buyers had to remain vigilant against fraudulent practices, not just tampered or incorrect instruments. The colourful instances of fraud perpetuated in the measurement of coal (Chapter 4) stand in contrast with those encountered in the measurement of wire sizes (Chapter 5). Due diligence by the purchaser could not be substituted by metrological standardisation or weights and measures legislation. Caveat emptor was applicable where measurements could be easily and precisely made, as in the case of coal and wire, but this principle could only work as long as the measurement practices were transparent and reliable. Where measurements remained opaque, or where the measured attributes were not evident to the buyer, third-party guarantees had to be invoked, as in the case of measurements of wheat quality.

If individual freedom of contract did increase during this period, as Atiyah claimed,[4] accompanied by the rise of legal formalism, it was also accompanied by changes in local practices that made mensuration a more reliable process. Reliable mensuration processes meant better due diligence, which in turn made for an effective deterrent to opportunism. In the language of economics, reliable mensuration processes diminished the need to resort to costly ex post mechanisms such as arbitration, adjudication or litigation. The moral thermometer of 'fair' measurements, where some authority ensured this fairness, was replaced by institutionally acceptable business practices.

---

[4] P. S. Atiyah, *The rise and fall of freedom of contract* (Oxford, Clarendon Press, 1979).

Changing existing measurement practices, many of them centuries old, required lobbying, negotiation, cooperation and, at times, coercion. Often new institutions had to be developed, while existing institutions were altered, to accommodate these changes. This is captured in the events surrounding the centralised grading systems for imported wheat or the abolition of the public metage system in the London coal trade. Heaped measurements, for example, which had been acceptable for several hundred years in British markets, and which inevitably were the source of opportunistic behaviour, required intense lobbying, political manoeuvring and several parliamentary acts to abolish; even then it persisted in many parts of the country throughout the nineteenth century. Centralised grading and measurements, which made integration of transatlantic markets possible, required agreements between trade associations and commodity exchanges. Accepting standards set by other institutions, in the case of the wheat trade, took nearly fifty years.

Institutional changes were born through the politics of the market, which weighed the economic logic against the political power of the various business groups.[5] The ability of certain groups to move the state machinery more than other rival groups, thus shaping the changes to the measurement practices that they favoured, is starkly evident. The lobbying power of coal merchants and wire manufacturers, and the consequent state participation in reconfiguring local practices, is an attestation of how porous the boundary actually was between state and market action. These considerations transcended the centre's need to enchain local activities to its metrological aspirations of uniformity, predictability and traceability. They were not reason for the state to become involved in reconfiguring local measurement practices, though the state did so when it felt its involvement was necessary, and only to the extent to which intervention was considered necessary. In the case of grain markets, the state, after circa 1860, resisted attempts to be drawn into introducing legislation that favoured any one measurement practice over another (e.g. sale of wheat by weight as opposed to by volume). The state solved the measurement problems that it faced concerning corn returns rhetorically by arbitrarily fixing a density measurement – a bureaucratic procedure that was largely divorced from the various local market practices.

Many of the measurement standards that resulted from such episodes were what Henson and Humphrey term *public voluntary standards*,

---

[5] M. J. Daunton and M. Hilton (eds), *The politics of consumption: material culture and citizenship in Europe and America* (Oxford, Berg, 2001). T. L. Alborn, *Conceiving companies: joint-stock politics in Victorian England* (London, Routledge, 1998). P. Johnson, 'Market disciplines', in P. Mandler (ed.) *Liberty and authority in Victorian Britain* (Oxford, Oxford University Press, 2006).

although private businesses and merchants initiated them.[6] The public nature of these standards, some of them with legal backing, was on occasion crucial in preventing opportunistic behaviour, as in the case of coal or wire. However, the nonobligatory nature of some of these standards, making them voluntary in adoption, meant that businesses had the flexibility to alter product quality, design or specifications as they considered appropriate. No one was obligated to use only specific measurement practices to measure, say, wire sizes or wheat grades in their contracts; however, most voluntarily did so. Brunsson and Jacobsson term such privately set but legally mandated standards *optional laws*.[7]

In Chapter 1, I drew a distinction between the science of metrology and the practice of mensuration. Metrology represents the system of weights and measures and the infrastructure that surrounds this system, including the structures, organisations and people who are involved in maintaining this system. In this regard, metrology is the infratechnology that a society develops.[8] Mensuration, in contrast, represents the act of making measurements and obtaining information from these measurements. The case studies on mensuration within the commercial sectors of the British economy in this book show that the study of local practices is crucial in understanding how businesses sought solutions to measurement issues and what those localised solutions were. Nineteenth-century metrological centralisation and standardisation were only part of the solution, as far as commercial measurements were concerned. As Bruce Curtis argues, social codes (i.e. regulations) should not be understood as *unitary* expressions of social practices that relate to those codes.[9] Understanding how various groups took up the metrological codes and translated them into reliable practices must become an indelible part of economic history of markets in the nineteenth century.

This leads to the second distinction that I introduced in Chapter 1 – that between the two types of measurement problems that historical markets faced. The one on which much of the literature on British history

---

[6] S. Henson and J. Humphrey, 'Understanding the complexities of private standards in global agri-food chains', paper presented at the International Workshop on Globalization, Global Governance and Private Standards, Leuven (2008).

[7] N. Brunsson and B. Jacobsson, 'The contemporary expansion of standardisation', in N. Brunsson and B. Jacobsson (eds) *A world of standards* (Oxford, Oxford University Press, 2000).

[8] P. Temple and G. Williams, 'Infra-technology and economic performance: evidence from the United Kingdom measurement infrastructure', *Information Economics and Policy* 14 (2002). G. Tassey, 'The role of government in supporting measurement standards for high-technology industries', *Research Policy* 11 (1982). R. D. Huntoon, 'Concept of a national measurement system', *Science* 158 No 3797 (1967).

[9] B. Curtis, 'From the moral thermometer to money: metrological reform in pre-confederation Canada', *Social Studies of Science* 28 No 4 (1998): p. 567.

focuses is the absence of a unified metrology prior to the nineteenth century. Markets faced measurement problems due to the lack of a uniform
metrology, that is, the presence of diverse measurement units that were
largely local in origin and use. The other source of measurement problems, the one that much of the historical literature has so far ignored,
arose due to the institutional constraints of selecting a finite set of attributes to measure from amongst a virtually limitless number of possible
attributes. Making measurements, particularly economic measurements,
is not simply a way of abstracting information that is out there with
a very precise instrument. They require agreement on attributes to be
measured, instruments to be used and the meaning of the observations
within a given context.[10]

The case studies show that while metrological standardisation addressed the first historical measurement problem, the solution to the
second institutional problem required changes to local practices. Such
practices were embedded within the context of the historical micromar-
kets. Firms and other business groups struggled to develop practices that
were relevant to their particular contexts. Standardising measurement
practices was a context-specific process, in contrast to conforming to
an abstract ideal that metrological standardisation sought to achieve. I
submit that in the process, merchants and businesses addressed some of
the fundamental problems of economic exchange that they encountered
during the nineteenth century; problems of defining the commodity, of
detecting fraud and opportunism (monitoring), of manufacturing interchangeable parts, of trading fungible commodities and so on. Measurement practices and market transactions are inextricably linked in an
historical and institutional sense.

Historical (re)interpretation

It is possible to interpret the rich historical material presented here in
several ways. I offer the following interpretation. Pre-nineteenth-century
markets generally relied upon decentralised, highly contextual and thus
numerous local measurement units. Many of these units had legal sanction, although they were relevant only in the context of the localised
measurement practices in which they were used. The diversity of measurement units, along with localised practices, *potentially* created barriers

[10] J. Searle, *The construction of social reality* (London, Allen Lane, 1995). Searle makes a
distinction between 'brute facts' and 'institutional facts' (p. 2). According to him, an
institutional fact is considered a fact because we all have agreed to do so. This is an
essential difference between scientific facts (such as the distance from the earth to the
sun) and economic facts (such as the price of a commodity in terms of money).

to trade and movement of goods between different markets and regions. Information anomalies created uncertainties, compounded agency problems and complicated internal trade. Business groups (firms, merchants, entrepreneurs etc.) dealt with such uncertainties and imperfections by developing highly specific measurement practices along established trade routes. In this way, markets were able to alleviate the disruptive influence of contextual measurement units.

At the beginning of the nineteenth century, a centralised, decontextualised system of weights and measures was introduced in Western Europe, particularly in Britain. This gradually replaced the numerous local measurement units and potentially created an environment in which measurements could be made reliably, irrespective of the context in which they were made or used. This solved the historical measurement problem. However, businesses continued to grapple with several institutional issues, for example, who was ultimately responsible for making the measurements, what properties or attributes should be measured, what instruments or tools should be used, who could guarantee these measurements and so on. Decontextualisation of the measurement units may have even compounded such institutional issues by delinking the context from the measurement units. The act of measuring continued to be context driven, despite metrological reform. With measurement units no longer lending the context, the older measurement practices – which had helped to overcome the institutional issues – had to be reformed or altered. At the same time, most businesses found themselves operating within an environment that was rapidly reshaped by the industrialisation process. The economic, social and political changes accompanying industrialisation created other transactional issues, for which it was necessary to have reliable measurements – both of the commodity and of the transactions involving the commodity. Notwithstanding the reasons, the changing economic context required a redefinition of traditional relationships and existing practices.

The impetus for changing measurement practices came largely from the merchants and businesses and rarely from the state. The motivation for change was economic; however, the process of change was steeped in the micropolitics of the industry, the commodity or the region. Involved in this process were diverse groups such as merchants and businesses; industry and trade associations; producers and buyers; local governments and central state agencies; politicians, parliaments and bureaucrats; scientists, engineers and entrepreneurs and so on. Powerful interests vied with each other, often clashing openly and lobbying for legal sanction to ensure that the standards that were established and practices that became dominant would further their own economic interests. These struggles were parallel to, and independent of, the heated metrological debates between circa 1860 and 1880 that were occurring at the centre. The arena for the 'battle of the standards' – the Imperial versus the metric systems – was quite distinct from the localised debates involving such questions as the adoption of one standard size over another or the use of weight measures or measures of volume. The politically charged arguments for or against metrication – which continued until recent years, symbolised by the so-called metric martyrs – did not, and could not, resolve all the measurement problems that businesses faced in the nineteenth century.[11]

Implications

What are the implications of this research? The most evident implication is that there need not be an unambiguous or straightforward way in which superior practices or standards replace inferior practices or standards. In other words, there may be limitations to analysing changes to market practices in a systematic manner in which the system will tend to forget its history and/or converge towards some steady state or equilibrium. Path dependency need not diminish with the passage of time. If we replace the terms *superior* and *inferior* with *efficient* and *inefficient*, respectively, then the implication becomes still more profound. We are left with historical events where efficient practices (or standards) do not replace inefficient practices (or standards) in a straightforward or guaranteed manner. The practices or standards that emerged in the nineteenth-century markets – whether efficient or inefficient – persisted subsequently because they worked well with other practices or standards. They became part and parcel of an institutional bundle that most groups found acceptable and that allowed the markets to function.

These observations are not at odds with the self-interest hypothesis that Adam Smith and his nineteenth-century successors held. According to classical economists and several early Victorian thinkers, individuals were driven by economic self-interest, which in turn encouraged market activity. This does not imply that markets became more efficient as a result of increased activity. The economic institutions and public goods such as standards that supported this increased market activity were equally likely to have been *in*-efficiency reinforcing, not only efficiency

---

[11] E. F. Cox, 'The metric system: a quarter-century of acceptance (1851–1876)', *Osiris* 13 (1958). M. Spiering, 'The Imperial system of weights and measures: traditional, superior and banned by Europe?' *Contemporary British History* 15 No 4 (2001).

promoting. Markets could fail the efficiency test even when they worked to promote individual self-interest.

Nineteenth-century markets often failed the efficiency test. The confusing array of measurement units used in the London coal trade was certainly not efficiency promoting. Neither was the diversity of measurement units in the coal-producing pits eliminated as a result of reform at the London end of the trade route. But there is no evidence that trade was disrupted entirely as a result, and diversity did not act as an impediment to the trade's expansion. As they had over the previous four centuries, nineteenth-century coal markets expanded substantially, even though transactions continued to be highly inefficient. Similarly, the market transactions in wire would fail the efficiency test not because of taxes or government intervention. In fact, the efficiency-promoting, compatible and uniform standards required state intervention. Johnson and other historians present other examples in which Victorian markets failed and had to be disciplined in similar ways.[12] My research contributes towards overturning the myths of efficient and free markets of the nineteenth century.

This leads to the second implication of my research, that is, the provision of public goods to mitigate the market's failures or excesses. Historians of the modern British state show how the boundary between laissez-faire and state intervention was porous and constantly renegotiated.[13] While the state intervened in the form of laws, arbitration and so on, the cases in this book show the importance of meso-level institutions – industry associations, trade bodies, scientific societies – to provide public goods in the form of standards. Such privately formed public goods, voluntarily adopted, provided a more measured alternative to regulation and control of markets. They functioned like instruments of coordination, not control. The state was involved, perhaps tacitly, in letting such private–public goods emerge. The Victorian state may not have been entirely laissez-faire, but it certainly was not a disciplinarian. Its participation in the market was that of an arbitrator or a stakeholder.

But just how independent was it as an arbitrator? When arbitrating between the interests of consumers versus the producers, it would certainly be sympathetic to their grievances, as is discernible in the case

---

[12] Daunton and Hilton, *Politics of consumption*. Alborn, *Conceiving companies*. Johnson, 'Market disciplines'.

[13] P. Harling, 'The powers of the Victorian state', in P. Mandler (ed.) *Liberty and authority in Victorian Britain* (Oxford, Oxford University Press, 2006). M. J. Daunton, *Progress and poverty: an economic and social history of Britain 1700–1850* (Oxford, Oxford University Press, 1995). W. J. Ashworth, *Customs and excise: trade, production, and consumption in England, 1640–1845* (Oxford, Oxford University Press, 2003).

of the measurements in the London coal trade.[14] But it is difficult to ignore that the state – or rather, the officials representing the state – often had strong ties with several sections of trade and industry. Joseph Chamberlain, as president of the Board of Trade, is unlikely to have been totally unsympathetic to particular producers in the wire industry, many of whom were his colleagues in his erstwhile political and business career in Birmingham. Similarly, major reforms of the coal tax in the 1820s and 1830s were mainly initiated by coal owners who were themselves powerful politicians. The view of the state as a disinterested arbitrator must be held with much caution.

The implication of all this is that networks of individuals mattered in shaping nineteenth-century markets and economic activity. The networks included scientists and engineers working with merchants and businesses as well as politicians and bureaucrats. The politics within and between these networks shaped practices, influenced negotiations and bargaining and generated solutions to problems at a practical level. Certainly this was the case with the reform of Britain's metrology. In comparison with the rest of Europe at the time, the manner in which the nation's metrology and commercial practices were reformed sets Britain apart. The reformers – an eclectic mix of career politicians, bureaucrats, engineers and scientists – were keen to preserve the propriety of local customs. The metrological centres were not all-powerful, and local practices were shaped by the intersection of networks and the interests they represented.

People changed the way they measured things and phenomena in the nineteenth century. The metrological tools that they could henceforth use also changed dramatically, despite the vestigial remains of older measurement units (e.g. the Winchester bushel). They became the same everywhere in Britain. Nevertheless, how people made their measurements reliable and trustworthy continued to be determined by their local contexts, not by the metrological centres.

---

[14] Daunton and Hilton, *Politics of consumption.*

Appendix 2.1: Milestones in the international acceptance of the metric system

1851	French Conservatoire des Arts et Metiers exhibits metric standards at the First International Exhibition in London. The exhibition also highlights the widespread metrological diversity in the industrialising nations of the time.
1853	British Society for the Encouragement of Arts, Commerce and Manufacturers declares that the introduction of decimal measures would be an important step for the United Kingdom's industry and commerce.
	International Statistical Conference in Brussels proposes to include metric equivalents of weights and measures in government statistics.
1855	Second International Exhibition held in Paris includes another exhibit by Conservatoire des Arts et Metiers of the metric standards. Judges strongly urge the adoption of universal measures based on the decimal scale.
	International Association for Obtaining a Uniform Decimal System of Measures, Weights and Coins (IA) is formed, with branches in fifteen countries, including Britain.
1859	IA becomes one of the first international organizations to actively promote the international acceptance of metric measures.
	British Branch of IA recommends the metric system for use in the United Kingdom.
	Ecuador, Venezuela, Mexico, Costa Rica and Guatemala adopt the metric system for official government usage.
1860	Fourth International Statistical Congress is held. Statisticians propose that all government statistics be expressed in metric units.
	Cobden–Chevalier Treaty between the United Kingdom and France is signed, boosting international trade and strengthening demands for universal measures based on the metric units.
1861	US Congress investigates the possibility of adopting decimal metric units, but the Civil War interrupts any further consideration of the issue.
	Italy adopts the metric units as part of its political unification, to be effective within a few years, and to replace the multitude of customary units used by the nation's former kingdoms and states.
	Numerous petitions by the IA to the House of Commons (HC) results in the formation of a parliamentary select committee to investigate conversion to the metric system in the United Kingdom.
1862	Latin American countries, including Brazil, Argentina and Chile, adopt metric measures.

(continued)

(continued)

1863	IA drafts a bill for introduction in the HC. The bill passes the vote despite Cabinet opposition, but it lapses as it does not pass to the Lords in that parliamentary session. The widespread international expectation is that Britain is likely to adopt the metric system eventually.
	International Postal Congress in Paris recommends use of the metric system for international postage purposes.
	Fifth International Statistical Congress in Paris urges metric units for obligatory use in nonmetric countries, in customs duties and for instruction in schools.
1864	Connecticut in the United States directs school officials to commence instruction of the metric system immediately in all public schools.
	British Parliament passes a bill for permissive use of the metric system in the country; however, use was not encouraged and remained unlawful in commercial contracts.
1866	After the end of the Civil War, a committee of scientists recommends the adoption of the metric system to the US Congress. The use of metric units becomes legal in all contracts in the United States.
1867	At the Fourth International Exhibition in Paris, IA urges nonmetric countries to introduce the study of metric measures in schools and their use in government publications, statistics, post offices, customs houses, public works etc.
	Sixth International Statistical Congress in Florence urges nonmetric countries to form national associations for the promotion of metric measures.
	International Geodetic Association in Berlin selects the metric system as a uniform system to initiate an international and scientific measurement of the figure and size of the earth. New metric standards are devised, and a permanent International Bureau of Weights and Measures (BIPM) is proposed.
1868	Legislature of newly founded North German Confederation introduces the obligatory use of the metric system in aid of its political unification. The Zolleverin had been using some metric-based units in the commercial sector since 1854.
	In Britain, the Royal Standards Commission (RSC) begins a comprehensive review of British weights and measures. Parliament considers and passes a bill to establish compulsory use of the metric system. However, delay in the commission's report results in withdrawal of the bill and ensures victory for the antimetric lobby.
1869	Second report of the RSC asserts that Britain is not ready for acceptance of the metric system but recommends introducing it in permissive form.
1870	French Bureau des Longitudes et Academie des Sciences and the Academy of Sciences of St Petersburg, Russia, support various resolutions of the International Geodetic Association to set up an international metrological organization. France invites the major nations of the world to send delegates to an international conference to meet in Paris. The first session of the Commission Internationale du Metre (CIDM) was attended by representatives of twenty-seven nations, including the United Kingdom and the United States. The Franco-Prussian War interrupts the work of CIDM until the end of the conflict.
1871	UK Parliament tries to secure compulsory adoption once again, but under Cabinet opposition, it loses the bill in the HC by a margin of five votes.

1873	CIDM reconvenes with delegates from twenty-nine nations. This organization confirms that the metric system would form the basis of an international system of weights and measures.
	BIPM is established as a permanent organization located in France. This organization is expected to coordinate research and international cooperation on metrology and related scientific fields.
1875	Convention du Mètre, an international treaty incorporating the recommendations of CIDM and ratifying the establishment of BIPM, is signed by seventeen nations initially, with Portugal and the United States following soon after.
1878	United Kingdom passes legislation that authorizes the use of metric weights and measures for all purposes, except for use in commercial contracts.
1879	US House Committee on Coinage, Weights and Measures delivers a strongly pro-metric report; however, no further legislative action is taken. The use of metric units remains permissive, not obligatory.
1897	Metric system is fully legalized in the United Kingdom, and its use in commercial contracts is finally permitted. Nevertheless, the use of these units remains permissive, not compulsory.
c. 1900	Nearly all European and Central and South American countries adopt the metric measures as the basis for their national metrological systems. Among the major industrial nations, Japan and Russia remain nonmetric by c. 1900, in addition to the United States and the United Kingdom.

Source: Table constructed by the author based on published material and other archival sources. See text for details.

Appendix 4.1: Analysis of local practices and measurement inconsistencies in the London coal trade

Heaped measures and the ingrain were the major sources of inconsistencies surrounding the quantity measured using the LCh, vat and bushel. Assuming that the measurer used the correct artefacts, the likely extent of variation can be derived as follows.

Suppose q_c to be the quantity delivered in LCh and q_v to be the quantity in vats. Then,

$$q_c = q' + q^h$$
$$q_c = 4q_v \quad \text{(by definition)},$$

where q' is the quantity measured by the internal dimensions of the measuring vessel and q^h is the quantity contained within the cone of the heap. Similarly, $q_v = q'_v + q^h_v$, where q'_v is the quantity contained within the vat and q^h_v is the quantity within the cone of the heap on top of the vat. Now suppose $q^h = 0.3q'$ and $q^h_v = 0.3q'_v$. Thus

$$q_c = q' + 0.3q' = 1.3q'$$
$$q_v = q'_v + 0.3q'_v = 1.3q'_v.$$

Suppose buyer A purchases twenty chaldrons from the seller, a shipowner. According to custom, the quantity that is actually delivered from the collier, including the ingrain, into the lighter is $Q_a = 21q_c = 21(4q_v) = 84q_v = 84(1.3\ q'_v) = 109.2\ q'_v$, that is, a quantity that is 109.2 times the volume measured by the dimensions of the vat.

If buyer B, another merchant, purchases five chaldrons from buyer A, the quantity that A should deliver to B is

$$Q_b = 5q_c + q_v,$$
$$Q_b = 5(4q_v) + q_v,$$
$$Q_b = 21q_v = 21(1.3q'_v), \quad \text{(by the ingrain given on twenty vats)}$$
$$Q_b = 27.3q'_v.$$

Thus the quantity that buyer B should receive is 27.3 times the volume measured by the dimensions of the vat measure, consistent with our earlier result above, that is, one-fourth part of 109.2 units that A purchased. However, A can deliver less than $27.3q'_v$ to B in three ways. One, the ingrain is withheld and a score of twenty vats is given instead of the expected twenty-one vats; two, the ingrain is given but the vat is measured stricken and not heaped; and three, the ingrain is withheld and the vat is measured stricken.

If the ingrain is withheld,

$$Q_b = 5q_c,$$
$$Q_b = 20q_v = 20(1.3q'_v),$$
$$Q_b = 26q'_v,$$

that is, about 5 per cent less than the required quantity. If the measure is stricken and not heaped,

$$Q_b = 5q_c + q_v$$
$$Q_b = 5(4q_v) + q_v = 21q_v,$$

but now $q_v = q'_v$, and so

$$Q_b = 21q'_v,$$

that is, 23 per cent less than the required quantity. If the measure is not heaped and the ingrain is withheld,

$$Q_b = 5q_c = 20q'_v,$$

that is, about 27 per cent less than the required quantity.

If we consider another scenario in which another buyer C purchases a quantity smaller than five chaldrons from A, in this case, no ingrain is to be provided, and the quantity to be delivered is then $Q_c = 4q_c = 4(4q_v) = 16q_v = 16(1.3q'_v) = 20.8q'_v$. If the seller then provides a stricken measure, the maximum amount of short measure that C will receive will be $16q'_v$ instead of $20.8q'_v$, that is, 23 per cent less.

Empirical evidence to confirm this is not easily available. However, instances of measurement fraud reported to the Parliamentary Select Committees in 1800 show that the extent of short measure could be as low as 5 per cent to as much as 33 per cent (see *Report on Coal Trade*, 1800, appendices 34 and 37). Table 4.1A.1 presents an illustration of the fraud reported. Thus, assuming that the proper physical artefacts were used to measure the quantity, the merchant sellers could and did provide a substantial short measure to the buyers.

Table 4.1A.1. *Reports of measurement fraud in London (c. 1800)*

Report no	Nominal quantity delivered			Shortfall detected			% Shortfall
	LCh	Bushels	Sacks	LCh	Bushels	Sacks	
1	5	180	60			7	12
2	5	180	60			7	12
3	20			1			5
4	5	180	60			7	12
5	20			1.5			8
6	5	180	60			12	20
7	10.5	378		1			10
8	10.5			1			10
9	7			2			29
10	5	180	60			7	12
11	1	36	12		6		17
12	1	36	12		6		17
13	20			4			20
16	10			1.5			15
17	20			1			5
19	5			1			20
21	2.5	90	30		30		33
22	2.5	90	30			7	23

Source: First report of the Committee on Coal Trade, PP Vol. X 1800, appendix 34.

Variability due to conversion

Variability in quantity as a result of conversion from weight to volume would have been of concern primarily to merchants who sold on the basis of weight (coal owners and shipmasters), if the variation tended to be mostly positive, and to merchants who purchased on the basis of volume (first buyers), if the variation tended to be mostly negative. The extent of variation due to the weight:volume conversion can be examined as follows.

Suppose q_n to be the quantity of coal measured using the NCh and q_l to be the quantity measured using the LCh. The relation between the two units is $q_l = rq_n$, where r is the ratio of conversion between the two units and varies between $0.47 < r < 0.53$.

Suppose q_n^i is the quantity in NCh of a particular type or quality of coal i and d_i is the density in weight per cubic capacity of coal of type i. Since q_n^i is measured in terms of weight, its volume equivalent can be expressed as q_n^i/d_i, that is, weight divided by the density giving volume in cubic capacity units. Expressing this volume quantity in terms of LCh units, we then have

$$q_l^i = r\left(q_n^i/d_i\right).$$

Table 4.1A.2. *Estimate of ratios used to convert quantities of coal from Newcastle chaldron to London chaldron*

Name of ship	Quantity in Newcastle chaldrons	Quantity in London chaldrons		Ratio of LCh:NCh
		Certified	Delivered	
Kate	107	220	225.75	2.06
Kate	108	216	228.75	2.00
Kate	108	216	225.50	2.00
Kate	108	216	229.75	2.00
Kate	107	216	237.50	2.02
Kate	108	216	231.00	2.00
Malta	120	240	270.75	2.00
Malta	114	224	247.75	1.96
Malta	116	232	246.00	2.00
Malta	116	230	248.50	1.98
Malta	116	232	249.75	2.00
Percy	132	272	286.25	2.06
Percy	132	272	288.00	2.06
Percy	132	272	285.75	2.06
Perseverance	85	176	190.00	2.07
Perseverance	85	176	172.75	2.07
Perseverance	85	174	186.00	2.05
Recovery	123	260	270.25	2.11
Recovery	125	256	276.25	2.05
Recovery	125	256	275.50	2.05
Recovery	126	256	269.30	2.03
Recovery	125	256	271.25	2.05

Note: All voyages are c. 1827–1829, carrying the variety known as Pelaw Main.
Source: PP Vol. VIII 1830, p. 12 and appendix 13.

An error term ε captures the extent of variation in r and d_i from some initial values, say, r' and d_i'. Thus

$$q_l^i = r'\left(q_n^i/d_i'\right) + \varepsilon.$$

The error term is composed of $\varepsilon = \varepsilon_r + \varepsilon_d$, where ε_r is the variation due to the changing conversion ratio and ε_d is the variation accounted for by the density of coal. The density term captures the variation due to the varying specific gravity as well as due to breakages during transportation. Under ideal circumstances, the average of these errors should be null or negligible, that is, $\bar{\varepsilon}_r = 0$. An analysis of twenty-two observations (summarized in Table 4.1A.2) suggests that the variation in quantity due to conversion, that is, ε_r was very small: a variation of 2 percentage points around the average ratio of 2:1 between the LCh and the NCh.

Table 4.1A.3. *Analysis of the difference between certified quantity and measured quantity of coal delivered from colliers in the Port of London (1827–1829)*

	Dataset 1	Dataset 2
No of ships	10	6
No of voyages	28	46
No of coal varieties	4	10
Max. variation by individual ship (%)	7	5
Min. variation by individual ship (%)	−5	−2
Total observed variation (%)	4	2

Source: PP Vol. VIII 1830, dataset 1 from appendix 13 and dataset 2 from p. 140.

To test if $\varepsilon_d = 0$ variation within the same voyage and across different voyages, controlling for initial quantity, the type of coal and the individual ship were examined. Data reported in appendix 13 and the evidence provided by James Bentley included in the select committee report on the coal trade (PP Vol. VIII, 1830), comprising twenty-eight and forty-six individual voyages, respectively, were analyzed. Table 4.1A.3 provides a summary of this analysis. The overall variation in the first set of twenty-eight voyages was 4 per cent and from the second set of forty-six voyages was 2 per cent. As the extent of uncertainty in quantities delivered due to conversion from weight to volume units was relatively modest, it is reasonable to expect the minor variations to be adjusted within the price mechanism, given a tightly controlled market by a small number of merchants.

Appendix 4.2: Financial details of the metage system operated by the city of London

	Sea meters			Land meters[a]		
	Revenue	Expenditure	Surplus	Revenue	Expenditure	Surplus/deficit
1810	18,754	6,174	12,580	4,222	4,167	55
1811	18,698	6,074	12,624	4,215	4,189	26
1812	18,015	6,079	11,936	3,936	4,023	−87
1813	16,280	5,579	10,701	3,512	3,911	−399
1814	19,062	6,476	12,586	4,017	3,934	83
1815	18,720	6,350	12,370	4,089	3,923	166
1816	20,356	6,765	13,591	4,313	3,890	423
1817	19,052	6,452	12,600	4,162	3,844	318
1818	20,146	6,697	13,449	4,183	3,836	347
1819	19,834	6,937	12,897	4,102	3,976	126
1820	21,987	7,144	14,843	4,539	4,246	293
1821	21,297	7,396	13,901	4,313	4,187	126
1822	21,020	7,818	13,202	4,083	4,191	−108
1823	23,954	8,059	15,895	4,398	4,246	152
1824	25,910	9,080	16,830	4,254	4,260	−6
1825	24,638	9,038	15,600	4,020	4,311	−291
1826	26,624	9,613	17,011	4,301	4,102	199
1827	24,367	9,108	15,259	4,779	4,540	239
1828	25,893	9,166	16,727	4,891	4,990	−99
1829	26,559	9,499	17,060	4,962	5,628	−666

Note: All figures are in pounds sterling.
[a] These accounts do not include the figures for land meters employed in Westminster and Surrey districts.
Source: PP Vol. VIII 1830, *Report of the select committee on coal trade*, appendices 8 and 10.

Appendix 5.1: Comparison of sizes of various wire gauges

Size	Stubs gauge[a]	BWG[a]	RG[a]	CSG[b]	SSG[b]	Variation as compared to the Stubs gauge (%)			
						BWG	RG	CSG	SSG
1	300	312.5	300		302.5	−4	−		−1
2	284	281	274		275.5	1	4		3
3	259	265	250		256.5	−2	3		1
4	238	234	229	246	236	2	4	−3	1
5	220	218	209	226	217	1	5	−3	1
6	203	203	191	198	207.5	−	6	2	−2
7	180	187	174	183	184.5	−4	3	−2	−3
8	165	171	159	175	167.5	−4	4	−6	−2
9	148	156.25	146	160	153	−6	1	32	−3
10	134	140	133	136	134	−4	1	−1	−
11	120	125	117	128	116.5	−4	2	−7	3
12	109	109	100	107	106.5	−	8	2	2
13	95	93	90	100	96.5	2	5	−5	−2
14	83	78.125	79	92	89	6	5	−11	−7
15	72	70	69	79	73	3	4	−10	−1
16	65	62	62	70	60.5	5	5	−8	7
17	58	54	53	63	54	7	9	−9	7
18	49	46	47	57	49.5	6	4	−16	−1
19	42	42	41	47	41.5	−	2	−12	1
20	35	38	36	42	39	−9	−3	−20	−11
21	32	34	31		34	−6	3		−6
22	28	31.25	28		28.5	−12	−		−2
23	25	28			26	−12			−4
24	22	25			23	−14			−5
25	20	22			19.5	−10			3
26	18	19			16.5	−6			8
27	16	17			15.5	−6			3
28	14	15.625			14.5	−12			−4
29	13	14.5			11	−12			15
30	12	13.5			10.5	−13			13

	Stubs					Variation as compared to the Stubs gauge (%)			
Size	gauge[a]	BWG[a]	RG[a]	CSG[b]	SSG[b]	BWG	RG	CSG	SSG
31	10	12.5			10	−25			−
32	9	11.5			9.5	−28			−6
33	8	10.5				−31			
34	7	9.5				−36			
35	5	8.5				−70			
36	4	7.5				−88			

Note: Sizes are expressed in one-thousandth of an inch. Abbreviations are as follows: BWG, Birmingham wire gauge; CSG, Cocker steel gauge; RG, Rylands gauge; SSG, South Staffordshire gauge.
[a] Extract from John Watkins, 'A comparison of numbers and sizes of the new legal standard wire gauge...', British Library MS 1881.c.3 fo. 10 (1881).
[b] Ironmonger, 'The Birmingham wire gauge: being a collection of better known versions...', British Library 1882.d.2 fo. 126 (1905).

Appendix 5.2: Comparison of the standard wire gauge with other proposed gauges

Gauge no	SWG (1,000th of an inch)	Differences across gauges (1,000th of an inch)		
		SWG and ACC	SWG and ISWMA	ACC and ISWMA
1	300	–	–	–
2	276	−0.4	0.6	10
3	252	−0.8	0.2	10
4	232	−0.8	0.2	10
5	212	−0.8	0.2	10
6	192	−0.8	0.2	10
7	176	−0.4	0.1	5
8	160	−0.4	–	4
9	144	−0.4	−0.1	3
10	128	−0.4	−0.2	2
11	116	−0.4	−0.1	3
12	104	−0.4	0.4	8
13	92	−0.4	0.2	6
14	80	−0.4	–	4
15	72	–	0.2	2
16	64	–	0.2	2
17	56	–	0.2	2
18	48	–	0.2	2
19	40	–	–	–
20	36	–	–	–
21	32	–	–	–
22	28	–	–	–
23	24	–	−0.10	−1
24	22	–	−0.10	−1
25	20	–	−0.10	−1
26	18	–	−0.10	−1
27	16.4	0.04	−0.06	−1
28	14.8	0.08	−0.12	−2
29	13.6	0.06	−0.14	−2
30	12.4	0.04	−0.16	−2

Gauge no	SWG (1,000th of an inch)	Differences across gauges (1,000th of an inch)		
		SWG and ACC	SWG and ISWMA	ACC and ISWMA
31	11.6	0.06	−0.14	−2
32	10.8	0.08	−0.12	−2
33	10	0.10	−0.10	−2
34	9.2	0.12	−0.08	−2
35	8.4	0.14	−0.06	−2
36	7.6	0.16	−0.04	−2
37	6.8	0.18	−0.02	−2
38	6.0	0.20	−0.05	−2.5
39	5.2	0.22	−0.08	−3
40	4.8	0.28	−0.07	−3.5

Note: The measurements, including the differences, are reported in one-thousandths of an inch. Abbreviations are as follows: ACC, Associated Chambers of Commerce; ISWMA, Iron and Steel Wire Manufacturers Association; SWG, standard wire gauge.

Sources: The SWG gauge of August 1833 is taken from the National Archives, BT 101/133; the ACC gauge of March 1882 is taken from BT 101/114; and the ISWMA gauge of July 1882 is taken from BT 101/116.

Bibliography

Adams, C. A., 'Industrial standardization', *Annals of the American Academy of Political and Social Science* 82 No 1 (1919): 289–99.

Adell, R., 'The British metrological standardization debate, 1756–1824: The importance of parliamentary sources in its reassessment', *Parliamentary History* 22 No 2 (2003): 165–82.

Aitken, W. C., 'Brass and brass manufactures', in S. Timmins (ed.), *The resources, products and industrial history of Birmingham and the Midland hardware district* (London, Robert Hardwicke, 1866).

Alborn, T. L., *Conceiving companies: joint-stock politics in Victorian England* (London, Routledge, 1998).

Alder, K., 'A revolution to measure: the political economy of the metric system in the ancien régime', in M. N. Wise (ed.), *The values of precision* (Princeton, Princeton University Press, 1995).

Alder, K., 'Innovation and amnesia: engineering rationality and the fate of interchangeable parts manufacturing in France', *Technology and Culture* 38 No 2 (1997): 273–311.

Alder, K., 'Making things the same: representation, tolerance and the end of the ancien régime in France', *Social Studies of Science* 28 No 4 (1998): 499–545.

Alder, K., *The measure of all things: the seven-year odyssey and hidden error that transformed the world* (New York, Free Press, 2003).

Allen, R. C., 'International competition in iron and steel, 1850–1913', *Journal of Economic History* 39 No 4 (1979): 911–37.

Anon. 'An account of a comparison lately made by some gentlemen of the Royal Society, of the standard of a yard, and the several weights lately made for their use; with the original standards of measures and weights in The Exchequer, and some others kept for public use, at Guild-Hall, Founders-Hall, The Tower, &c', *Philosophical Transactions* 42 (1742): 541–56.

Antonelli, C., 'Localized technological change and the evolution of standards as economic institutions', *Information Economics and Policy* 6 Nos 3–4 (1994): 195–216.

Arthur, W. B., 'Competing technologies, increasing returns, and lock-in by historical events', *Economic Journal* 99 No 394 (1989): 116–31.

Artman, H., and Waern, Y., 'Distributed cognition in an emergency coordination centre', *Cognition, Technology and Work* 1 (1999): 237–46.

Ashton, T. S., and Sykes, J., *The coal industry of the eighteenth century* (Manchester, Manchester University Press, 1929).

Ashworth, W. J., 'The calculating eye: Baily, Herschel, Babbage and the business of astronomy', *British Journal for the History of Science* 27 No 4 (1994): 409–41.

Ashworth, W. J., *Customs and excise: trade, production, and consumption in England, 1640–1845* (Oxford, Oxford University Press, 2003).

Atiyah, P. S., *The rise and fall of freedom of contract* (Oxford, Clarendon Press, 1979).

Atkinson, N., *Sir Joseph Whitworth: 'the world's best mechanician'* (Gloucestershire, Sutton, 1996).

Austin, M. T., and Milner, H. V., 'Strategies of European standardization', *Journal of European Public Policy* 8 No 3 (2001): 411–31.

Axelrod, R., Mitchell, W., Thomas, R. E., Bennett, D. S., and Bruderer, E., 'Coalition formation in standard-setting alliances', *Management Science* 41 No 9 (1995): 1493–1508.

Bagwell, P. S., *The Railway Clearing House in the British economy 1842–1922* (London, Allen and Unwin, 1968).

Baker, D., 'The marketing of corn in the first half of the eighteenth century: north-east Kent', *Agricultural History Review* 18 No 2 (1970): 126–50.

Bald, A., *The farmer and corn-dealer's assistant; or, the knowledge of weights and measures made easy, by a variety of tables, etc.* (Stirling, 1780).

Balmer, R. T., 'The operation of sand clocks and their medieval development', *Technology and Culture* 19 No 4 (1978): 615–32.

Barbrow, L. E., and Judson, L. V., *Weights and measures standards of the United States: a brief history* (Washington, DC, US Department of Commerce, National Bureau of Standards, 1976).

Barry, A., 'The history of measurement and the engineers of space', *British Journal for the History of Science* 26 No 4 (1993): 459–68.

Barty-King, H., *The Baltic story: Baltic coffee house to Baltic Exchange, 1744–1994* (London, Quiller Press, 1994).

Barzel, Y., 'Measurement cost and the organization of markets', *Journal of Law and Economics* 25 No 1 (1982): 27–48.

Bell, L., *The iron trade of United Kingdom* (London, British Iron Trade Association, 1886).

Bennett, G., Clavering, E., and Rounding, A., *A fighting trade: rail transport in Tyne coal, 1600–1800* (Gateshead, County Durham, Portcullis, 1990).

Berg, M., 'From imitation to invention: creating commodities in eighteenth-century Britain', *Economic History Review* 55 No 1 (2002): 1–30.

Berg, S., 'The production of compatibility: technical standards as collective goods', *Kyklos* 42 No 3 (1989): 361–83.

Besen, S. M., and Farrell, J., 'Choosing how to compete: strategies and tactics in standardization', *Journal of Economic Perspectives* 8 No 2 (1994): 117–31.

Beveridge, W., 'A statistical crime of the seventeenth century', *Journal of Economic and Business History* 1 No 4 (1929): 503–33.

Beveridge, W., *Prices and wages in England: from the twelfth to the nineteenth century*, Vol. 1 (London, Longmans, Green, 1939).

Biggs, N., 'A tale untangled: measuring the fineness of yarn', *Textile History* 35 No 1 (2004): 120–29.

Blake-Coleman, B. C., *Copper wire and electrical conductors – the shaping of a technology* (Reading, Harwood Academic, 1992).

Boumans, M. (ed.), *Measurement in economics: a handbook* (London, Elsevier, 2007).

Bowbrick, P., *The economics of quality, grades and brands* (London, Routledge, 1992).

Brackenborough, S., Mclean, T., and Oldroyd, D., 'The emergence of discounted cash flow analysis in the Tyneside coal industry c1700–1820', *British Accounting Review* 33 No 2 (2001): 137–55.

Broomhall, G. J. S., and Hubback, J. H., *Corn trade memories: recent and remote* (Liverpool, Northern, 1930).

Brunsson, N., and Jacobsson, B., 'The contemporary expansion of standardisation', in N. Brunsson and B. Jacobsson (eds), *A world of standards* (Oxford, Oxford University Press, 2000).

Bullen, A., *Drawn together: one hundred and fifty years of wire workers' trade unionism* (Wigan, Wire Workers Section of the Iron and Steel Trades Confederation, 1992).

Carnevali, F., '"Crooks, thieves and receivers": transaction costs in nineteenth-century industrial Birmingham', *Economic History Review* 57 No 3 (2004): 533–50.

Chang, H., *Inventing temperature: measurement and scientific progress* (New York, Oxford University Press, 2004).

Chattaway, C., 'Arbitration in the foreign corn trade in London', *Economic Journal* 17 No 67 (1907): 428–31.

Child, J., *A new discourse on trade* (Glasgow, 1751).

Clark, L., 'On the Birmingham wire gauge (paper presented to the British Association in 1867)', *Journal of the Society of Telegraph Engineers* 7 (1878): 332–35.

Clark, L., 'On the Birmingham wire gauge (paper presented to the British Association in 1869)', *Journal of the Society of Telegraph Engineers* 7 (1878): 336–44.

Connor, R. D., *The weights and measures of England* (London, HMSO, 1987).

Cowan, R., 'Nuclear power reactors: a study in technological lock-in', *Journal of Economic History* 50 No 3 (1990): 541–67.

Cox, A. B., 'Relation of the price and quality of cotton', *Journal of Farm Economics* 11 No 4 (1929): 542–49.

Cox, E. F., 'The metric system: a quarter-century of acceptance (1851–1876)', *Osiris* 13 (1958).

Cromar, P., 'The coal industry on Tyneside 1771–1800: oligopoly and spatial change', *Economic Geography* 53 No 1 (1977): 79–94.

Cunningham, B., *Cargo handling at ports: a survey of the various systems in vogue, with a consideration of their respective merits* (London, Chapman and Hall, 1923).

Curtis, B., 'From the moral thermometer to money: metrological reform in pre-confederation Canada', *Social Studies of Science* 28 No 4 (1998): 547–70.

Cusumano, M. A., Mylonadis, Y., and Rosenbloom, R. S., 'Strategic maneuvering and mass-market dynamics: the triumph of VHS over beta', *Business History Review* 66 No 1 (1992): 51–94.

Dale, H. B., *The fellowship of woodmongers: six centuries of the London coal trade* (London, repr. from the *Coal Merchant and Shipper*, 1923).

Dane, E. S., *Peter Stubs and the Lancashire hand tool industry* (Altrincham, John Sherratt, 1973).

Danvers, F. C., *On coal – with reference to its screening, transport, etc.* (London, W. H. Allen, 1872).

Daunton, M. J., 'The material politics of natural monopoly: consuming gas in Victorian Britain', in M. J. Daunton and M. Hilton (eds), *The politics of consumption: material culture and citizenship in Europe and America* (Oxford, Berg, 2001).

Daunton, M. J., *Progress and poverty: an economic and social history of Britain 1700–1850* (Oxford, Oxford University Press, 1995).

Daunton, M. J., and Hilton, M. (eds), *The politics of consumption: material culture and citizenship in Europe and America* (Oxford, Berg, 2001).

David, P. A., 'Clio and the economics of QWERTY', *American Economic Review* 75 No 2 (1985): 332–37.

David, P. A., and Greenstein, S., 'The economics of compatibility standards: an introduction to recent research', *Economics of Innovation and New Technology* 1 Nos 1 and 2 (1990): 3–41.

Daviron, B., 'Small farm production and the standardization of tropical products', *Journal of Agrarian Change* 2 No 2 (2002): 162–84.

Davis, J., 'Baking for the common good: a reassessment of the assize of bread in medieval England', *Economic History Review* 57 No 3 (2004): 465–502.

Deane, P., and Cole, W. A., *British economic growth: 1688–1959 – trends and structures* (Cambridge, Cambridge University Press, 1962).

Dendy, F. W. (ed.), *Records of the company of hostmen of Newcastle-upon-Tyne* (Durham, Surtees Society, 1901).

Denzau, A. T., and North, D. C., 'Shared mental models: ideologies and institutions', *Kyklos* 47 No 1 (1994): 3–31.

Desrosières, A., 'How real are statistics? Four possible attitudes', *Social Research* 68 No 2 (2001): 339–55.

Dickinson, H. W., and Rogers, H., 'Origin of gauges for wire, sheets and strip', *Transactions of the Newcomen Society* 21 (1943): 87–98.

Dietz, B., 'The north-east coal trade, 1550–1750: measures, markets and the metropolis', *Northern History* 22 (1986): 280–94.

Driel, H. V., and Schot, J., 'Radical innovation as a multilevel process: introducing floating grain elevators in the Port of Rotterdam', *Technology and Culture* 46 No 1 (2005): 51–76.

Dumbell, S., 'Early Liverpool cotton imports and the organization of the cotton market in the eighteenth century', *Economic Journal* 33 No 131 (1923): 362–73.

Dumbell, S., 'The sale of corn in the nineteenth century', *Economic Journal* 35 No 137 (1925): 141–45.

Dutton, H. I., and Jones, S. R. H., 'Invention and innovation in the British pin industry, 1790–1850', *Business History Review* 57 No 2 (1983): 175–93.

Edington, R., *Essay on the coal trade* (London, 1803).

Ellis, B., *Basic concepts of measurements* (Cambridge, Cambridge University Press, 1966).

Ellison, T., *The cotton trade of Great Britain: including a history of the Liverpool cotton market and of the Liverpool cotton brokers' association* (London, E. Wilson, 1886).

Farrell, J., 'Should competition policy favour compatibility?', in S. M. Green-stein and V. Stango (eds), *Standards and public policy* (Cambridge, Cambridge University Press, 2007).

Farrell, J., and Saloner, G., 'Coordination through committees and markets', *RAND Journal of Economics* 19 No 2 (1988): 235–52.

Farrell, J., and Saloner, G., 'Installed base and compatibility: innovation, product preannouncements, and predation', *American Economic Review* 76 No 5 (1986): 940–55.

Farrell, J., and Shapiro, C., 'Standard setting in high-definition television', *Brookings Papers on Economic Activity. Microeconomics* 1992 (1992): 1–93.

Favereau, O., Biencourt, O., and Eymard-Duvernay, F., 'Where do markets come from? From (quality) conventions!' in O. Favereau and E. Lazega (eds), *Conventions and structures in economic organization* (Cheltenham, Edward Elgar, 2002).

Fay, C. R., 'The London corn market at the beginning of the nineteenth century', *American Economic Review* 15 No 1 (1925): 70–76.

Fay, C. R., 'The sale of corn in the nineteenth century', *Economic Journal* 34 No 134 (1924): 211–18.

Feenstra, R. C., 'Integration of trade and disintegration of production in the global economy', *Journal of Economic Perspectives* 12 No 4 (1998): 31–50.

Feinstein, C. H., 'Pessimism perpetuated: real wages and the standard of living in Britain during and after the Industrial Revolution', *Journal of Economic History* 58 No 3 (1998): 625–58.

Ferguson, R. B., 'The adjudication of commercial disputes and the legal system in modern England', *British Journal of Law and Society* 7 No 2 (1980): 141–57.

Fisher, F. J., 'The development of the London food market, 1540–1640', *Economic History Review* 5 No 2 (1935): 46–64.

Fleischman, R. K., and Macve, R. H., 'Coals from Newcastle: an evaluation of alternative frameworks for interpreting the development of cost and management accounting in Northeast coal mining during the British Industrial Revolution', *Accounting and Business Research* 32 No 3 (2002): 133–52.

Flinn, M. W., *The history of the British coal industry*, Vol. 2, *1700–1830* (Oxford, Clarendon Press, 1984).

Floud, R. C., 'The adolescence of American engineering competition, 1860–1900', *Economic History Review* 27 No 1 (1974): 57–71.

Foray, D., 'Users, standards and the economics of coalitions and committees', *Information Economics and Policy* 6 Nos 3–4 (1994): 269–93.

Forrest, D. M., *A hundred years of Ceylon tea: 1867–1967* (London, Chatto and Windus, 1967).

Forrester, R. B., 'Commodity exchanges in England', *Annals of the American Academy of Political and Social Science* 155 No 1 (1931): 196–207.

Frangsmyr, T., Heilbron, J. L., and Rider, R. E. (eds), *The quantifying spirit in the 18th century* (Berkeley, University of California Press, 1990).

Gambles, A., *Protection and politics: conservative economic discourse 1815–1852* (London, Royal Historical Society, 1999).

Garside, A. H., *Cotton goes to market: a graphic description of a great industry* (New York, Frederick A. Stokes, 1935).

Gereffi, G., 'The organization of buyer-driven global commodity chains: how US retailers shape overseas production networks', in G. Gereffi and M. Korzeniewicz (eds), *Commodity chains and global capitalism* (Westport, Praeger, 1994).

Gereffi, G., Humphrey, J., and Sturgeon, T., 'The governance of global value chains', *Review of International Political Economy* 12 No 1 (2005): 78–104.

Gooday, G. J. N., *The morals of measurement: accuracy, irony and trust in late Victorian electrical practice* (Cambridge, Cambridge University Press, 2004).

Gordon, R. B., 'Who turned the mechanical ideal into mechanical reality?', *Technology and Culture* 29 No 4 (1988): 744–78.

Greenstein, S. M., and Stango, V. (eds), *Standards and public policy* (Cambridge, Cambridge University Press, 2007).

Greif, A., 'The fundamental problem of exchange: a research agenda in historical institutional analysis', *European Review of Economic History* 4 No 3 (2000): 251–84.

Greif, A., Milgrom, P., and Weingast, B. R., 'Coordination, commitment, and enforcement: the case of the merchant guild', *Journal of Political Economy* 102 No 4 (1994): 745–76.

Hall, N., 'The emergence of the Liverpool raw cotton market, 1800–1850', *Northern History* 38 No 1 (2001): 65–81.

Hall, T. Y., 'Remarks on the coal trade', *Transactions of the North of England Institute of Mining and Mechanical Engineers* II (1853–1854): 104–236.

Hallström, K. T., *Organizing international standardization: ISO and the IASC in quest in authority* (Cheltenham, Edward Elgar, 2004).

Harley, C. K., 'Coal exports and British shipping, 1850–1913', *Explorations in Economic History* 26 No 3 (1989): 311–38.

Harley, C. K., 'Ocean freight rates and productivity, 1740–1913: the primacy of mechanical invention reaffirmed', *Journal of Economic History* 48 No 4 (1988): 851–76.

Harrison, G. V., 'Agricultural weights and measures', in J. Thirsk (ed.), *The agrarian history of England and Wales*, Vol. VII, *1640–1750 (agrarian change)* (Cambridge, Cambridge University Press, 1985).

Hatcher, J., *The history of the British coal industry*, Vol. 1, *Before 1700* (Oxford, Clarendon Press, 1993).

Hausman, W. J., 'Cheap coals or limitation of the vend? London coal trade, 1770–1845', *Journal of Economic History* 44 No 2 (1984): 321–28.

Hausman, W. J., 'The English coastal coal trade, 1691–1910: how rapid was productivity growth?', *Economic History Review* 40 No 4 (1987): 588–96.

Hausman, W. J., 'Market power in London coal trade: the limitation of the vend, 1770–1845', *Explorations in Economic History* 21 No 4 (1984): 383–405.

Havinga, T., 'Private regulation of food safety by supermarkets', *Law and Policy* 28 No 4 (2006): 515–33.

Heilbron, J. L., 'Introductory essay', in T. Frangsmyr, J. L. Heilbron and R. E. Rider (eds), *The quantifying spirit in the 18th century* (Berkeley, University of California Press, 1990).

Heilbron, J. L., 'The measure of enlightenment', in T. Frangsmyr, J. L. Heilbron and R. E. Rider (eds), *The quantifying spirit in the 18th century* (Berkeley, University of California Press, 1990).

Helgesson, C.-F., Hultén, S., and Puffert, D. J., 'Standards as institutions: problems with creating all-European standards for terminal equipment', in J. Groenewegen, C. Pitelis and S.-E. Sjöstrand (eds), *On economic institutions: Theory and applications* (Cheltenham, Edward Elgar, 1995).

Henson, S., and Humphrey, J., 'Understanding the complexities of private standards in global agri-food chains', paper presented at International Workshop on Globalization, Global Governance and Private Standards, Leuven (2008).

Henson, S., and Reardon, T., 'Private agri-food standards: implications for food policy and the agri-food system', *Food Policy* 30 No 3 (2005): 241–53.

Hewitt, J., *The corn dealer's assistant* (London, 1736).

Higgins, W., and Hallström, K. T., 'Standardization, globalization and rationalities of government', *Organization* 14 No 5 (2007): 685–704.

Hill, L. D., *Grain, grades and standards: historical issues shaping the future* (Urbana, University of Illinois Press, 1990).

Hodgkins, E., *A series of mercantile letters, with the weights, measures and monies reduced into the English Standard, etc.* (London, 1815).

Holtzapffel, C., *Turning and mechanical manipulation*, Vol. 2 (London, Holtzapffel, 1847).

Hoppit, J., 'Income, welfare and the Industrial Revolution in Britain', *Historical Journal* 31 No 3 (1988): 721–31.

Hoppit, J., 'Reforming Britain's weights and measures, 1660–1824', *English Historical Review* 108 No 426 (1993): 82–104.

Horwitz, M. J., 'The rise of legal formalism', *American Journal of Legal History* 19 No 4 (1975): 251–64.

Hounshell, D. A., *From the American system to mass production 1800–1932: the development of manufacturing technology in the United States* (Baltimore, Johns Hopkins University Press, 1984).

Hughes, T., *The English wire gauge* (London, E. and F. N. Spon, 1879).

Hunt, B. J., 'Doing science in a global empire: cable telegraphy and electrical physics in Victorian Britain', in B. Lightman (ed.), *Victorian science in context* (Chicago, University of Chicago Press, 1997).

Hunt, B. J., 'The ohm is where the art is: British telegraph engineers and development of electrical standards', *Osiris* 9 (1994): 48–63.

Huntoon, R. D., 'Concept of a national measurement system', *Science* 158 No 3797 (1967): 67–71.

Hutchins, E., *Cognition in the wild* (Cambridge, MA, MIT Press, 1996).

Jacobides, M. G., Knudsen, T., and Augier, M., 'Benefitting from innovation: value creation, value appropriation and the role of industry architectures', *Research Policy* 35 (2006): 1200–1221.

Jaffe, J. A., 'Competition and the size of firms in the north-east coal trade, 1800–1850', *Northern History* 25 (1989): 235–55.

Jago, W., and Jago, W. C., *The technology of bread-making* (London, Kent, 1911).

Janes, H., *Rylands of Warrington: 1805–1955* (London, Harley, 1956).

John, H., *General view of the agriculture of the county of Lancaster . . .* (David and Charles, 1795; repr. Newton Abbot Devon, 1969).

Johnson, P., 'Market disciplines', in P. Mandler (ed.), *Liberty and authority in Victorian Britain* (Oxford, Oxford University Press, 2006).

Johnston, S. F., 'From eye to machine: shifting authority in colour measurement', in B. Saunders and J. Van Brakel (eds), *Theories, technologies and instrumentalities of colour* (Lanham, Maryland, University Press of America, 2002).

Jones, E., 'The role of information in US grain and oilseed markets', *Review of Agricultural Economics* 21 No 1 (1999): 237–55.

Jones, G., *The millers: a story of technological endeavour and industrial success, 1870–2001* (Lancaster, Carnegie, 2001).

Jones, S. R. H., 'Price associations and competition in the British pin industry, 1814–40', *Economic History Review* 26 No 2 (1973): 236–53.

Kaplan, S. L., *Provisioning Paris: merchants and millers in the grain and flour trade during the eighteenth century* (Ithaca, Cornell University Press, 1984).

Katz, M. L., and Shapiro, C., 'Network externalities, competition and compatibility', *American Economic Review* 75 No 3 (1985): 424–40.

Kelly, P., *Metrology; or an exposition of weights and measures chiefly those of Great Britain and France . . .* (London, 1816).

Kennelly, A. E., *Vestiges of pre-metric weights and measures persisting in metric-system Europe 1926–1927* (New York, Macmillan, 1928).

Kenwood, A. G., 'Capital investment in docks, harbours, and river improvements in north-eastern England 1825–1850', *Journal of Transport History* 1 No 2 (1971): 69–84.

Kilburn, T., *Joseph Whitworth: toolmaker* (Cromford, Derbyshire, Scarthin Books, 1987).

Kindelberger, C., 'Standards as public, collective and private goods', *Kyklos* 36 No 3 (1983): 377–96.

Kircher, P., 'Measurements and managerial decisions', in C. W. Churchman and P. Ratoosh (eds), *Measurement: definition and theories* (New York, John Wiley, 1959).

Kirkland, J., 'The relative prices of wheat and bread', *Economic Journal* 6 No 23 (1896): 475–84.

Konrad, K. A., and Thum, M., 'Fundamental standards and time consistency', *Kyklos* 46 No 4 (1993): 545–68.

Koski, H., and Kretschmer, T., 'Entry, standards and competition: firm strategies and the diffusion of mobile telephony', *Review of Industrial Organization* 26 (2005): 89–113.

Kula, W., *Measures and men*, R. Szreter (trans.) (Princeton, Princeton University Press, 1986).

Laman, N. K., 'The development of the wire-drawing industry', *Metallurgist* 3 No 6 (1959): 267–70.

Landes, D. S., 'Watchmaking: a case study in enterprise and change', *Business History Review* 53 No 1 (1979): 1–39.

Langlois, R. N., 'Competition through institutional form: the case of cluster tools standards', in S. M. Greenstein and V. Stango (eds), *Standards and public policy* (Cambridge, Cambridge University Press, 2007).

Langton, J., 'The Industrial Revolution and the regional geography of England', *Transactions of the Institute of British Geographers* 9 No 2 (1984): 145–67.

Latour, B., *Science in action: how to follow scientists and engineers through society* (Cambridge, MA, Harvard University Press, 1987).

Lazer, D., 'The free trade epidemic of the 1860s and other outbreaks of economic discrimination', *World Politics* 51 No 4 (1999): 447–83.

Lean, C., 'Wire drawing and steel wire, and its uses', in S. Timmins (ed.), *The resources, products and industrial history of Birmingham and the Midland hardware district* (London, Robert Hardwicke, 1866).

Leonelli, S., 'Packaging small facts for re-use: databases in model organism biology', in M. S. Morgan and P. Howlett (eds), *How well do facts travel? The dissemination of reliable knowledge* (New York, Cambridge University Press, 2010).

Levi, L., *The theory and practice of the metric system of weights and measures* (London, Griffith and Farran, 1871).

Liebowitz, S. J., and Margolis, S. E., 'The fable of the keys', *Journal of Law and Economics* 33 No 1 (1990): 1–25.

Linebaugh, P., *The London hanged: crime and civil society in the eighteenth century* (London, Allen Lane, 1991).

Macrosty, H., 'The grainmilling industry: a study in organization', *Economic Journal* 13 No 51 (1903): 324–34.

Mallock, H., and Preece, W. H., 'On a new telegraph wire gauge', *Journal of the Society of Telegraph Engineers* 1 (1872): 79–83.

Marshall, A., *Principles of economics* (London, Macmillan, 1891).

Mattli, W., 'The politics and economics of international institutional standards', *Journal of European Public Policy* 8 No 3 (2001): 328–44.

Mavor, J., 'The English railway rate question', *Quarterly Journal of Economics* 8 No 3 (1894): 280–318.

McCarthy, M., and Garcia, R., 'Screw threads on the SS Xantho Engine: a case of standardization in the 19th century Britain', *International Journal of Nautical Archaeology* 33 No 2 (2004): 330–37.

Merrill, J. C. F., 'Classification of grain into grades', *Annals of the American Academy of Political and Social Science* 38 No 2 (1911): 58–77.

Miller, G. A., 'Contextuality', in J. Oakhill and A. Garnham (eds), *Mental models in cognitive science: essays in honour of Phil Johnson-Laird* (Hove, Psychology Press, 1996).

Miller, G. A., 'On knowing a word', *Annual Review of Psychology* 50 (1999): 1–19.

Mokyr, J., *The gifts of Athena* (Princeton, Princeton University Press, 2002).

Mokyr, J., 'Technological inertia in economic history', *Journal of Economic History* 52 No 2 (1992): 325–38.

Morgan, D., *Merchants of grain* (New York, Viking Press, 1979).

Morgan, M. S., 'Making measuring instruments', *History of Political Economy* 33 Suppl. (2001): 235–51.

Morgan, M. S., and Howlett, P. (eds), *How well do facts travel? The dissemination of reliable knowledge* (New York, Cambridge University Press, 2010).

Mott, R. A., 'The London and Newcastle chaldrons for measuring coal', *Archaeologia Aeliana* 40 4th Ser. (1962): 227–39.

Murphy, C. N., and Yates, J., *The International Organization for Standardization (ISO): global governance through voluntary consensus* (New York, Routledge, 2009).

Murphy, G. L., 'Comprehending complex concepts', *Cognitive Science* 12 (1988): 529–62.

Musson, A. E., 'Joseph Whitworth and the growth of mass-production engineering', in R. P. T. Davenport-Hines (ed.), *Capital, entrepreneurs and profits* (London, Frank Cass, 1990).

Musson, A. E., and Robinson, E., 'The origins of engineering in Lancashire', *Journal of Economic History* 20 No 2 (1960): 209–33.

Nasmyth, J., 'Remarks on the introduction of the slide principle', in R. Buchanan (ed.), *Practical essays on mill work and other machinery* (London, John Weale, 1841).

Nef, J. U., *The rise of the British coal industry*, Vol. 2 (London, George Routledge, 1932).

Nelson, R. R., 'Co-evolution of industry structure, technology and supporting institutions, and the making of comparative advantage', *International Journal of the Economics of Business* 2 No 2 (1995): 171–84.

North, D. C., *Institutions, institutional change and economic performance* (Cambridge, Cambridge University Press, 1990).

O'Brien, P. K., 'The political economy of British taxation, 1660–1815', *Economic History Review* 41 No 1 (1988): 1–32.

Ogilvie, S., '"Whatever is, is right"? Economic institutions in pre-industrial Europe', *Economic History Review* 60 No 4 (2007): 649–84.

Olmstead, A. L., and Rhode, P. W., 'Hog-round marketing, seed quality, and government policy: institutional change in US cotton production, 1920–1960', *Journal of Economic History* 63 No 2 (2003): 447–88.

O'Rourke, K. H., and Williamson, J. G., 'When did globalisation begin?', *European Review of Economic History* 6 No 1 (2002): 23–50.

Palladino, P., and Worboys, M., 'Science and imperialism', *Isis* 84 No 1 (1993): 91–102.

Pasley, C. W., *Observations on the expediency and practicability of simplifying and improving the measures, weights and money* (London, Egerton's Military Library, 1834).

Pearson, R., 'Moral hazard and the assessment of insurance risk in eighteenth- and early-nineteenth-century Britain', *Business History Review* 76 No 1 (2002): 1–35.

Percival, J., *Wheat in Great Britain* (Reading, 1934).

Perren, R., 'Structural change and market growth in the food industry: flour milling in Britain, Europe and America, 1850–1914', *Economic History Review* 43 No 3 (1990): 420–37.

Petersen, C., *Bread and the British economy, c1770–1870* (Aldershot, Solar Press, 1995).

Pirrong, S. C., 'The efficient scope of private transactions-cost-reducing institutions: the successes and failures of commodity exchanges', *Journal of Legal studies* 24 No 1 (1995): 229–55.

Pöll, J. S., 'The story of the gauge', *Anaesthesia* 54 No 6 (1999): 575–81.

Pollard, S., 'Capitalism and rationality: a study of measurements in British coal mining, ca. 1750–1850', *Explorations in Economic History* 20 No 1 (1983): 110–29.

Poni, C., 'Standards, trust and civil discourse: measuring the thickness and quality of silk thread', *History of Technology* 23 (2001): 1–16.

Ponte, S., and Gibbon, P., 'Quality standards, conventions and the governance of global value chains', *Economy and Society* 34 No 1 (2005): 1–31.

Poppo, L., and Zenger, T., 'Testing alternative theories of the firm: transaction cost, knowledge-based, and measurement explanations for make-or-buy decisions in information services', *Strategic Management Journal* 19 No 9 (1998): 853–77.

Porter, M. E., 'Technology and competitive advantage', *Journal of Business Strategy* 5 No 3 (1985): 60–78.

Porter, T. M., 'Objectivity as standardization: the rhetoric of impersonality in measurement, statistics, and cost-benefit analysis', in A. Megill (ed.), *Rethinking objectivity* (London, Duke University Press, 1994).

Porter, T. M., 'Precision', in M. Boumans (ed.), *Measurement in economics: a handbook* (London, Elsevier, 2007).

Porter, T. M., *Trust in numbers: the pursuit of objectivity in science and public life* (Princeton, Princeton University Press, 1995).

Power, M., 'Counting, control and calculation: reflections on measuring and management', *Human Relations* 57 No 6 (2004): 765–83.

Puffert, D. J., *Tracks across continents, paths through history: the economic dynamics of standardization in railway gauge* (Chicago, University of Chicago Press, 2009).

Quinn, T., and Kovalevsky, J., 'The development of modern metrology and its role today', *Philosophical Transactions of the Royal Society of London, Series A* 363 No 1834 (2005): 2307–27.

Riello, G., 'Strategies and boundaries: subcontracting and the London trades in the long eighteenth century', *Enterprise and Society* 9 No 2 (2008): 243–80.

Romer, P. M., 'Endogenous technological change', *Journal of Political Economy* 98 No 5, Part 2 (1990): S71–S102.

Rosenberg, N., *Perspectives on technology* (Cambridge, Cambridge University Press, 1976).

Rosenberg, N., 'Technological change in the machine tool industry, 1840–1910', *Journal of Economic History* 23 No 4 (1963): 414–43.

Rothstein, M., 'Centralizing firms and spreading markets: the world of international grain traders, 1846–1914', *Business and Economic History* 17 (1988): 103–13.

Rothstein, M., 'Multinationals in the grain trade, 1850–1914', *Business and Economic History* 12 2nd Ser. (1983): 85–93.

Samuelson, P. A., 'The pure theory of public expenditure', *Review of Economics and Statistics* 36 No 3 (1954): 387–89.

Santos, F. M., and Eisenhardt, K. M., 'Organizational boundaries and theories of organization', *Organization Science* 16 No 5 (2005): 491–508.

Saul, S. B., 'The market and the development of the mechanical engineering industries in Britain, 1860–1914', *Economic History Review* 20 No 1 (1967): 111–30.

Schaffer, S., 'Metrology, metrication and Victorian values', in B. Lightman (ed.), *Victorian science in context* (Chicago, University of Chicago Press, 1997).

Schatzberg, E., *Wings of wood, wings of metal: culture and technical choice in American airplane materials, 1914–1945* (Princeton, Princeton University Press, 1999).

Schumpeter, J. A., *The theory of economic development*, R. Opie (trans.) (Cambridge, MA, Harvard University Press, 1912).

Scott, J. C., *Seeing like a state: how certain schemes to improve the human condition have failed* (New Haven, Yale University Press, 1998).

Searle, G. R., *Morality and the market in Victorian Britain* (Oxford, Clarendon Press, 1998).

Searle, J., *The construction of social reality* (London, Allen Lane, 1995).

Seth-Smith, M., *Two hundred years of Richard Johnson and Nephew* (Manchester, Richard Johnson and Nephew, 1973).

Shapiro, C., and Varian, H. R., 'The art of standards wars', *California Management Review* 41 No 2 (1999): 8–32.

Shapiro, C., and Varian, H. R., *Information rules: a strategic guide to the network economy* (Cambridge, MA, Harvard Business School Press, 1998).

Sheldon, R., Randall, A., Charlesworth, A., and Walsh, D., 'Popular protest and the persistence of customary corn measures: resistance to the Winchester bushel in the English west', in A. Randall and A. Charlesworth (eds), *Markets, market culture and popular protest in eighteenth-century Britain and Ireland* (Liverpool, Liverpool University Press, 1996).

Sherman, W. A., 'Standardizing production – what has been done and what can be done', *Annals of the American Academy of Political and Social Science* 142 (1929): 419–24.

Simpson, A. D. C., 'Grain packing in early standard capacity measures: evidence from the Scottish dry capacity standards', *Annals of Science* 49 No 4 (1992): 337–50.

Simpson, A. D. C., 'The pendulum as the British length standard: a nineteenth-century legal aberration', in R. G. W. Anderson, J. A. Bennett and W. F. Ryan (eds), *Making instruments count: essays on historical scientific instruments presented to Gerard L'Estrange Turner* (Aldershot, Ashgate, 1993).

Sinclair, B., 'At the turn of the screw: William Sellers, the Franklin Institute, and a standard American thread', *Technology and Culture* 10 No 1 (1969): 20–34.

Smith, J. B., *Wire, its manufacture and uses* (London, John Wiley, 1891).

Smith, J. G., *Organised produce markets* (New York, Longmans, Green, 1922).

Smith, R., *Sea-coal for London: history of the coal factors in the London market* (London, Longhams, 1961).

Spiering, M., 'The imperial system of weights and measures: traditional, superior and banned by Europe?' *Contemporary British History* 15 No 4 (2001): 111–28.

Spring, D., 'The Earls of Durham and the great northern coal field, 1830–1880', *Canadian Historical Review* 33 No 3 (1952): 237–53.

Spruyt, H., 'The supply and demand of governance in standard-setting: insights from the past', *Journal of European Public Policy* 8 No 3 (2001): 371–91.

Staudenmaier, J., 'Problematic stimulation: historians and sociologists constructing technology studies', in C. Mitcham (ed.), *Social and philosophical constructions of technology* (London, Jai Press, 1995).

Stern, W. M., 'The first London dock boom and the growth of the West India docks', *Economica* 19 No 73 (1952): 59–77.

Stevens, S. S., 'On the theory of scales of measurement', *Science* 103 No 2684 (1946): 677–80.

Stewart, J., 'Marketing wheat', *Annals of the American Academy of Political and Social Science* 107 (1923): 187–92.

Stones, F., *The British ferrous wire industry* (Sheffield, J. W. Northend, 1977).

Swann, P., Temple, P., and Shurmer, M., 'Standards and trade performance: the UK experience', *Economic Journal* 106 No 438 (1996): 1297–1313.

Sweezy, P. M., *Monopoly and competition in the English coal trade: 1550–1850* (Cambridge, MA, Harvard University Press, 1938).

Tann, J., and Jones, G., 'Technology and transformation: the diffusion of the roller mill in the British flour milling industry, 1870–1907', *Technology and Culture* 37 No 1 (1996): 36–69.

Tassey, G., 'The role of government in supporting measurement standards for high-technology industries', *Research Policy* 11 No 5 (1982): 311–20.

Tavernor, R., *Smoot's ear: the measure of humanity* (New Haven, Yale University Press, 2007).

Taylor, J. T., *The archaeology of the coal trade* (Newcastle, Frank Graham, 1858).

Teece, D. J., 'Profiting from technological innovation: implications for integration, collaboration, licensing and public policy', *Research Policy* 15 No 6 (1986): 285–305.

Teece, D. J., and Sherry, E. F., 'Standards setting and antitrust', *Minnesota Law Review* 87 No 6 (2003): 1913–94.

Temple, P., and Williams, G., 'Infra-technology and economic performance: evidence from the United Kingdom measurement infrastructure', *Information Economics and Policy* 14 (2002): 435–52.

Tenny, L. S., 'Standardization of farm products', *Annals of the American Academy of Political and Social Science* 137 (1928): 205–12.

Thévenot, L., 'Organized complexity: conventions of coordination and the composition of economic arrangements', *European Journal of Social Theory* 4 No 4 (2001): 405–25.

Thirsk, J. (ed.), *The agrarian history of England and Wales*, vol. VII, *1640–1750 (agrarian change)* (Cambridge, Cambridge University Press, 1985).

Thomas, L., *The development of wire rod production* (Cardiff, Guest, Keen, and Nettlefolds, 1949).

Thompson, E. P., 'The moral economy of the English crowd in the eighteenth century', *Past and Present* 50 No 1 (1971): 76–136.

Thompson, G. V., 'Intercompany technical standardization in the early American automobile industry', *Journal of Economic History* 14 No 1 (1954): 1–20.

Timmins, S. (ed.), *The resources, products and industrial history of Birmingham and the Midland hardware district* (London, Robert Hardwicke, 1866).

Tirole, J., *The theory of industrial organization* (Cambridge, MA, MIT Press, 1988).

Tooze, J. A., *Statistics and the German state, 1900–1945: making of modern economic knowledge* (Cambridge, Cambridge University Press, 2001).

Velkar, A., 'Caveat emptor: abolishing public measurements, standardizing quantities, and enhancing market transparency in the London coal trade c1830', *Enterprise and Society* 9 No 2 (2008): 281–313.

Velkar, A., 'Transactions, standardisation and competition: establishing uniform sizes in the British wire industry c.1880', *Business History* 51 No 2 (2009): 222–47.

Ville, S., 'Defending productivity growth in the English coal trade during the eighteenth and nineteenth centuries', *Economic History Review* 40 No 4 (1987): 597–602.

Ville, S., 'Total factor productivity in the English shipping industry: the northeast coal trade, 1700–1850', *Economic History Review* 39 No 3 (1986): 355–70.

Walton, J. R., 'Varietal innovation and the competitiveness of the British cereals sector, 1760–1930', *Agricultural History Review* 47 No 1 (1999): 29–57.

Webb, S., and Webb, B., 'The assize of bread', *Economic Journal* 14 No 54 (1904): 196–218.

Weiss, M. B. H., and Sirbu, M., 'Technological choice in voluntary standards committees: an empirical analysis', *Economics of Innovation and New Technology* 1 No 1 (1990): 111–33.

Wengenroth, U., *Enterprise and technology: the German and British steel industries, 1865–1895*, S. H. Tenison (trans.) (Cambridge, Cambridge University Press, 1994).

White, F., *Commercial and trades directory of Birmingham*, Vol. 2 (Sheffield, Francis White, 1875).

Whitworth, J., *Papers on mechanical subjects* (London, E. and F. N. Spon, 1882).

Wilkinson, J., 'A new paradigm for economic analysis?' *Economy and Society* 26 No 3 (1997): 305–39.

Wilson, A. S., *A bushel of corn* (Edinburgh, David Douglas, 1883).

Wise, M. N. (ed.), *The values of precision* (Princeton, Princeton University Press, 1995).

Wrigley, E. A., *People, cities and wealth: the transformation of traditional society* (Oxford, Basil Blackwell, 1987).

Zupko, R. E., *Revolution in measurement: Western European weights and measures since the age of science* (Philadelphia, American Philosophical Society, 1990).

PARLIAMENTARY PAPERS

Report of the Carysfort Committee on weights and measures, HC Reports (1738–1765) Vol. II 1758.

Second report of the Carysfort Committee on weights and measures, HC Reports (1738–1765) Vol. II 1759.

Report from the Committee on Coal Trade, HC Reports (1785–1801) Vol. X 1800.

Second report from the Committee on Coal Trade, HC Reports (1785–1801) Vol. X 1800.

Report of the Select Committee on Import and Export of Corn, PP Vol. III 1805.

Report from the Committee on Weights and Measures, PP Vol. III 1813–1814.

Account of coals shipped from the ports of Great Britain, PP Vol. XIV 1818.

First report of the commissioners on weights and measures, PP Vol. XI 1819.

Second report of the commissioners on weights and measures, PP Vol. VII 1820.

Report from the Committee on Weights and Measures, PP Vol. IV 1821.
Number of chaldrons imported into London: 1801–1827, PP Vol. XVIII 1826–1827.
Appointment of Select Committee on Coal Trade, HL Journal Vol. 61 1829.
Report from the Committee on Coal Trade, HL Journal Vol. 61 1829.
Report of the Select Committee on Coal Trade, PP Vol. VIII 1830.
Account of duties charged on coals in London, PP Vol. XXXIII 1833.
Report from Select Committee on the Sale of Corn, PP Vol. VII 1834.
Returns from corn inspectors, PP Vol. XLIX 1834.
Report of the Select Committee on Coal Trade, PP Vol. XI 1836.
New York Industrial Exhibition Reports, PP Vol. XXXVI 1854.
Report from the Committee on Weights and Measures, PP Vol. VII 1862.
Account of coals brought coastways and by inland navigation, PP Vol. LXIV 1867.
Royal Commission to inquire into condition of Exchequer standards (of weights and measures) second report, PP Vol. XXIII 1868–1869.
Report from Select Committee on the Metropolis Gas, PP Vol. VI 1876.
Memorandum by comptroller of corn returns, PP Vol. LXV 1878–1879.
Summary of returns by corn inspectors, PP Vol. LXV 1878–1879.
Return showing total quantity for wheat in 1880, PP Vol. LXXXIII 1881.
Return of total quantity of various kinds of grain and flour imported into the UK in each year from 1828, PP Vol. LX 1886.
Quantities and average price of wheat as sold in the towns of England and Wales between 1815 and 1888, PP Vol. LXIII 1889.
Report of Select Committee on Corn Sales, PP Vol. XI 1893–1894.
Report of the Select Committee on Weights and Measures, PP Vol. XIII 1895.

STATUTES

Act for ascertaining the coal measure, 12 Anne Stat. 2 C. 17, 1713.
Act for regulating the importation and exportation of corn, 31 George III C. 30, 1791.
Act for regulating the delivery of coals, 47 George III C. 68, 1807.
Act for ascertaining and establishing on uniformity of weights and measures, 5 George IV C. 74, 1824.
Act for regulating delivery of coal, 1 & 2 William IV C. 76, 1831.
Act to discontinue duties upon coals, 1 & 2 William IV C. 16, 1831.
Weights and measures (amendment) act, 5 & 6 William IV, C. 63, 1835.
Weights and measures act, 41 & 42 Victoria C. 49, 1878.
Weights and measures in the sale of corn act, 11 & 12 George V C. 35, 1921.

ARCHIVAL SOURCES

Council papers of Association of Chambers of Commerce, Guildhall Library, London.
Council papers of Birmingham Chamber of Commerce, Birmingham City Archives.
The records of the Standards, Weights and Measures Department of Board of Trade Papers, National Archives, London.
Council reports and committee papers of City of London, Corporation of London Records Office, London.

Sub-committee reports and minutes of London Corn Trade Association, Corporation of London Records Office, London.[1]
Council papers of Society of Telegraph Engineers, Institution of Engineering and Technology Archives, London.

OTHER OFFICIAL PUBLICATIONS

Census of England and Wales, 1871, 1881 and 1891.
Statistical Abstracts for the United Kingdom, Nos 37 and 38.
Final report on the first census of production of the United Kingdom (1907), HMSO, London, 1912.
Review of the rationale for and economic benefit of the UK national measurement system, National Measurement System Policy Unit, Department of Trade and Industry, 1999.
The forty-seventh annual report of the trade and commerce of Chicago, Chicago Board of Trade, 1905.

NEWSPAPERS AND PERIODICALS

Ironmonger and Metal Trades Advertiser
Miller
The Times

---

[1] At the time of research for this book, these records were kept at the Guildhall Library, London. They are now held by the Corporation of London Records Office, London.

Index

absolute standard, 48, 49, 172
abstract principle, 38, 43, 47, 53, 72, 88,
    153, 167, 218
accuracy. *See also* precision
    definition, 73
    of instruments, 79
    of measurements, 15, 45, 55, 70, 73,
    122, 152, 219
Adams, John Quincy, 65
Alder, Ken, 5, 56
ambiguity, 32, 131, 150
anthropocentric measures, 31, 66
arbitration, 25, 84, 166, 212
Argentina, 175
artefact, 39, 43, 78, 88, 108, 119
assizes, 35, 40, 76, 197
Associated Chambers of Commerce, 156
Australia, 64, 175

bakers, 35, 176, 186
Barzel, Yoram, 72
Beveridge, William, 74
BIPM or Bureau International des Poids et
    Mesures, 83
Bird, John, 42
Birmingham, 138, 147
Birmingham Chamber of Commerce, 155
Birmingham wire gauge. *See* wire gauges
Board of Trade, 52, 156–157, 167, 194
    Standards Department, 136, 166
Boumans, Marcel, 73, 219
bread, 35, 76, 176, 181, 185, 191, 195,
    199
Buddle, John, 113, 121
bushel, 32, 35, 48, 53, 74, 77, 108–110,
    113, 124, 184, 189, 203, 204, 205,
    206. *See also* measurement, units

Canada, 64, 147, 180
capacity, 43, 46, 65, 138, 161. *See also*
    volume measures

Carysfort Committee, 42, 51. *See also*
    parliamentary committee
Carysfort, Lord, 42, 48
caveat emptor, 23, 167, 220
cental, 59, 207
centralisation, 9, 46, 84, 201
chaldron, 32, 107, 125
Chamberlain, Joseph, 167, 227
Chicago, 180
Chicago Board of Trade, 187, 189
Clark, Latimer, 149, 152
classification, 22, 32, 81, 187, 219
coal
    bushel, 108
    measurements, 114, 221
    trade, 101, 115
coastal shipping, 100
Cobden-Chevalier treaty, 63
colliers, 103, 105, 108, 117
commodity exchange, 187, 208, 209. *See
    also* industry association
competition, 56, 86, 119, 159, 162,
    199
conformity, 21, 46, 74, 155, 182
consistency, 34, 74, 110, 154, 183, 197,
    205, 232
context, 31, 34, 74, 91, 207
    contextualising, 76
    decontextualise, 38
contracts, 39, 62, 149, 185, 195
Convention du Mètre, 57
conventions, 34, 55, 68, 74, 79,
    90
cooperation, 57, 165
Corporation of London, 106

debates, 23, 58, 155–159, 206
decimal division, 51, 57, 59, 152
decimal measures, 55, 58, 153. *See also*
    cental; metre (measurement unit)
density. *See* specific gravity, wheat

259

Printed in the United States
By Bookmasters